JULES LAFORGUE

and the Ironic Inheritance

JULES LAFORGUE
Unter den Linden, 1885

JULES LAFORGUE
and the Ironic Inheritance

WARREN RAMSEY

New York · OXFORD UNIVERSITY PRESS

1953

For Elizabeth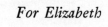

FOREWORD

THE name of Jules Supervielle inevitably appears in a study of Laforgue and the Ironic Inheritance, and it might well be written in large print at the beginning of the present book. For it was due to the friendly offices of M. Supervielle that in the summer of 1950, soon after the death of Georges Jean-Aubry, editor of the *Oeuvres complètes*, I was granted access to Laforgue's manuscripts.

These papers have had a varied history since a December day in 1887 when Leah Laforgue wrote a 'télégramme' to Téodor de Wyzewa, asking that he stop by her hotel the next day because she was leaving for Menton in the evening and had a favor to ask regarding her husband's papers. The writings she left with the Polish critic passed through many hands before finding their way back, considerably reduced in number, to Wyzewa, who finally entrusted them to Jean-Aubry. Although a great deal is lost, much remains, including unpublished material, for French editors, like French poets, have their 'rules for the eye,' and tend to reject what is not in finished form. Needless to say, what is unfinished can be highly revealing of an artist and a man, and I am particularly grateful to Mme Paule Aubry for permission to reproduce unpublished verse and prose in the following pages, as well as for her graciousness in opening her husband's library to me at a difficult time, and for her many other courtesies. My thanks go also to M. Lucien Jaïs for advice and services cordially rendered and for the gift of extremely rare Laforguiana privately printed for *Nous Quatre* by Daragnès. I further wish to express my appreciation to the editors of the *Mercure de France* for allowing me to consult Volume VII of the *Oeuvres complètes* in manuscript.

Mr. Henri Peyre has been unfailingly sensitive in his encouragement of this project since its beginnings as a Ph.D. thesis at Yale University; my debt to him is great. Mr. René Wellek and Mr. Norman Holmes Pearson of Yale and Miss Margaret Gilman of Bryn Mawr have made valuable suggestions. I owe special thanks also to Mr. Kenneth Cornell and Mr. Andrew Morehouse of Yale, Mr. John Edwards of the University of California, and Mm. Fernand and Michel Mohrt, all of whom have been most helpful.

The author of the *Cantos* and Dorothy Shakespear Pound gave generously of their time and recollections, and I am grateful for the opinions of Mr. Malcolm Cowley and Mr. Allen Tate. Among earlier writers on Laforgue, I owe most to Jean-Aubry, and to François Ruchon, René Taupin, and Edmund Wilson. Acknowledgments are also due to the editors of *Comparative Literature*, the *Sewanee Review*, and *Yale French Studies*, in which portions of this work have appeared. Permission has been granted by Mr. Samuel Loveman for the use of 'Locutions des Pierrots,' translated by Hart Crane. And I should certainly not fail to express my appreciation to the staffs of many libraries, especially those of Yale and Columbia Universities, the New York Public Library, and the Bibliothèque Nationale. Photographs of manuscripts, sketches, and the frontispiece portrait of the poet are published with permission of Mme Aubry.

Finally, I wish to express my sincere gratitude to the members of the committee which selected this book for the Modern Language Association-Oxford University Press Award: Professors Orie William Long, Williams College; Henri M. Peyre and René Wellek, Yale University; Ernest J. Simmons, Columbia University; and Ernest Hatch Wilkins, President of Oberlin College; and to the officers and editors of the Oxford University Press for thoughtful services since this book won that award. Along with those I have named and others I have not, they have helped to make possible what I now present, 'un livre de bonne foi.'

W. R.

Berkeley, California
March 1953

CONTENTS

ILLUSTRATIONS

JULES LAFORGUE

and the Ironic Inheritance

Aber das Wehende höre,
die ununterbrochene Nachricht, die aus Stille sich bildet.
Es rauscht jetzt von jenen jungen Toten zu dir.

RAINER MARIA RILKE

I

New Dimensions

THE works of Jules Laforgue acquire new dimensions with the passage of time. Of course, the poet himself remains what he has been ever since 1887, when his brief life ended before it had properly begun—an evasive moonlit presence peering over the tops of doors and laughing at his forebears, as Paul Verlaine wrote of Pierrot in a poem that ranks next to Laforgue's in the writings about that well-loved clown. There are times—perhaps a trick of light, a cloud across the moon, or the pathos of distance—when it seems to us that the wraith-like figure has changed. Then Verlaine's sonnet comes to mind:

> Ce n'est plus le rêveur lunaire du vieil air
> Qui riait aux aïeux dans les dessus de porte;
> Sa gaîté, comme sa chandelle, hélas! est morte,
> Et son spectre aujourd'hui nous hante, mince et clair. . .

It may seem to us at these times that Laforgue, like Pierrot, whom he brought to literary perfection, has taken on tragic dimensions, once unsuspected, and we are haunted by a pale and slender specter. But then, after a moment, we find his gaiety intact, his candle still alight, and we are very glad that we were wrong. Laforgue, the essential Laforgue, will never change. He will simply have, for his amusement, a lengthening line of literary descendants to add to his literary antecedents.

The number of his published writings has increased, however. So much additional verse and prose has come to light in the

3

last half-century that the 'two small volumes, one of prose, the other of verse,'[1] to which Arthur Symons rashly sought to confine all of the poet's works, have somehow been transformed into eight quite bulky ones. It turns out that Laforgue produced more verse than most poets since Baudelaire—verse, moreover, that reflects continual development and falls into at least three periods. He was the author of tales in experimental prose, in addition to an early *novella* and many fragments that demonstrate how easily and well he could write in a realistic vein. Potentially a literary critic of the first order, in his remarks on Baudelaire particularly Laforgue has commanded respect from hard-bitten historians who have found his creative work bewildering. If his art criticism falls somewhat below his usual level, that is because it was tampered with by overcautious editors while the author was still very young and unknown; its value as evidence of a strong plastic sense is considerable. There is a whole volume of vivid criticism of Germany, where Laforgue spent nearly five years of productive exile. Finally, and in some ways most significantly of all, this young poet had an uncommon flair for speculative thought—which, because it was genuine, was never ponderous, heavy-footed or forbidding. His copious notes toward an aesthetics kept coming out in the reviews for years after his death; many must still be consulted in manuscript. It is not difficult to find contradictions in jottings that the author lacked the time to sift, to align. Nevertheless, these jottings represent an attempt of a kind made by no other poet of the period—an effort to come to grips with contemporary philosophical and scientific ideas at first hand.

All this is no slender accomplishment for a moonstruck dreamer dead at twenty-seven, one who complained so often of ennui, 'fruit of dull lack of curiosity,' as Baudelaire defined it, and who has usually been counted with the Symbolists, poets not conspicuous for their intellectual endeavor. But then Laforgue is full of surprises, disavowals, and his work, whether in two volumes or in eight, has never fit neatly into familiar pigeonholes. Born in 1860, he was a contemporary of the men who gathered round Mallarmé; he knew their aims and contributed to their magazines. He was only five years older than William Butler

Yeats, and hardly more the senior of Proust, Valéry, and Gide, who put Symbolist lessons to account in the twentieth century. He was exposed to and had his own way of describing the forces that shaped the Symbolists: the 'packed and blinding' [2] poems of Leconte de Lisle and his Parnassians, who made their readers see things clearly, all too clearly; the 'plaintively nervous' [3] poetry of Baudelaire, point of departure for all modern poets; the 'technical cunning' [4] of the most gifted of singers, Verlaine. Rather late in his career he read Rimbaud, 'precocious, absolute flower without before or after.' [5] And yet Laforgue, who read and responded to the older poets during formative years, takes his place among these initiators of the Symbolist movement, rather than with the true Symbolists among whom he has been ranged and the problems of whose poetry he raises.

Mallarmé wrote that the pure poet 'yields the initiative to the Word.' [6] His disciples tried to do just that. And Albert Thibaudet, one of the best critics of Symbolism, took up Mallarmé's thought in an effort to formulate the distinctive quality of the greatest of the Symbolists. In Mallarmé's verse, he said, the initiative is left to the Word as, in the mystique of pure love, the initiative is left to God. In the beginning of the poem there exists a frame, an emotive tone, a receptive void, an availability, as, in the beginning of pure love, there exists the individual. Upon this frame, consummating it, acts the enchanting and transfiguring power of words which the poet summons up, to whose operation he surrenders himself.[7] There is probably confusion here between mystic and magician. For the mystic summons nothing. He merely waits. And Mallarmé conceived the poet as one possessing magical, quasi-divine powers:

> Le Maître, par un oeil profond, a, sur ses pas,
> Apaisé de l'éden l'inquiète merveille
> Dont le frisson final, dans sa voix seule, éveille
> Pour la Rose et le Lys le mystère d'un nom.

> The Master, with his deep eye, has, in his path,
> Appeased the restless mystery of that Eden
> Whose final shudder in his voice awakens
> For Lily and Rose the mystery of a name.

Yet this vision of the poet as one who waits with a mystic's receptivity for the word that binds a spell, the word that will really have power to call up, to create by bestowing a name, to create even man and woman (for that is the meaning of Lily and Rose in Mallarmé's 'Toast funèbre'), applies to Mallarmé at his most intense, and to Valéry at his best; and this is the ideal that other Symbolists sought to approximate. Language was regarded with a long-lost reverence. The magical word religiously awaited had, for the Symbolists, something in common with the divine Word, the Logos. A fine critic such as Charles Du Bos [8] could quote, apropos of the language of Stefan George, a German Symbolist, the opening verse of St. John's Gospel, and the effect is not nearly so incongruous as we might have expected.

It would be too much to say that Laforgue experienced any such shudder as this before the Word thus held sacred. He revised a good deal on occasion, but the corrections seem to have come as the first draft came, with a quite un-Mallarméan facility. He was capable of writing carelessly, and sometimes we wish that there were a little more mystical receptivity or prophetic seriousness about him. Underneath there is always the abundance, the facility, the sheer uninhibited gift of language. That is why he never attains certain intensities to be found in the work of lesser men, intensities induced only by resistances, by hindrances of one kind or another. And yet Laforgue was, in the sober estimate of the best judges of his time, a genius— not one of those who slowly and painfully discover their personal vision of the world, but one who naturally, with little effort, opens new windows on reality.

When Thibaudet observed that Victor Hugo's words overflow in a powerful stream, that Théodore de Banville's spread out in an easy river, but Mallarmé's 'ooze forth in an inhuman climate, slowly form the stalactites of marvelous poetry,' [9] he was touching on another essential characteristic of Symbolism. From Baudelaire onward, poets gave a prominent place to jewels, metals, stony, treeless landscapes, and such 'dehumanized' imagery. In part this was only an apparent rejection of the accustomed lush imagery of nineteenth-century poetry. The devil—the fallen angel—of sentiment came back with seven other spirits more wicked than himself to repossess a house that he found thus swept and garnished. Man's noble emotions were thrown into higher relief by the rejection of trivial or facile ones that found their readiest equivalents in a humanized landscape. To some extent, however, it must be admitted that the Symbolists were simply not interested in that general fund of feelings which had furnished the subject matter of Romantic poetry. In this respect, they resemble their immediate predecessors, the Parnassians; and they are the poorer for this.

Laforgue was aware of the poetic utility of the dehumanized, could find images to fit a wasteland of his own. The moon is given a climate and geographical features such as these:

> Oui, c'est l'automne incantatoire et permanent
> Sans thermomètre, embaumant mers et continents,
> Etangs aveugles, lacs ophtalmiques, fontaines
> De Léthé, cendres d'air, déserts de porcelaine. . .[10]

> Yes, this is autumn permanent and fixed,
> Thermometerless, balm of seas and lands,
> Blind pools, ophthalmic lakes, oblivious
> Fountains, ashes of air, porcelain badlands. . .

Here he is writing in a style that was to be cultivated extensively until about 1925. This passage, however, is not typical of Laforgue's verse, which is, in the main, human, all too human, deriving some of its most characteristic effects from the moods and meters of popular songs. In neither the good nor the bad sense is his verse 'dehumanized.' Neither an overruling passion nor a simulated concern for form throws his subject matter into a position of secondary importance.

In speaking of the musical qualities of Symbolist poetry, we are on familiar ground, Valéry having written that 'what was christened Symbolism can be summed up quite simply in the common intention of several groups of poets (hostile to one another, incidentally) to take back from music their own.'[11] This utterance of Valéry had been preceded, as was so often the case, by a similar one of Mallarmé: 'Music rejoins the verse to form, since Wagner, poetry.' [12] It might be difficult to decide which exactly among the properties of poetry, lost a while to music, were found again during the Symbolist period. Verlaine was that *rara avis*, a discoverer of original rhythmic patterns, new vowel melodies that have sung in the ears of poets ever since. René Ghil was persuaded that poets had neglected the resources and technique of instrumentation, that vowels and consonants, each with its own timbre, could have instrument-like effects. This was an instructive error in that it showed how music and poetry overlapped in the average poetic mind of 1886. Gustave Kahn, Laforgue's friend and a Symbolist of the kind that flourished during the brief official life of the school, wrote imprecise, vaguely sonorous, Wagnerian verse. Mallarmé endeavored to bring to poetry a quality it had never before possessed, an abstractness that would have invested words —no longer signs, no longer pointers to things—with the self-sufficiency of musical notes.

Valéry's often-quoted formulation of the Symbolist aim is valuable though vague. The musical intention was fundamental, and closely related to the aim of a poet from whose attitudes and techniques Valéry held himself aloof. 'Que ton vers soit la chose envolée,' Verlaine had written. Music is the art of the thing in flight, the essentially dynamic art contrasting radically with the pictorial, the static. And pure poetry seems to share with music the dynamic quality. It is the province of the plastic arts, of painting and sculpture, to present contours and colors, to repro-duce in some measure. And it was the intention of Parnassian poets to describe, to present the clearest possible images of ma-terial objects. But imaginative writing at its most concentrated, when it is doing the task most uniquely its own, tends to avoid telling how things look or are otherwise perceived by the senses. It neglects description and instead shows objects in action. In the verse of Mallarmé's mature period we are conscious that he had outgrown Parnassian emphasis on the pictorial, the sculp-tural, that he is describing less and dramatizing more, till *Un Coup de Dés* is the barest, most skeletal representation possible of the lunges and recoils, the *Antösse,* of the ego developing self-consciousness. To the extent that Valéry relies on more or less laborious description, as he does in sections of *La Jeune Parque*, his verse is less purely poetic than Mallarmé's.

Symbolist poetry is musical in that it is dynamic. It is musical in other ways, too, has rare rhythmical and melodic qualities, perhaps even unusual tone color; for the Symbolists were the most self-conscious of poets, bent on realizing all the potentialities of their medium. Laforgue's poetry was certainly dynamic, in its own special way; but it lacks some of the more obvious musical traits. It is not very melodious, for example, except when the imitation of Verlaine is close, or the modeling on a popular air is patent, or when the alexandrine is of the traditional, conventional variety. Laforgue discovered new rhythmic patterns —he was the only authentic French poet of his time who wrote any considerable amount of free verse; but as his contemporaries rightly observed, he was not interested in his free-verse lines as musical units. Rather, he was concerned with their 'psychological' unity. There is no particular experimentation with tone color, or with the still less tangible musical resources.

On the other hand, there is more static imagery here than in most Symbolist poetry. Laforgue paints, or etches, memorable word pictures that remind us of Imagist verse of the Anglo-American poetic renascence:

A travers le lacis des branches dépouillées
Dont l'eau-forte sabrait le ciel bleu-clair et froid,
Solitaire et navrant, descendait l'astre-roi. . .

Across the network of denuded boughs
Whose etchings carved the cold and clear-blue sky,
Lonely and heart-breaking declined the sovereign star. . .

en ce Paris, jardin
Obtus et chic, avec son bourgeois de Jourdain
A rêveurs, ses vitraux fardés, ses vieux dimanches
Dans les quartiers tannés où regardent des branches
Par-dessus les murs des pensionnats . . .

                                           in this Paris, obtuse
And stylish garden, with its bourgeois Jordan
Haunted by dreamers, primped windows, stodgy Sundays
In wearied quarters where the branches peer
Over the walls of girls' dormitories . . .

   —*Un fin sourire (tel ce triangle d'oiseaux
   D'exil sur ce ciel gris!) peut traverser mes heures.*

   —A delicate smile (like that bird-triangle
   Of exile on gray sky!) can traverse my hours.

Such lines have their share of the verbs that lend vividness to
verse: naked branches carve the sky, others stare over walls, a
delicately traced smile persists through the hours. And yet this
is verse in which the plastic traits predominate. This is description, though far from ponderous—swift impressionistic description. The attention to plastic detail is the kind that Rilke learned
from close association with Rodin. Some of the objects are 'small,
dry things' of the kind to which T. E. Hulme turned poets'
attention. These lines of Laforgue are, in other words, eminently
modern, and take their place in the main current of nineteenth-
and twentieth-century poetry. But they do not sing, or they sing
in no ordinary fashion. We must try to clarify the difference
from the true Symbolists that both Laforgue and his contemporaries recognized.

   Historically speaking, Laforgue began to write a little earlier
than the men who, after his main work was done, began to
call themselves Symbolists. His particular subjects of admiration
were the young Paul Bourget (author of delicate descriptive
verse inspired in part by the English Lake Poets), the Goncourt
brothers, and Joris-Karl Huysmans. Bourget confirmed in him
his natural impulse to probe surgically into the passions of the
eternal masculine and feminine, in dramatic lyrics that always
verge on verse drama (and once found that form), or in prose
narratives—and to tell of his findings unmistakably and explicitly
rather than symbolically. Unhappily, Laforgue also picked up
from Bourget some of his 'à-quoi-bonisme,' his fashionable and

facile 'what's the good of it all' attitude, which did not seriously cripple his activity but which is often, on the face of it, disagreeable. The Goncourts passed on to Laforgue their passion for the eighteenth century, its painters and their landscapes, the stylized figures of its comedy and pantomime; even, for a time, their naturalism, their conviction that heredity and environment shape human beings in inevitable, scientifically observable ways. Moreover—alack, and rue the day—the Goncourts contaminated Laforgue with their 'écriture artiste,' their twisted, snarled, and altogether deplorable manner of writing prose. From Huysmans the young Laforgue acquired a whole aesthetics, ultimately traceable to Baudelaire and the Romantics, it is true, a theory of the beautiful that led him to welcome into his verse urban and suburban imagery, grotesqueries of modern industry that self-respecting Symbolists regarded as unfit for poetry. It is noteworthy that the Goncourts and Huysmans had strong ties with painters, and none of these three masters of Laforgue felt any special attraction to music.

For all these reasons, Laforgue did not participate in that complex revulsion against mid-century modes of thought, feeling, and expression which was Symbolism. The climate of ideas that helped to form him, about 1880, was distinctly different from that of 1886. At the Ecole des Beaux-Arts, Taine was delivering lectures—applications of his deterministic method in its extreme form—which at once fascinated and repelled Laforgue. Ernest Renan was apparently still busy with his study of the history of religions, maintaining some remnant of his faith in the future of science. It had not yet become clear, as it did with the publication of the *Souvenirs* in 1883, that Renan was an aged and undiscriminating skeptic who did not really believe in anything. At the Collège de France, Théodule Ribot was expounding philosophical and scientific ideas, subsequently writing them down with a clarity and vigor reminiscent of Thomas Huxley and Herbert Spencer—whose works, full of faith in evolution, Laforgue also pondered.

In the domain of art, the Impressionists were painting pictures calculated to 'make a cab-horse rear,' as a conservative critic put it, and certain to make an enthusiastic disciple of a young poet who was no mean draftsman himself. If it were equitable to borrow a painter's term for a man of letters, Laforgue might be described as an Impressionist, for he set out, like Manet and Degas, Renoir and Seurat, to capture the beauty of the commonplace under ever-changing light. He became one of the embattled advocates of these artists, wrote about them with an excitement that is bound to remind the English reader of George Moore—the first to write about Laforgue in English, incidentally —not to mention James Gibbons Huneker, whose first flight to Paris coincided with Laforgue's earliest years there.

The literary world of 1880 was a world On the Eve. As we look backward, it is easy enough to see that the sign had already been given, that Mallarmé had been publishing conspicuously for some fifteen years. However, the Mallarmé of 1880 was apparently whiling away his time in trifling pursuits. The publication of Huysmans' *A Rebours* in 1884, with its aesthete-hero proclaiming his devotion to all that was 'decadent' and to Mallarmé, changed everything so far as Mallarmé was concerned and brought the young men flocking round to form one of those groups without which a literary movement can never get under way in France. Mallarmé's apartment in the Rue de Rome became a rallying point.

Laforgue flourished somewhat in advance, his course took him a little to one side of the main movement, partly because early experience had deepened personal qualities that made it difficult for him to give himself to any literary movement, partly because circumstances led him to spend his most productive years outside France.

But Laforgue, who was not quite a Symbolist, was consummately himself. His verse is free of some of the faults, the excesses, the blur of the Symbolists'. Now, nearly three quarters of a century after Laforgue's death, the lessons of Symbolism have been learned, applied, and, so far as active poets are concerned, largely forgotten. Once more poets discourse openly on actions, situations, ideas. A symbol, according to the useful definition given by Jules Lemaître, is a prolonged comparison of which the first term is suppressed—a system of sustained metaphors. The symbol, the truncated and mysterious comparison, is rare in

Anglo-American poetry since Eliot, in French since Fargue, in
Spanish since Alberti. The younger poets are more direct, sometimes perhaps for lack of the intensity that gives multiple meanings to language, but sometimes, too, because of the conflicting
urgencies of things to say. For the poetry on this side of Symbolism is not, any more than was Laforgue's on the other, out of
touch with life and contemporary ideas. Once more, as in 1880,
concepts are expressed in verse whose quality depends on its
style, which in turn usually relies on one or another of the
varieties of wit. Laforgue has much to teach the interested student of verse at the present time.

'The poetry's the thing' where any poet is concerned, and
this study is focused on two volumes of verse and a book of
tales closely appertaining thereto. For reasons already suggested,
however, Laforgue would suffer seriously from an examination
limited to his poetry alone. His verse is far from being 'pure,'
self-sustaining, analyzable in and for itself. It carries a rich freight
of ideas worthy of examination. Furthermore, his career having
been cut off so soon, the question of influence becomes something like a question of prolongation, of observing how discoveries he made have found their application in the works of
other men. Finally, Laforgue's life is as interesting as that of
most pure poets is dull, and it would be a lifeless tome that would
neglect what Miguel de Unamuno called 'intimate biography'—
especially in the light of many facts not previously committed
to print.

This book represents an attempt to tell a poet's story, to dis-
cuss his thought, verse, and imaginative prose, his literary criticism, and the impact of his work, all without undue fragmentation. Accordingly, Chapters II, III, V, and X are mainly devoted
to Laforgue's life, and portions of intervening chapters fill in the
account. The fourth chapter is concerned for the most part with
reactions to the idealistic philosophy of the century and to such
scientific and pseudo-scientific ideas as the poet drew into his
verse. Chapter VI deals with notes on aesthetic questions, with
Laforgue as disciple of the Romantic philosophers, especially
Eduard von Hartmann, philosopher of the Unconscious, and
Friedrich Schelling. In the seventh chapter, Laforgue is discussed

as a literary critic, and in VIII and IX as ironic poet and story-teller. Nearly all verse and prose passages are translated, except when the point is one of prosody.

Later chapters center on certain lunar syntheses achieved in France and America. Laforgue's daemonic possession of T. S. Eliot is reasonably familiar, although the consequences bear closer scrutiny. Less well known are the lunar influences on Hart Crane, the good giant James Huneker, and Frances Newman, a librarian-critic-novelist from Atlanta, Georgia, who translated Laforgue's *Moral Tales*, dedicated them to the moonlit memory of their author, and had them bound in deep-mourning violet because, as Laforgue said more than once,

Le violet grand-deuil, c'est ma couleur locale.

II

'For the Eye's Delight'

And yet it is just this, this intimate biography, which explains the most to us.

MIGUEL DE UNAMUNO

'A GOOD Breton, born below the Tropics,' [1] Laforgue wrote of himself at a time when Taine had made some mention of an author's racial strain indispensable, and when a widely read essay by Renan had lent more prestige than ever to Breton origins. But Laforgue spent a good deal of his time demurring to Taine's deterministic doctrines, and evidently he took Renan and 'The Poetry of the Celtic Peoples' *cum grano salis*, for he wrote elsewhere that he 'was born—and this is no joke—of a Bretonne who was really a bit of a Gasconne, and of a Gascon who was misanthropic, footloose and pure of heart like a Breton. Make what you can out of that. . .' [2]

It was once rumored that the poet's ancestors came from Saint-Brieuc on the English Channel and had connections with the legendary Counts of Villiers de l'Isle-Adam, whose ultimate off-shoot was the Symbolist of that name. But this, according to a South American Laforguian who talked with members of the poet's family living in and around Montevideo, was pure invention. The Laforgues were peasant folk from the neighborhood of Brest. Early in the nineteenth century, part of the family moved to Tarbes, in that southwestern corner of France which has seen much shuttling to and from South America. Isidore-Lucien Ducasse, self-styled 'Comte de Lautréamont,' one of the most mysterious and powerful of modern poets, was born in Montevideo of a Tarbais father. Jules Supervielle, the poet of our own time who bears the greatest resemblance to Laforgue,

15

was born in the same city of a family from Orthez. And untold numbers of plain bourgeois, from the eighteenth century right down to the present, respectable citizens of the Béarn and Navarre, have gone off to South America to seek their fortunes, planning to return and spend their declining years in their province, there to be known picturesquely as 'Americans.'

Charles Laforgue, the misanthropic, footloose, pure-hearted Gascon, did not make his fortune, exactly. He became, after a few preliminary hesitations, a teacher. Taken to Montevideo in 1842 at the age of eight, he was brought up and educated there, turning into a serious, reserved young man devoted to the poetry of Lamartine and the ideas of Jean-Jacques Rousseau. He named his eldest son Emile, and his second son Jules, after one of those Roman heroes whom Rousseau revered. Charles Laforgue became an expert penman, but lost his right hand as the result of a hunting accident, and in 1858 founded a little French *lycée* in the Calle Rincón in Montevideo. The same year he married one of his pupils, Pauline Lacolley, who had been born in Cherbourg eighteen years before. Her father, Louis Lacolley, had been a French légionnaire in the long and savage war of independence fought by Uruguay against Argentina, and had distinguished himself in one of its principal battles before settling down as a bootmaker—*the* bootmaker of the town, by all accounts—with a fine shop in the Calle 25 de Mayo. Grandfather Lacolley's military recollections were vivid, and when another war broke out in 1865, between Uruguay and Paraguay this time, and the boys played soldiers in the marshland outside the city, he had heroic tales to tell of the nine years' siege of Montevideo.

Jules Laforgue was born in the dead of a South American winter, on 16 August 1860, in a house bearing the name La Sirena, on the corner of the Calle Juncal and the west side of the Plaza de la Independencia. He was to die in Paris on 20 August 1887, and a generation of critics liked to maintain that he had been born just twenty-seven years before, on 20 August. But since the certificate of baptism was turned up among the papers of the Church of San Francisco de Asís, there has been no room for doubt as to the real birth date of 'un párvulo . . . Julio, que nació el día diez y seis del presente, hijo legítimo de don Carlos Laforgue y de doña Paulina Lacolley, naturales de Francia.'

The poet was to retain clear memories of a checkerboard city with the regular, rectangular streets characteristic of colonial towns, a city built on a granite peninsula, sloping down on three sides to the broad Río de la Plata. He would remember the winds that howled over the exposed point of land: 'In Montevideo the windy weeks rushed by. Sundays we would go a long way with grandmother, all dressed up, peeling bananas, to eat a galette with distant relatives who kept a bakery. There were rats behind the sacks.' [3] The proprietor of the Panadería del Sol, for so the bakery was called, was a not-so-distant relative, Pascal Darré, a first cousin of Charles Laforgue who was shortly to retire to Tarbes, where he would play a considerable part in the subsequent lives of the Laforgues. 'Another Sunday,' Jules would recall, 'we might go to the uncle's who owned a factory. How rich everything seemed! Two boy cousins, adolescents, would already be off horseback riding. Two girl cousins would be on hand. . .' [4] These relatives are unidentified, but the poor-relation sentiments have their interest.

Jules attended, briefly and desultorily, his father's *lycée*. There, as in the two schools he attended later on, he was dreamy and listless, and the wartime atmosphere was encouraging to truancy. He used to wander off toward the green shade of a suburb called the Paso del Molino. A little further on was another inviting retreat, a park belonging to a rich German, José Buschenthal.

American experiences were brief, however. Grandfather and grandmother Laforgue wanted to see the homeland again before they died. Moreover, the little school, which had never prospered, now collapsed entirely, and Charles Laforgue had to go to work as a bookkeeper in the Calle Cerrito. In 1866 he decided to send his parents, wife, and five children—Emile, Jules, Marie, Madeleine, and Charles—off to Tarbes, planning to join them there in a year.

It was from the deck of a sailing vessel (the captain was

an acquaintance of Charles Laforgue) that Jules saw disappearing behind him the low and level coast line broken by the
Cerro, the abrupt hill west of the city, with its out-of-date
dungeon on top. In mid-Atlantic the ship was becalmed for three
weeks, and the voyage to Bordeaux took no less than seventy-
five days. One after another the children fell ill—'with ennui,' [5]
said the ship's doctor, who could offer no better diagnosis. The
captain traced the general ill luck to the breaking of a mirror
soon after the passengers had come aboard. Jules saw sunsets
that he never forgot. Nor did he forget his fits of depression
during the interminable voyage. 'I am prodigiously bored,' he
wrote from Germany in 1883. 'Since I crossed the Atlantic I
have never experienced such black fits of spleen.' [6]

Tarbes in the *département* of the Hautes-Pyrenées is, as Stendhal observed in his *Voyage dans le Midi*, 'a horizontal town if
there ever was one.' On unusually fine days, the snow-covered
Pic du Midi de Bigorre can be seen to the south—but the Tarbais
consider such visibility ominous, a sign of rain. Twenty kilo-
meters up the valley of the Adour is Bagnères-de-Bigorre, one
of the greenest of mountain resorts. But the lower valley lacks
the interest of the Landes, the heath and pine country to the
north, or the country sloping down toward Biarritz and Saint-
Jean-de-Luz on the west, or the vine-growing valleys of the
eastern Pyrenees. It is chiefly distinguished for the growing of
field corn. Tarbes in 1866 (it has not changed greatly since)
was a dun-walled, red-tiled town of twenty thousand, a self-
sufficient provincial center of the kind one finds scattered over
France, with small businesses and industries ministering to broad
farmlands, an ingrown, small-minded place long untouched by
wars, food shortages, or ideas. Here Jules Laforgue was to
spend some of his most susceptible years. As he wrote in a bit
of verse heretofore unpublished:

> *J'ai passé l'âge timide*
> *Dans un stagnant pays*
> *Où pèse un ciel torride*
> *Sur rien que des champs de maïs*

Tuiles, choux, commères du voisinage,
  C'est là que j'ai passé mon bel âge
    Et lan lan là,
      C'est là!
Ces beaux ramiers de l'incurie . . .[7]

I passed the timid age
In a stagnant country-side
Where endless cornfields bear
The hot weight of the sky

Tiles, cabbages, tongue-wagging old goodwives—
  And there I passed my young life,
    There, there, nowhere
      But there!
Those gentle ringdoves of indifference . . .

'J'AI PASSÉ L'ÂGE TIMIDE'
Unpublished verse

That first year the Laforgues lived in the modest rue Saint-Louis, now the rue Abbé Torné, just across from the present entrance to the Lower School. In 1868 Charles Laforgue arrived, not to stay with his family, but to take all except the two oldest boys back with him to Montevideo, where living was after all, he had decided, cheaper. Emile and Jules were left behind, to become boarding pupils at the Collège Impérial.

Jules was enrolled at the Collège—where Théophile Gautier and Isidore Ducasse had been pupils and Ferdinand Foch still was—from 1869 till 1876. During these years he received only one first prize, in religious instruction. He won three seconds, in natural science, history, and penmanship. A principal of the school summed it up this way: 'Dreamy, not very diligent, but remarkably intelligent, young Laforgue was not what at the *lycée* is called a good pupil.' [8] But the centers of interest, religion, science, and history, are significant.

We can approach Jules' life at Tarbes by way of references in his own writings and through testimony of those who knew him. His published verse and later prose are relatively barren of recollections. There are generalized memories:

Voici venir les pluies d'une patience d'ange [9]

C'est la toux dans les dortoirs du lycée qui rentre,
C'est la tisane sans le foyer . . . [10]

Now do the unremitting rains descend

The cough down corridors where school resumes,
The potion tendered by no friendly hand . . .

But these might be the feelings of almost any impressionable schoolboy.

Laforgue's early works include one revealing tale, long buried and not published until 1946. *Stéphane Vassiliew* is the story of a miniature exile in a *lycée* of southwestern France. Stéphane's parents are somewhere in Russia, instead of South America, and they are rich, so that Stéphane is the slightly etiolated outgrowth of luxury. He is all alone instead of having cousins on the rue

Massey in Tarbes, and at the end of the narrative he dies somewhat too rapidly of galloping tuberculosis. But these are minor
transpositions, and in all important respects *Stéphane Vassiliew*,
an early tale by a poet, is transparently autobiographical.

Young Stéphane is utterly desolate within the ugly precincts of
his school. 'Son spleen lui vient de tout': the rigid routine, the
bare stone walls, the graveled courtyard, planted with meager
plane trees, where he does not join in the games. We find the
first mention of Philoctetes, a figure that is to reappear at every
stage of Laforgue's work. Suffering from an advanced case of
chilblains (as a boy coming from Russia would not be, but as
Jules actually was), an affliction that makes it impossible for him
to go outdoors, Stéphane confides to the teller of the tale that
a single book comforted him, Fénelon's *Télémaque*, 'especially
the pages in which Philoctetes tells how he was abandoned on
the Isle of Lemnos because of the contagion spread abroad in
the Greek camp by the wound that was devouring his foot.
Stéphane feels rushes of infinite consolation as he reads and re-
reads the words: "I was alone for almost the whole time of
the siege of Troy, without help, without hope, without relief . . . !" ' And he has underlined the following passage: 'This
wild, uninhabited island where I heard only the sound of the sea
breaking against the rocks . . . For I was asleep when the Greeks
abandoned me. Imagine my terror when I awoke and saw the
ships disappearing across the waves! . . . O shores! O promon-
tories of this island! To you I make my lament. Who else would
hear me? You are accustomed to my lamentations.' *

* The myth of Philoctetes, the hero who derived a mysterious virtue
from his suffering, has attracted much attention from critics. See (besides
André Gide's version of the legend and 'Philoctetes: the Wound and the
Bow' in Edmund Wilson's *The Wound and the Bow*) 'The Ghost of Henry
James,' by Saul Rosensweig, in *The Partisan Review* for Winter, 1944. Mr.
Rosensweig finds what he calls 'the sacrificial roots' of James' literary power
in the obscure injury he suffered at the age of eighteen—thus rediscovering
the pattern of Wilson's book, to which he refers. In the next issue of
The Partisan Review, Lionel Trilling objects (as he has continued to do
since then) to the notion that power springs from pain and neurotic sacri-
fice. Literary men make their difficulties public, as doctors, for example,
do not; but the writer's talents are as independent of his experience as
the surgeon's. The Philoctetes myth, Trilling maintains, is not explanatory
but moral: 'It tells us, in its juxtaposition of the wound and the bow,

The term 'unconscious' recurs in this tale with a persistence that already suggests the Unconscious of Eduard von Hartmann's *Philosophie des Unbewussten*. Left alone at the *lycée* during the long vacations, Stéphane wanders in the countryside. He 'bakes gently in the burning sun . . . absorbed in the unconscious fixity of things.' He meditates all afternoon beside a pond: 'At the surface of the pool swarms of midges danced, suddenly cut through by flights of swallows that drank as they flew. A cool wind rose over the meadows, bringing with it the healthy smell of freshly mown hay. The poplar leaves danced with a silvery sound. In the distance, herds turned homeward in huge clouds of dust. Carts passed, their axles grinding. Stéphane rose, drunken, almost weaving from this day passed utterly absorbed in the vast unconscious life of nature.'

Stéphane is like Shelley's poet in *Prometheus Unbound:*

> He will watch from dawn to gloom
> The lake-reflected sun illume
> The yellow bees in the ivy-bloom. . .

He is like Lamartine (Charles Laforgue's favorite poet), bent above the brook in his native valley:

> *La fraîcheur de leurs lits, l'ombre qui les couronne,*
> *M'enchaînent tout le jour sur les bords des ruisseaux;*
> *Comme un enfant bercé par un chant monotone,*
> *Mon âme s'assoupit au murmure des eaux. . .*

> The coolness of their beds, by shadow crowned,
> Binds me all day above the waters' brim;
> Like a child lulled by a monotonous round
> My soul grows drowsy with the sound of them. . .

Again, Stéphane is like George Moore's model writer, who reads one book and sits on a stone in the sun. (Moore is certain to have

that we must be aware that weakness does not preclude strength nor strength weakness.' So far as Stéphane-Laforgue is concerned, it would seem that the myth afforded, precisely, 'infinite consolation'—the moral virtue that must have rendered the other kind available, strengthened the will, and so on. Was it La Fontaine who said, 'C'est le fonds qui manque le moins'?

read some of Laforgue's notes on 'unconscious' contemplation, published in periodicals of the 'nineties, and can help us understand just what Laforgue meant by surrender to the Unconscious. Nineteenth-century philosophies of the Unconscious are only restatements of Romantic doctrines of enthusiasm. Man is absorbed by a god that is virtually nature.)

Toward the end of the story come Stéphane's infatuation with a circus and its clowns, his falling in love with a pale circus lady, his desperate break toward unattainable freedom, his swift tubercular death. All this is curiously prophetic, as we shall see. *Stéphane Vassiliew* is interesting because of its Romantic attitudes—abdication of intellect, absorption in nature, pursuit of the impossible, suicidal impulse. The figure of the Romantic sufferer is enhanced by its merging into the more fundamental figure of Philoctetes. And in view of Laforgue's literary development, it is worthy of notice that these attitudes and their dramatic resolutions in the narrative are presented without irony, straightforwardly, and—at the end—with pathos.

Nor is there irony in the fabric of the prose, with its manifest reverence for the pure Platonic imagery of Fénelon. Half a dozen years later, Laforgue was to satirize the basalt-monumental, exotic-inventorying aspects of Flaubert's style, the style of 'Hérodias,' *Salammbô*, and the hunting episode in 'La Légende de Saint Julien l'Hospitalier.' But his own style in *Stéphane Vassiliew* is heavy with Flaubert—the perdurable Flaubert. Stéphane is traced in these strokes: '. . . toujours des mines souffreteuses, en toute saison des foulards délicats au cou, très frileux, montant pour un rien à l'infirmerie . . .'—the very rhythms with which Flaubert achieved the same concision.

The relationship between Stéphane's underlying attitudes and those of his creator is clear. It is unlikely, however, that this work gives an accurate impression of Laforgue's day-to-day existence at the Collège Impérial de Tarbes. We have the testimony of an observing school friend, Jean Pérès, a future psychologist, who paints a quite un-Vassiliew-like portrait of Laforgue as a schoolboy: 'He had his share of mischief . . . showed no lack of spontaneity, the repartee that makes one somebody in the schoolboy world. I can even say more: these youngsters [Jules and Emile] who had come from the other side of the ocean to pass their boyhood within the walls of a French *lycée* . . . enjoyed a certain prestige in the eyes of their comrades because of a touch of newness, freshness difficult to describe, and because of the vision of another world they conjured up in the Crusoesque minds of the schoolboys of those days.' [11]

There was a profound reserve about the temperament of Jules Laforgue—the ultimate cause of his defensive irony. Friends whom he saw almost daily in Berlin did not know that he wrote verse until they found him correcting proof for the *Complaintes*. It is not surprising, indeed quite true to character, that during his school days he should have kept his deeper feelings to himself.

Unlike Stéphane, Jules and Emile had someone to be responsible for them on Thursdays, *fête* days, and during vacations. This was Pascal Darré, the retired Montevidean baker, their father's first cousin, now living a leisurely life on an acacia-planted property across from the Massey Gardens. Pascal was on the horny-handed side and assuredly did not spoil his young relations. On the other hand, he saw to it that they had regular painting lessons, encouraging a bent for plastic art in both boys. It is hard to think of the poet as having been uncommonly miserable during these years.

At least one teacher took an interest in him, a young study-hall master named Théophile Delcassé, in spite or because of an inauspicious event. One day Jules, turning around suddenly as the monitor came up behind, knocked off his eyeglasses, was thunderously reprimanded and sent to detention room. He took to calling the young man 'Cafardinet' (Snoopy), but student and teacher became good friends nonetheless. Later on in Paris, Delcassé did his best by dint of private lessons to get Jules through the baccalaureate. It was long supposed that the one-time teacher was the author of a friendly review of the *Complaintes*, though it now appears that Laforgue wrote it himself. At least Delcassé let his name be used! And it was becoming a well-known name. Having tried his hand unsuccessfully at play-writing, Delcassé turned to politics, where he did much better, serving several times as foreign minister and becoming the architect of the Anglo-French Entente Cordiale.

Jules fell in love. Her name was Marguerite. A story of somewhat later vintage than *Stéphane*, 'Amours de la quinzième année,' [12] relates 'how at fifteen one changes! I skipped class to go
far from town, to roll on the grass and weep causelessly. And
every Sunday morning, regularly, I found myself standing outside
the church after mass was over, watching the girls fly off on
wings of white dresses. A critical period, as Joseph Prudhomme
well observes, and it was precisely at this time that a novel by
Balzac took it into its head to fall into my hands: *Un Grand
Homme de province à Paris*. I devoured it, I dreamed of it, I had
an intuitive vision of Paris. That faraway inferno fascinated me;
for its sake I forgot to eat and drink. Lucien de Rubempré was
a poet. I would be a painter!

'And immediately I broke with my comrades, whom I thence-
forth regarded as vile seed of grocers and pettifoggers. I spent my
spare time sketching, either at the library or at the museum.
Then I began to paint. . . At night I worked very late copying
Julien's models, and on Sundays, from eight in the morning till
six in the evening, I was at the shop of a little plaster-molder
whom I had come to know, clear at the other end of town.
While he poured plaster in his old strung-up molds, I copied the
Dancing Faun, Diana of Gabii, all the ancients. It was a real
crisis of work and ambition. You can imagine that love soon
joined in the dance. I had already found my Dulcinea. At a certain window in a certain street—I can shut my eyes and see it
now!—I had found her. It was she.

Je ne te connais pas, mais je t'ai reconnue!

'She must have been at least three years older than I, but she
was exquisite in her wisteria-framed window, with her fine pallor,
her great bright eyes, the eternal blue ribbon in her blond tresses,
and her ample embroidered collar molding her shoulders. That
was all I could see from the street. But one day I had a glimpse
of her from close at hand. I trembled to see in her chin a soft and
rosy dimple, a very nest for kisses. A look that she cast upon me,
a gaze like a dying gazelle's, finished me. I became quite mad.
The night was spent in projects. Everything was over. I would
love her from afar. I would kill myself with work. I would go to

Paris. I would become famous. And I saw myself in the triumph of my return, laying down my love and glory at her feet.

'I would have liked her to be a trifle more elegiac—her birdlike brain, her great bursts of laughter, intimidated me; yet I adored her—yes, to the point of weeping with rage sometimes, at night before falling asleep. . .'

After months of stubborn and devoted toil, during which time Marguerite pays little attention to him and appears to be on excellent terms with a cousin of hers, one rainy, chilly Sunday evening on the way home from the plaster-molder's, thinking of Marguerite, of her cousin, of his ambitions, of Paris, of the frigid cell in his uncle's house to which he is returning, he sees Marguerite's window brightly lit and hears music and laughter. A party is going on. He throws a rock through the pane and spends the night in jail—an unlikely conclusion to an otherwise engrossing confession.

At the end of the 'Amours' the author remarks that *they* are married and that *they* will no doubt have numerous offspring. On a vacation from Germany, visiting Tarbes in August 1883, he was to note in another vein: 'Evening, music in the park—Marguerite glimpsed in the crowd, pale, her head high, lost, talking with a fat and vulgar gentleman.' [13]

In May 1875, Charles and Pauline Laforgue came back from Montevideo with eight children, for the family now included, besides the five brothers and sisters who had arrived in Tarbes nine years before, Pauline, Louise, Adrien, Charlotte, and Edouard. An eleventh child, Albert, was born in November. The following year the whole family moved to Paris. There is no record of the reasons, but the education of Jules and Emile was undoubtedly a factor. The Laforgues settled down in a house with a garden at 66 rue des Moines in the Batignolles quarter; but they were not all together for long. On 6 April 1876, Mme Laforgue died giving birth to a twelfth child, who did not live. 'J'avais presque pas connu ma mère,' Jules was to write in the opening poem of *Des Fleurs de bonne volonté*.

Two years after his wife's death, the elder Laforgue took his children over to the Left Bank so that Emile could be near the Ecole des Beaux-Arts, where he was a student, and Jules could be within walking distance of the Bibliothèque Sainte-Geneviève. The family moved into a first-floor apartment at 5 rue Berthollet, a pleasant enough street, some allegations to the contrary notwithstanding, running north off Boulevard Port-Royal. On one side of rue Berthollet windows looked over the broad gardens of the military hospital of the Val-de-Grâce. Poems, letters, notebooks, all bear witness to the poet's affection for this street.[14] Charles Laforgue did not sink into discouraged indigence after his wife's death. For four years, at least, until his health broke in 1881, he managed to support eleven children; and it was not his fault if Emile remained a perpetual art student and Jules never succeeded in becoming a *bachelier*.

Jules attended the Lycée Fontanes (now Condorcet) for a while, during the years when Henri Bergson was a pupil there. He took the stiff state examination for the baccalaureate three times and once passed the written part, but foundered in the oral while his father looked on and suffered. The rigid educational system had now done its worst for the intractable, creative pupil.

Laforgue's earliest preserved writings are a bundle of notes dating from this period when the schoolboy was turning into the creative writer. They include a passage extolling passive surrender to the Unconscious, rather like the one quoted from *Stéphane Vassiliew*, only this time set in a Paris park. The motif of the young ladies' boarding school, already hinted at in 'Amours de la quinzième année,' makes its appearance. And we find this description of a sunset: 'In the evening through the window a sky of deep-mourning violet . . .' This is the 'violet grand-deuil,' Laforgue's *couleur locale*, as he is to tell us over and over.

One of the most interesting of these fragments deals with the celebration that followed the dedication of the Lion de Belfort in the Place Denfert-Rochereau. This was the day, 20 September 1880, on which Laforgue first thought of writing *Complaintes*, poems on the order of the *complaintes populaires*, ballads of a kind sung by the people ever since the Middle Ages. The idea was to bear fruit in his first real book,[15] several years later. Entitled 'Fête de nuit, inauguration du lion de Belfort,' the passage begins, characteristically, with a few words about the clowns and mountebanks on hand. Then come lines which may

'FÊTE DE NUIT. INAUGURATION DU LION DE BELFORT'

or may not record the precise moment when the poet thought of writing verse to hurdy-gurdy rhythms, but which are certainly essential Laforgue: 'A woman of the party vomiting puddles of wine, a dog lapping away at it. A second female, tapping the first one on the back maternally, to facilitate matters, muttering meanwhile that it just wasn't sensible to go for a ride on the merry-go-round after eating and drinking all day long. . . Whole families higher than a kite. . . A pimp shepherding along a band of girls, one of them adorable and sad, with a black eye—all drinking wine. . . The smell of Argand lamps, cries of barkers, the melancholy of barrel organs playing tunes heard in public squares in autumn. And high up, the virgin and eternal stars. Strange, strange planet!' [16]

The carnival was to become an image of humanity for Laforgue, who had read Baudelaire's great prose poem on the old saltimbanque and had seen the circus pictures of Manet and Degas. He felt the vulgarity of people massed together, inevitably drawn toward what is most garish, ignoring or striking down that which is less so—the aged showman to whom Baudelaire likens the worn-out writer or the prostitute not quite as tough as her fellows. One of his bitterest poems is 'Complainte du soir des comices agricoles,' in which he is thinking not only of an agricultural show that he saw at Baden-Baden but also of that section of *Madame Bovary* into which Flaubert put so much of his hatred of the exploiter and his compassion for the victim. In most of the poems, prose passages and pictures presenting the carnival as microcosm, some face, figure, or sketched-in detail reminds us of human aspiration. Thus in the poem about the agricultural show a nostalgic horn-call stands for the Absolute, and in the excerpt above we have 'the virgin and eternal stars.'

There is great variety in the rhythms of these prose fragments. We pass from Romantic mingling of the grotesque and the sublime, as illustrated above, to such Pascalian analysis as the following:

> *Berce-moi, roule-moi, vaste fatalité—*
> *On se laisse aller.—Votre mère meurt,*
> *Vous perdez au jeu, un ami vous lâche,*

une femme vous accable de son indifférence
. . . vous tombez malade, la mort est là peut-être. . .

Lull me, cradle me, vast fatality.—
You let yourself go.—Your mother dies,
You lose at gambling, a friend cuts you off,
a woman overwhelms you with her indifference
. . . you fall ill, death is at hand perhaps. . .

One passage is worth quoting in its entirety as evidence of the poet's nascent wish that the work of art should be truly new. The following is probably his earliest art criticism, written in a free-flowing, rapid hand: 'The landscape across the way, a splendid twilight scene—but too much the picture—a fine sky flecked with soft cinnabar—those two regular hills bristling with black fir trees, curving—green places for the young firs—above, the rosy ruin—and further, on the steep wavy descents of green hills with the serpentine of a dusty road, trees, with little white vermilion-tiled houses set among them—windows sparkling in the last desperate rays of the picturesque star—then the church bell in the valley—this is Calame, Canon Schmidt, etc.—the weather is fine and this is fine and there is nothing to say—these Fénelon-like landscapes composed for the eye's delight—this nature is too much arranged—oh, the sickly Bièvre, the meager vine-shoots, and those vacant lots. . .' [17]

This is criticism of a picture seen in a gallery, and of much else besides—of literary works such as *Stéphane Vassiliew*, for instance, composed chiefly 'for the eye's delight.' Unimpressed by the conventionally idyllic landscape on the gallery wall, the critic ends with words of longing for the Bièvre, the little stream, pathetic even in that day, trickling past the Gobelins factory into the main sewer of Paris. He would like to see the spindly vine-yards and vacant lots that mark its course brought into art. However pleased his readers may be with *Stéphane*, its smiling or frowning landscapes and predictable cadences, Jules Laforgue was speedily dissatisfied with it, probably before he had finished writing it.

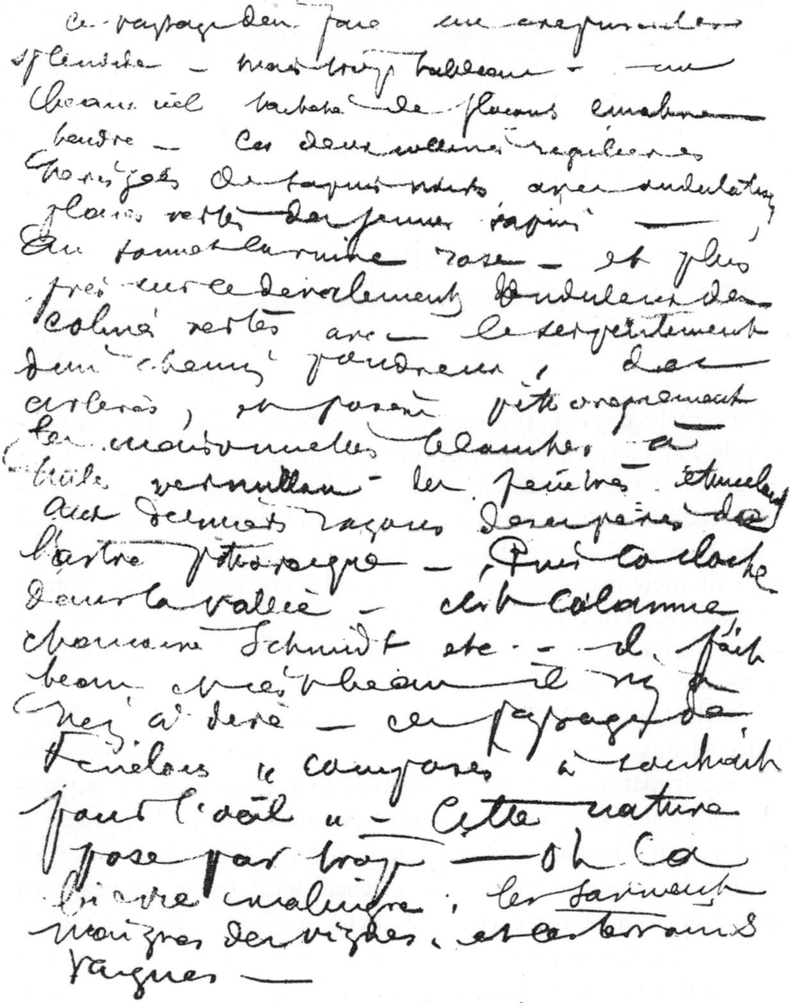

'CE PAYSAGE D'EN FACE'

III

Presences and Absences

In the early days of the recent occupation, the German censorship in Paris agreed to permit publication of a volume of fifty-six letters on condition that its title be changed from *Lettres à Gustave Kahn* to *Lettres à un ami*, and that the salutations should read 'Mon cher ami' rather than 'Mon cher Kahn.' After some hesitations of their own, the editor and publishers accepted the minor mutilations. They did well, since otherwise this record of one of the memorable literary associations might have continued inaccessible for some time.

Nearly forty years before, in *Symbolistes et Décadents*, Kahn had told how, one spring day in 1880, at a meeting of the Club des Hydropathes—one of those tentative groupings of writers that preceded the flood tide of Symbolism—he had noticed a young man 'd'aspect un peu clergyman,'[1] somewhat too well dressed for the occasion, who listened with great attention to the unremarkable verse that was being recited. 'His quiet gray eyes lighted up and his cheeks grew pink whenever the poems offered the slightest interest.' Since the author happened to be Kahn, he took note of the appreciative listener, and after the reading of his verse was over, while another Hydropathe was declaring iambically that henceforth he would love only women of stone, he struck up a conversation. He was as much impressed by the scope of Jules Laforgue's knowledge and the delicacy of his feelings as by his artistic fervor. 'He told me that he wanted to devote himself to the history of art, and was further contem-

plating a drama on Savonarola. It was agreed that we should see
each other again; we showed each other our literary baggage, his
consisting of a little lyrical study of Watteau and some quite
impeccable sonnets, sketches of street scenes, children with faded
blouses, and the main points of a serious cosmogony.'

The two young men were almost of an age, and their aims
and inclinations were similar enough. During the spring and
summer they took long walks in the ugly industrial outskirts of
Paris, under the influence of the naturalistic novels of the time.
Laforgue 'always carried a book, some miserable art treatise by
Taine, or a philosophical tome.' His sonnets were, according to
Kahn, pale Buddhistic protestations, and he took the credit for
introducing his new friend to the poetry of Corbière. Unfortunately, Kahn managed to suggest in later years that Laforgue
owed more to his hints and suggestions, than was actually the
case. Yet he admitted that he counted among his best memories
'those summer afternoons of 1880.' And, he said, 'This young
sage's mind, astonishingly receptive, extremely fine in its capacity
to grasp relationships, analogies, interested me immensely.'

Conversations were cut short. In the fall Kahn was drafted and
went off to North Africa for four years of military service, something from which Laforgue's fragile health exempted him. Jules
still went to the café where they had sat together, and in mid-
December he wrote the first of his letters to his friend, letters
valuable for the light they shed on several months of his life
about which nothing had been known.

Laforgue complains about Sundays in the crowded, family-
ridden apartment in the rue Berthollet. He mentions the Pont
Saint-Michel of a Saturday evening, 'with the tumult of the
bells of Notre-Dame in the two sonorous towers; the noise of the
Boul' Mich' drowns out the voices of the bells—and how philosophical that is. It symbolizes the end of Christianity. This has
killed that. This = the tramway horns; that = the voices of the
melancholy bells.' [2] Here is the subject of a prose poem that he
had just finished, 'Les Fiancés de Noël': 'Christmas! Christmas
in Paris! Sad and cold the wind blows, and the bells intone
toward the black and rainy sky; but the incessant coming and
going of pedestrians in the mud of the sidewalks, the eternal

lumbering of ponderous omnibuses and broken-down cabs, the din of cafés and restaurants, the cries of the merchants of *Bel' Valence!*—the whole inferno of the boulevard drowns the voice of the lonely bells.' [3]

It was apparently a few months earlier that 'this' had killed 'that' for Jules Laforgue, the din of the Boulevard drowning the voices of the bells, the spirit of the age crushing orthodox belief. In March 1882, he was to look back from Germany on what he called his 'religious neurosis.' 'For two years now I have believed in nothing. I am a mystic pessimist. For five months I played at being an ascetic, a little Buddha with two eggs and one glass of water a day and five hours in the libraries. I yearned to go and weep on the Holy Sepulchre. Now, a dilettante, omniscient, I would be happy to smoke a cigarette on Golgotha and there contemplate a sunset of unusual hues.' [4] Allowing for the fact that Laforgue is not writing to Kahn here but to a poetess with pretensions, Madame Mullezer, it seems clear nonetheless that his religious faith was shaken conclusively in his twentieth year. He is able to write in this way about religion because he knows very well what is at stake, because he has experienced rather deep religious emotion. Belief precedes blasphemy.

It was probably about the Christmas of 1880 that he wrote the following:

Noël Sceptique

Noël! Noël? J'entends les cloches dans la nuit . . .
Et j'ai, sur ces feuillets sans foi, posé ma plume:
O souvenirs, chantez! tout mon orgueil s'enfuit,
Et je me sens repris de ma grande amertume.

Ah! des voix dans la nuit chantant Noël! Noël!
M'apportent de la nef qui, là-bas, s'illumine,
Un si tendre, un si doux reproche maternel
Que mon coeur trop gonflé crève dans ma poitrine. . .

Noël! Noël? I hear the church bells in the night . . .
And on this faithless print lay down my pen:
O memories, carol! all of my pride takes flight
And I am plunged in bitterness again.

Ah! Voices in the night singing Noël! Noël!
Bringing me from the lighted church nave yonder
A motherly reproof so mild and gentle
My overburdened heart can bear no more. . .

Early in 1881, in the rue Berthollet, Laforgue wrote the 'Complainte de la vigie aux minuits polaires':

>Le Globe, vers l'aimant,
>Chemine exactement,
>Teinté de mers si bleues
>De cités tout en toits,
>De réseaux de convois
>Qui grignotent des lieues.
>
>O ma côte en sanglots!
>Pas loin de Saint-Malo,
>Un bourg fumeux vivote,
>Qui tient sous son clocher,
>Où grince un coq perché,
>L'Ex-voto d'un pilote!
>
>The globe toward the magnet
>Its steady course has set,
>Tinted with seas so blue,
>With cities all of roofs,
>With networks of convoys
>That nibble up the miles.
>
>O my coast in sorrow!
>Not far from Saint-Malo
>A smoky hamlet struggles,
>Having beneath its steeple
>Crowned by a creaking cock
>A pilot's votive gift.

The votive offering is nothing less than a young Madonna holding up a ruby-colored heart,

Qui, du soir à l'aurore,
Et de l'aurore au soir,
Se meurt, de ne pouvoir
Saigner, ah! saigner plus encore!

Which, from dark till day
And dawn till dark again
Languishes because it cannot
Bleed, ah, bleed its secret life away.

By the spring of 1881, Charles Laforgue was beginning to suffer from shattering coughing fits alternating with periods of exhaustion. Like the poor and harassed man he had always been, he tried to treat himself out of medical books. Then he made a wiser decision, decided to leave the capital that had brought him nothing but bereavement and disappointment, to take all his children except the two eldest back to Tarbes and the chilly but secure house of Pascal Darré. Emile was off doing his military service. Jules could be left behind because he was working, as he had been since late in 1880, as assistant to Charles Ephrussi, one of the editors of the *Gazette des Beaux-Arts*. Marie stayed on with Jules in the rue Berthollet until August, but after her brother's birthday she, too, left for Tarbes, and one evening Jules made his way out of the Gare d'Orléans feeling for the first time like Lucien de Rubempré, the provincial left to his own devices in Paris.

From August till November he lived in a furnished room at 21 rue Monsieur-le-Prince, near where that none too fashionable street slants up to meet the Boulevard Saint-Michel. Baudelairian dandy that he was, Jules had no good to say of that 'sad and banal room where nothing belongs to me, where so many others have passed before me.' His uneasiness among the unfriendly furnishings of his room reminds us of the feelings of another young poet, Rainer Maria Rilke, who was to endure the mute hostility of Paris lodgings a few years later. The first night after his sister's departure, Jules could not bring himself to stay in the hotel at all, but ran off to a friend's room, where he spent the night bundled up in a chair. And almost every day for weeks he found his

way back through the Latin Quarter to the rue Berthollet to pick
up forgotten books (one volume he abandoned definitely, to the
concierge's son: a cram-book for the baccalaureate).

In the mornings he worked for Ephrussi, mostly on details of
that art historian's formidable volume on Albrecht Dürer. A native of Odessa emigrated to Paris, Charles Ephrussi took up the
Impressionist cause early, encouraging the new painters in the
Gazette and, *mirabile dictu*, buying their canvasses. After an in-
considerate curator drove Jules out of the Louvre he worked
regularly in Ephrussi's room. Raising his eyes he could see on the
wall 'two Pissarro fans, built up solidly with little patient touches
. . . Sisleys—the Seine with telephone poles and springtime sky,
or a river bank in the neighborhood of Paris, with a
tramp poetizing in the pathways. . . And the apple trees in
blossom climbing a hill, by Monet. . . And Renoir's shock-
headed wild creature and Berthe Morisot's deep, cool forest shade
with a woman seated, her child, a black dog, a butterfly net . . .
And the red-lipped Parisienne in a blue jersey, by Renoir again.
And that quite contrary lady with a muff, a lake rose in her
buttonhole, against a background cleverly whipped with snow.
And Mary Cassatt's dancer in yellow, green, light, russet, red
armchairs, bare shoulders. And Degas' nervous dancers, and
Degas' Duranty . . . And Manet's Polichinelle with Banville's
verses!' [5] Thus Laforgue, writing nostalgically from Germany
afterward. The value for an apprentice poet-critic of having
such works before his eyes could hardly be overestimated, especially a poet who was to write better about Pierrot than Banville
did about Polichinelle, who tried in every line of his more mature verse for Impressionist vibrancy, whose aesthetics is a
systematization of Impressionist intuitions, and who was to be
one of the first to bring telephone poles into verse.

Through Ephrussi, Laforgue met most of the Impressionists
personally. Thanks to Ephrussi he became a practicing art critic
for the *Gazette des Beaux-Arts* at a tender age. But one envies
him most of all for 'the good hours spent there, bent forgetfully
over the Contents of *Albert Dürer*, dreaming in the bright room
enlivened by the note of a yellow, oh-so-yellow armchair!' [6]

It has often been said that Jules was poorly paid for these

arduous labors, and pious biographers have woven a legend of poetic poverty around his months in Paris after the departure of his family. But Laforgue makes it abundantly clear that the editor was really very good to him. His salary, to be specific, was two hundred (gold standard) francs a month. Now two hundred francs a month in 1881 was the equivalent of fifty thousand francs at present, or three times the salary of an average librarian at the Bibliothèque Nationale. In 1881 the salary of a second lieutenant was one hundred and ninety francs a month. For a bachelor *non-bachelier* just turning twenty-one, two hundred a month was no mean figure.

The chief evidence for the hardness of Jules' lot at this time is a letter written to Marie in September. It is a delightful letter, telling of his life and habits with a mixture of aesthetic detachment and engaging self-pity: 'Yesterday, Sunday, I was so terribly bored, felt so utterly alone in the midst of these hordes of people, that it became a sort of artistic emotion. In the morning I had a chocolate bar, coffee, and a morsel of bread. Afterward I worked till five o'clock in my tiny room. And then in the evening! Oh, if you could only have seen me! I went for a walk alone, and saw the crowds dressed in their Sunday-best on their way home, taking the streetcars by storm. And—little things that made me feel my solitude all the more strongly—a woman, also dressed up, coming out of a delicatessen with a steaming roast wrapped up in a napkin, a family repast, and so on and on. —You couldn't even guess how I dined! Oh, I managed very well. All I needed was a bakery, a pork-butcher's and a fruit stand. As it happened there were three such places right at hand, just outside my door, in my street. But I didn't want my concierges to see me, and they might have, since they have a way of taking the air on the doorsill; so I went quite a long way, to a bakery where I bought two sous' worth of bread that quickly vanished into the cavernous depths of my pocket. As for the pork-butcher's, that was more difficult. I walked in front of one shop after another without daring to go in. Once I was intimidated because at the counter two young butcheresses with pink and shining cheeks were talking and laughing with one another; should I dare disturb the universe? . . . At another shop I didn't

have the same excuse because at the counter there was only
an elderly butcheress with an old fur neckpiece going bald in
patches. But I hesitated, wondering if a certain substance that I
spied was really galantine. Finally I did go into a shop. . . Then
I purchased at a fruit stand, for the modest sum of ten centimes, a
slice of melon, and went back up to my room. I locked and double
locked the door and munched away, thinking about life, about
you who don't write to me, and so on. When I had finished, not
wishing to leave the melon rind in my room, since that would
have revealed my poverty to the cleaning boy, I took my hat and
cane, donned my gloves, stuffed the rind into my pocket. I went
out, and pretending to be taking a stroll under the arcades of the
Odéon, took advantage of a favorable moment to let fall the
rind. . .' [7]

Like most of Jules' letters to his favorite sister, this one is full
of affection, good counsel, and vivid sketches of things seen and
done. We learn, too, that after disposing of the melon rind he
went up to Charles Henry's for coffee. But as far as his poverty is
concerned, we should have been more convinced if he had not,
in this same letter, told of being measured for a new suit of
English cheviot at a good round price.

Charles Henry, who for several years was to be a closer friend
than Kahn, deserves special mention. By 1881 he had already
served as assistant to Claude Bernard, and long after Laforgue's
death was to become head of the laboratory of experimental psychology at the Sorbonne. Henry's lasting bent was for science,
and he exemplified heroically a spirit of inquiry that Laforgue
shared in some degree. During Laforgue's lifetime, Henry's interests turned in half a dozen different directions, almost anywhere that manuscripts were to be uncovered, truths discovered.
He was the born private scholar, who, though suffering steady
privations, refused to take his university degrees for fear of
wasting his time and adulterating his results. Laforgue was to
spend part of every vacation from Germany with Henry and
his long-suffering amanuensis-mistress in a little cottage near
Chevreuse. While Kahn was away in Africa, Laforgue wrote
more often to the scientist than to the poet.

The early letters to Kahn include a sort of informal chronicle of literary and artistic events in Paris. Many of these have slipped below our horizons. We are not greatly concerned with the stage version of Daudet's *Jack*, even though there are reminiscences of Daudet in Jules' little prose poems, 'Fiancés de Noël'; and the fact that George Sand's correspondence was then appearing in the *Revue des deux mondes* leaves us unmoved. The publication of *Bouvard et Pécuchet* (Flaubert having died the previous May) is of more interest, and so is Laforgue's criticism of Maupassant's 'En Famille,' which had just appeared, as 'une nouvelle à la Mérimée.' [8]

Laforgue's project for his first novel sounds interesting if abortive: 'A charming disciple of Schopenhauer who kills himself on the verge of madness for being unable to bring off the following work: the macabre epic of humanity (history and the nineteenth century) in three grand tableaux corresponding to Hartmann's three stages of Illusion, plus a prologue (humanity of the first days), plus an epilogue (humanity of the last days, when Illusion will be dead, the cities deserted, when man, head shaven, bestrewn with ashes, will await the void), and so on and on. What plans! But life is short.' [9] The epilogue, as well as 'the three stages of Illusion,' is inspired by a book to which Paul Bourget had introduced Laforgue, Eduard von Hartmann's *Philosophy of the Unconscious*. No doubt the prologue would have been equally faithful to that treatise on popular pessimism, widely successful in Germany, translated into French in 1877. Laforgue was reading Hartmann before leaving Paris, a good two years earlier than was once believed.

Jules breaks off one of these early letters to Kahn by saying that he is leaving him for his 'friend H. Heine.' [10] There is a deep-seated relation betwen the work of the great German ironist and the verse that Laforgue was preparing to write. We are now concerned, however, with the verse he was actually writing, his 'volume de philosophiques' as he calls it, for which he reports that he has twenty-five sonnets ready. In February: 'I have 1800 lines of my volume. But I'm beginning to feel disgusted with it at times.' [11] He was to work on his philosophical poems for another two years before his distaste became insurmountable, before he abandoned a work that was not to be published until sixteen years after his death. If much of *Le Sanglot de la terre* is not really new, however, if some of it is mediocre and a portion distinctly bad, it is nevertheless remarkable for its responses to major intellectual developments.

IV

'The World Is My Idea'

Le Sanglot de la terre is appreciably more complex than the other sustained early work, *Stéphane Vassiliew*. It is the poetic record of thoughts acutely felt in the rue Berthollet, in a furnished room at 21 rue Monsieur-le-Prince, in comings and goings along many streets and quais, in the libraries of Paris. If *Stéphane* is a romantic transposition of provincial school days, *Le Sanglot de la terre* tells of a provincial arrived in the capital, a sort of intellectual Lucien de Rubempré pursuing an intense, haphazard self-education.

In words that reproduce rhythmically, almost syllable for syllable, Fénelon's version of Philoctetes' lament on Lemnos, Laforgue tells how the solitude of the Lycée de Tarbes turned into that of the Paris libraries. 'Two years of solitude in the libraries, without love, without friends, in fear of death.' ('I was alone for almost the whole time of the siege of Troy, without love, without friends, in fear of death,' Fénelon had Philoctetes say in the passage which Stéphane Vassiliew read and reread.[1]) Laforgue adds, 'Nights spent in meditation in an atmosphere like that of Mount Sinai.' It may well have been on such a night that he wrote the long and breathless prose fragment that contains, among many other things, the title of his first collection of verse. Apostrophizing a skull, he muses on all that the living man, plaything of universal laws, could not have known: 'What was the meaning of your life, you who knew nothing of the universe, the purpose of the whole, the faraway stars, history, the Law, universal evolution, nothing of the solemn splendors, anguishes, renunciations, prodigies, vertigoes, contemplations, fears, stupors, shudders, bedazzlements of the Unique Being, nothing about the universal misery, eternity, the infinite, nothingness, Life, the immense sorrows, time, space, the death of the suns, you departed knowing nothing of the outcries of the earth (*les sanglots de la terre*), its tragic odyssey, its history, its Gods, you suspected nothing—nothing even about your body, prodigious mechanism.' [2] What is interesting in this passage—besides the title phrase and the conception of the earth as something alive, capable of sobbing— is the reflection of the writer's interests. 'The universal misery,' 'the immense sorrows' are out of the atmospheric pessimism of the time. 'Renunciations,' 'prodigies,' 'bedazzlements of the Unique Being,' and the like suggest the Buddhism and primitive Christianity with which Schopenhauer found his ethical teachings in accord. Another set of words, 'the faraway stars,' 'universal evolution,' 'odyssey of the earth,' 'prodigious mechanism' of the body, is the residue of scientific readings and no doubt also of conversations with the scientist Charles Henry.

There is a fearful earnestness about the poems of *Le Sanglot de la terre*. Their philosophical cast reminds us of Alfred de Vigny's last and best book of poems, *Les Destinées*. But whereas the *Destinées* are sobered and silvery, full of the hard-won reflections of a poet who matured slowly, Laforgue's early verse is incandescent, as the ideas of books and textbooks take fire in a youthful mind. We have already seen that Laforgue could reproduce the rhythms of Pascal's interior debate. Here is 'Pascal's reaction,' man's dread before the enormousness and enormity of space, revitalized in terms of 1880:

> *Dans l'infini criblé d'éternelles splendeurs,*
> *Perdu comme un atome, inconnu, solitaire,*
> *Pour quelques jours comptés, un bloc appelé Terre*
> *Vole avec sa vermine aux vastes profondeurs.*
> —'Médiocrité'

> *Eternité! pardon. Je le vois, notre terre*
> *N'est, dans l'universel hosannah des splendeurs,*
> *Qu'un atome où se joue une farce éphémère.*
> —'Farce éphémère'

In the infinite riddled with eternal splendors,
Lost like an atom, unknown and solitary,
For certain counted days a block called Earth
Veers with its vermin toward the vast frontiers.

Eternity, pardon. I see it now. Our earth
In the general choir of splendors is no more
Than an atom where a passing farce is played.

Or, as Laforgue wrote in a prose note of the period, 'I am the atom in the infinite, the atom in the eternal, the sigh in the tempest, a force equivalent to a breath among the formidably brutal powers of the universal mechanism.' [3]

There are two kinds of influence, as André Gide remarked: that felt by an individual and that undergone by a group. The influence of Schopenhauer in France during the 'seventies and 'eighties was of the second sort. This philosopher's subjective idealism, his belief that investigation of the external world could not lead to truth were readily seconded because they were intimately related to fundamental nineteenth-century attitudes. The Romantics had been nothing if not self-centered, even though a second stage in the work of many a poet—and pessimistic philosopher, too, for that matter—had been a program for social betterment. Along with the scientific faith that knowledge would give power over the physical universe there had co-existed, often in the mind of a single man—Alfred de Vigny, for instance—a despairing awareness that such power had no truth in it, that control over physical forces could not bring contact with reality. Schopenhauer was the most formidable of Western Buddhists; but before he became known in France a number of writers, notably Leconte de Lisle and that physician friend of Mallarmé who called himself Jean Lahor, had proclaimed in Buddhistic terms the illusoriness of phenomena and found in this religion the hopelessness it usually engenders in a European mind. The Buddhists had been preceded by other anti-materialists who were vaguely Christian. Then there had been the mordant analysts of motives, heirs of the nihilistic eighteenth-century moralists. And beneath all, informing all, had been the pensive melancholy of

René, of which Chateaubriand would never have written without examples from beyond the Rhine.

Schopenhauer found refuge in contemplation, in the play of ideas, and in veneration of art. So had a French generation disappointed in more outward hopes by the failure of the mid-century revolution. Several of Taine's and Renan's works are as much monuments to 'pessimism' as Books I, II, and IV of *The World as Will and Idea;* and Book III of that work, 'The Object of Art,' is the major theoretical document in a European movement of art for art's sake.

The ground was well prepared when, in 1870, a liberal journalist and politician, Challemel-Lacour, published the record of his pilgrimage to Frankfurt, home of 'A Contemporary Buddhist in Germany: Arthur Schopenhauer.' [4] Challemel-Lacour knew little about metaphysics and communicated less. But he had visited Schopenhauer at home and at the Hôtel d'Angleterre, where the old philosopher took his meals and berated humanity, and he carried away enough acid to etch a good likeness. This anecdotic article set off the avalanche. A Sorbonne professor named Elme-Marie Caro dazzled his public with an eloquent, empty book on nineteenth-century pessimism. In 1874 appeared a model of lucid exposition, *La Philosophie de Schopenhauer* by Théodule Ribot, a philosopher-psychologist who was later to write significantly on the artistic imagination and the Unconscious. Thereafter came a spate of articles, some of them technical, and though *Die Welt als Wille und Vorstellung* was still untranslated, the key ideas of Schopenhauer were at hand for all to ponder. Here was what the age demanded: a system of thought based on withdrawal from society, on commitment to art, on contemplative zeal and heroism. With compelling force it gripped older men like Renan, younger men like Bourget, and there was no excuse for a still younger man like Laforgue to remain ignorant of it, even though his German was virtually non-existent.

Laforgue never carried Schopenhauer's work about with him, reading and rereading it all, as he did Eduard von Hartmann's *Philosophy of the Unconscious.* Schopenhauer's thought was for him something underlying and overshadowing. For that very reason it is well to look at some of the Schopenhauerian ideas

absorbed into the 'Catéchisme pessimiste,' Laforgue's most complete statement of his aims at the age of about twenty. For these
ideas, close kin to those he took from other sources, became the
felt thoughts of his poetry; while the ideas of Hartmann, studied
later, were the raw material for an aesthetics sometimes hauled
bodily into the verse.

'The world is my idea.' Schopenhauer begins his work with
this concise statement of the Idealist position. Such a view is far
from novel. One is reminded of the position taken by the ex-
pounder of Bishop Berkeley's philosophy to whom Samuel John-
son remarked, 'Pray, sir, do not leave us, for we may perhaps
forget to think of you, and then you will cease to exist.' It was
not from Berkeley, however, that the young Laforgue drew his
conviction that there is no object without a subject, no planet
without a perceiving eye:

> *L'homme, ce fou rêveur d'un piètre mondicule* . . .
>
> Man, mad dreamer of a petty planet . . .

In the most ambitious of his early poems, he addresses the earth
in these terms:

> *C'était un songe, oh! oui, tu n'as jamais été!*
> *Tout est seul! nul témoin! rien ne voit, rien ne pense.* . .
>
> It was a dream, ah! yes, and thou hast never been!
> All is alone! no witness! nothing sees or thinks. . .

If humanity should become extinct, a possibility envisioned
throughout the early poems, the earth would have been night-
mare.

We even find, in the verse of a later period, a poem about Time
and Space as forms of the faculty of knowledge. It has a saving
satirical title, 'Complainte du Temps et de sa commère l'Espace.'
But what other poet of that day (or this) would have presumed
to write about the categories, man's means of knowing about the
world that is his idea, 'fondement de la connaissance'? There is
no mention of causality in this poem. Since Schopenhauer main-

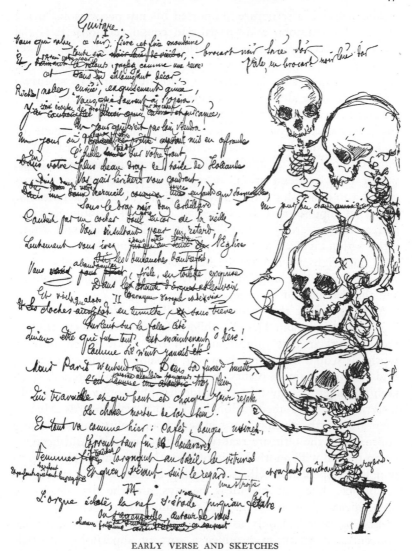

EARLY VERSE AND SKETCHES

tained, in opposition to Kant, that causal relation is as indispensable a condition of the world-idea as Time and Space, this poem is not Schopenhauerian; but no doubt it deserves the epithet of 'Kantian' which André Beaunier applied to it.

The world is a structure supported by my perceptions, made possible by temporal and spatial and causal relations. It is the cause-and-effect relation, the interlocking of events, that makes possible scientific inquiry. Schopenhauer, Hartmann, and their literary disciples such as Laforgue were not hostile to science— these three were all amateur scientists. They did, however, deny that science can deal only with the idea, with appearances. Within and everywhere around, 'objectifying' itself in phenomena of which the individual is one, is the ultimate reality, the Will. Philosophically, it is the thing-in-itself, the noumenon, with which only contemplation, never the measurement of things sensed, can establish contact. Psychologically, it is the potential of powerful impulses that dominate and dwarf all possible activities of reason, the 'ferocious and libidinous gorilla' which, said Taine, lurks within civilized man. Schopenhauer the moralist, who probably outweighs in importance Schopenhauer the metaphysician, was a writer who commented pithily on the power of the gorilla and the shakiness of its cage.

Men, especially the optimistic, socially minded, forward-looking bourgeois whom Hegel's philosophy flattered, were told to recognize their true condition, each one alone in an illusory world. It would be wrong, however, to suppose that man cannot find footing, attain to reality. Some of those who hastened to attach the label 'pessimism' to this Idealist philosophy were simply materialists, accustomed to looking for material rewards. Men, if they are worth anything, are in search of reality, of something approaching the ultimate reality, the thing-in-itself. And here we begin to deal with another kind of idea, the Platonic archetype, to which, Schopenhauer tells us, the thing-in-itself bears a strong resemblance. The Platonic ideas, he says, are 'the first degree of objectification' of the Will. And the human intelligence, evolved at first by the Will only as a tool for its own purposes, can by concentrated attention produce a sort of superfluity of itself capable of regarding the archetypal ideas, capable of aesthetic experience. The genius is the man who can lose himself utterly in objective contemplation. The talented artist and the amateur of art are, in different degrees, contemplatives. And the aim for everyone, as Laforgue writes in his Catechism, is serene contemplation, by which one 'escapes from oneself, is freed for an instant from Time, Space, and Numbers, dies to the consciousness of one's individuality, and attains to the great liberty, which is escape from the Illusory.' [5] It may have been arbitrary, as Ribot pointed out in 1874 and as many a critic has done since, for Schopenhauer to place the Platonic ideas first in the series of phenomena proceeding from that 'blind force' which is Will. One must fight down Will in order to contemplate something that is the outgrowth of Will. Nevertheless, this paradox within Schopenhauer's thought was, like his admirable prose style, evidence of the importance he attached to art and it helped to gain him some of his best disciples, Richard Wagner, Friedrich Nietzsche, Laforgue.

Escape from the multiplicity of phenomena by means of artistic experience is rare, however—the privilege of the few. So are those degrees of relative objectivity reached in philosophical and scientific inquiry. There is another route of escape, which Schopenhauer calls 'the most serious, since it relates to the action of men, the matter which concerns everyone directly and can be foreign or indifferent to none.' Moral perfection through suppression of the personal will is reached by several stages; and the individual progresses to the extent that he sees through the network of appearances. The just man has so far penetrated the Web of Maya as to perceive that he should not interfere with the interests of others, individuals like himself. But the truly virtuous man, realizing that all individuation is illusory, that all individuals are lost in the great whole, that one is simultaneously the slayer and the slain, will feel an active sympathy for all his fellows, victims of the same human limitations. So grievous is the state of man that love can only take the form of pity. 'The incentive to virtuous action is simply the *knowledge* of the suffering of others, directly understood from one's own suffering and placed on a level with it. . . Pure love (ἀγάπη, *caritas*) is by nature sympathy.' [6] As Laforgue writes in his Catechism, 'Sympathy, the first gift of the sage.' To the extent that the individual sees clearly, he will seek to share the sufferings of others, to mortify the will within himself. So the twenty year old poet sets down his rule: 'one must suffer for at least two years: fast, mortify oneself, bleed with pity and universal love, visit the hospitals, contemplate hideous and pitiful diseases, all forms of filthiness, become steeped in history in general and in detail, telling oneself that that is real, that all these billions of individuals had hearts, senses, aspirations to happiness; one must read history with *sympathy* . . . like Carlyle and Michelet.[7]

Remembering his 'two years in the libraries' [8] and his asceticism, we realize that Laforgue actually tried the more radical kinds of renunciation. We are in a better position to understand such passages as the following:

> *Je n'ai fait que souffrir, pour toute la nature,*
> *Pour les êtres, le vent, les fleurs, le firmament,*
> *Souffrir par tous mes nerfs, minutieusement,*
> *Souffrir de n'avoir pas d'âme encore assez pure.*
> —'Pour le Livre d'amour'

> I have done naught but suffer, for all nature,
> For the creatures, the wind, the flowers, the firmament,
> Suffer in bone and nerve and every fiber,
> Suffer for my soul's impediment.

When, in 'Pour la Mort de la terre,' the poet asks,

> *Où donc est Çakia, coeur chaste et trop sublime,*
> *Qui saigna pour tout être et dit la bonne Loi?*
> *Et Jésus triste et doux qui douta de la Foi*
> *Dont il avait vécu, dont il mourait victime?*

> Where now is Sakya, chaste heart that aimed too high,
> Who bled for all and spoke the saving Word?
> And melancholy Jesus who mistrusted
> The faith he lived and by which He would die?

We realize that the figure of Philoctetes, subject of early preoccupations with the discipline of suffering, is for the time being supplanted by other figures. Chief among these, for Laforgue as for Schopenhauer, is the Buddha, although Jesus is counted among the very great and good.

Of course Laforgue was not a Schopenhauerian only because of the metaphysics which demonstrates so beautifully that unseen things are real and that the vision of truth must be prepared by mortification. For him as for several generations of writers, Schopenhauer was the educator, the disquieter, whose sayings contained the cure for naïveté. Like the Swiss diarist Amiel, whose searching self-examinations were published when Laforgue was twenty-two, he began with Schopenhauer the aphorist; and since he did not remain a thoroughgoing philosophical pessimist for long, he may be said to have ended with the aphoristic Schopenhauer as well. Trenchant sayings in the minor works, some of them encountered second-hand, were assimilated and helped to shape a point of view. Woman as the 'undersized, narrow-shouldered, broad-hipped, short-legged' adversary, to quote the celebrated passage from the *Parerga*—a creature without metaphysical aspiration or capacity for objectivity, embodiment of perverse will seeking to perpetuate itself by the 'universal dupery'—woman thus understood comprises half the cast of characters in Laforgue's writings. True, such a view of womankind is in his case an ironic device rather than a heartfelt conviction. But from Pierrot to Lohengrin to Hamlet, his characters act on Schopenhauer's suggestion that chastity is the only solution and resolutely steer clear of further objectification. The refrain 'Célibat, célibat, tout n'est que célibat,' which runs like a pure silver thread through the verse and prose, is not so much a statement of fact as a program.

The poet may have learned something about irony from the philosopher, especially from the preface to the long-delayed second edition of *Die Welt als Wille und Vorstellung*, where Schopenhauer advises the Hegelians to continue their twenty-five-year conspiracy of silence indefinitely. Key words, including the all-important 'ennui,' have about the same meaning in the two writers. And the whole legend of Schopenhauer the man worked strongly on a youthful imagination. One of the two literary pilgrimages Laforgue made was to Frankfurt (the other being to Elsinore), at some inconvenience to himself and in spite of the Empress Augusta's outspoken aversion for 'that horrid man.'

Still another kind of idea, in addition to the world-idea and the

Platonic archetype, was to occupy Laforgue's imagination. He was to spend more and more time with Hartmann's *Philosophy of the Unconscious,* was to hold with this dissident Schopenhauerian that a Will which goes on objectifying itself cannot be purposeless, that present and co-ordinate with Will in the Absolute must be Idea: the creative Idea of Hegel working through history, through the manifold activities of the human mind, toward its own perfection. A systematic pessimist proceeding from the assumption that the ultimate reality is evil—that Laforgue emphatically was not. A temperamental pessimist like Leopardi,[9] able to abide the view of the darkness at the end of a philosophy of negation [10]—that he was not either. 'Un coeur tendre qui hait le néant vaste et noir,' he rebelled in various ways against such views of man's destination. Fertile in contrasts as he was, reacting to the thought of a century, he was even tinged with the religion of science, the positivism that Schopenhauer considered most pernicious. He neutralized a pessimistic world view, as did Vigny in 'La Bouteille à la mer,' by affirming that the individual's unlucky voyage leads somewhere: the observations one man makes will enable others to avoid his shipwreck. Laforgue writes of 'the cathedral of Herbert Spencer,' brings the evolutionary theory into his aesthetics. And from another positivist, Camille Flammarion, he seems to have taken the imagery of his longest early poem and the most striking imagery of *Le Sanglot de la terre* as a whole.

'If the innumerable creative floods,' wrote Lucretius in a passage quoted by Flammarion in his *Pluralité des mondes habités,* 'surge and flow in myriad varied forms through infinite space, should they have brought forth in their fecund strife only the orb of the earth and its celestial vault? Can we believe that beyond this world so vast a mass of elements is condemned to idle repose? . . . If the generative principles gave birth to masses whence have issued the heavens, the waves, the earth and its inhabitants, it must be supposed that in the remainder of the void the elements of matter have given birth to numberless animated beings, to skies, seas, earths, have sowed feet in the aerial floods. Wherever immense matter can find a space to contain it and no obstacle to its free expansion, it will give birth to life in various forms; and if the mass of elements is such that all ages and all beings together would be insufficient even to count them, and if nature has endowed these elements with the faculties which it has accorded to the generative principles of our globe, the elements, in the other regions of space, must have scattered other beings, mortals, and worlds.' [11]

It would be hard to prove that Laforgue read the curious monument to pseudo-scientific legend in which these sonorous words are quoted. But it is more than likely that he did. The poet of our time who has the most in common with Laforgue, Jules Supervielle, gives much of the credit for his first important volume of verse to a popular treatise on astronomy that he picked up in the early 'twenties. It had a liberating effect on his imagination, supplying him with striking dynamic imagery. Some work had such an effect on Laforgue, and it is a plausible guess that it was Flammarion's.

Published in 1862, *La Pluralité des mondes habités* was the first book of an astronomer with a flair for popularization and conjecture. In the preface to one of the numerous editions (twenty-five by 1876), the author expresses surprise, probably justified, at his success. Twenty years before, nothing astronomical would have been very popular. As the century progressed, however, the general imagination was stirred more and more by expanding knowledge of the heavens, and within a decade after its publication Flammarion's book had appeared in ten languages. There was literally a world-wide surge of curiosity about what the heavens might contain. On the part of one young poet there was certainty:

> *En tous sens, je le sais, sur ces mondes lointains,*
> *Pèlerins comme nous des pâles solitudes,*
> *Dans la douceur des nuits tendant vers nous les mains,*
> *Des Humanités soeurs rêvent par multitudes!*
> —'L'Impossible'

> *Songez! depuis des flots sans fin d'éternités,*
> *Cet azur qui toujours en tous les sens recule,*
> *De troupeaux de soleils à tout jamais pullule,*
> *Chacun d'eux conduisant des mondes habités. . .*
> —'Farce éphémère'

Un coin! et tout là-bas déroulement d'espaces
A l'infini! Peuples de frères plus heureux!
Qui ne retrouveront pas même, un jour, nos traces
Quand ils voyageront à leur tour par ces lieux!
                                    —'Curiosités déplacées'

On every side, I know, on those far worlds,
Pilgrims like us of the pale solitudes,
In the softness of the nights stretching toward us
            their hands,
Sister peoples dream in multitudes!

Consider, for unmeasured floods of time
This azure surging forth on every side
Has swarmed with troops of suns incessantly,
Each one among them with its peopled worlds.

This little world! And those deploying spaces
Ad infinitum! Races of happier brothers
Who one day will not even know we were,
When their path crosses where we crossed before.

The Vedas taught that the human soul sojourns in the stars
after its earthly incarnation. Xenophanes and Epicurus believed
in the plurality of worlds, and Christiaan Huygens wrote in
Cosmotheoros: 'It is not possible that those who are of the
opinion of Copernicus and believe truly that the earth we inhabit
is one of those that turn about the sun and receive light from it,
should not also believe that other planets are inhabited, cultivated
and adorned like ours.' [12] Kant not only had assumed that other
planets were inhabited but had also established a whole hierarchy
of the perfection of their inhabitants according to distance from
the sun. [13] Laforgue's first collection of verse provides us with
the only modern poetry on the subject.

Whether under the influence of the summary of evolutionary
doctrine that Flammarion undertakes in another place, or as a
result of readings in Spencer and Darwin, Laforgue also gives
poetic expression to what has frequently been called 'the key
idea of the nineteenth century.' A planet

après bien des siècles de jours lents,
Aux baisers du soleil sent tressaillir ses flancs.

La vie éclot au fond des mers des premiers âges,
Monades, vibrions, polypiers, coquillages.

Puis les vastes poissons, reptiles, crustacés
Râclant les pins géants de leurs dos cuirassés.

Puis la plainte des bois, la nuit, sous les rafales,
Les fauves, les oiseaux, le cri-cri des cigales.

Enfin paraît un jour, grêle, blême d'effroi,
L'homme au front vers l'azur, le grand maudit, le roi. . .
—'Litanies de misère'

after many ages of slow days,
Feels its flanks shudder at the sun's embrace.

Life spawns within the prehistoric sea,
Monads, vibriones, polyps, crustacea.

Then the vast fishes, reptiles, things with scales
Scrape giant pine trees with their armored tails.

And then the plaint of forests tempest-stirred,
Wild beasts and birds and the cicadas' chirr.

Until one day, frail and beset with fears,
Man the accursed, the struggling king appears.

In the same poem there is description of the birth of the planets, inorganic evolution:

Un lac incandescent tombe et puis s'éparpille
En vingt blocs qu'il entraîne ainsi qu'une famille.

An incandescent lake falls and is scattered
In twenty masses it leads family-like.

Another poem has an apostrophe to the mother-nebula:

O fleuve chaotique, ô Nébuleuse-mère,
Dont sortit le Soleil, notre père puissant . . .
        —'Crépuscule de dimanche d'été'

Chaotic river, mother-nebula
Whence sprang the sun, our puissant father . . .

In fact, imagery drawn from pseudo-scientific and scientific sources is in great part responsible for the quality of Laforgue's strange, troubled, technically fluent early poetry. Sully-Prudhomme was also writing melancholy 'scientific' verse during the last quarter of the century. But Sully-Prudhomme sadly lacked capacity for creating metaphors. Only Laforgue, in France, succeeded in making poetry out of objects revealed by 'the marvelous tube.'

His best sustained poem of this period is 'Pour la Mort de la terre.' The extinction of life upon the earth, or the extinction of the living earth, was much in his mind at this time. Perhaps the big work on Dürer [14] with which he was helping Ephrussi kept scenes of death and apocalypse before his eyes; or perhaps the palpitations of the heart he complained of late in 1880. 'Pour la Mort de la terre' is his nearest approach to the 'macabre epic of humanity' projected in his letter to Kahn. The opening quatrain is addressed to the suns:

O convoi solennel des soleils magnifiques,
Nouez et dénouez vos vastes masses d'or,
Doucement, tristement, sur de graves musiques,
Menez le deuil très lent de votre soeur qui dort.

O solemn progress of resplendent suns,
Wind and unwind your massive golden trails,
Mildly and sadly to religious hymns,
Conduct the mourning of your sister gone.

In eight stanzas of eight lines each the stages of the world's history are evoked. Six stanzas end:

Non, dors, c'est bien fini, dors pour l'éternité.

The line

> *O convoi solennel des soleils magnifiques*

returns between stanzas as a refrain. The poet foresees a time when the earth will be 'une épave énorme et solitaire . . . un bloc inerte et tragique,' quite different from what it was toward the other end of its history, when there were only:

> . . . *les pantoums du vent, la clameur des flots sourds,*
> *Et les bruissements argentins des feuillages.*

> . . . the wind's pantoums, the stubborn waves' complaint,
> And the silvery murmurs of the foliage.

However, the intruder appeared:

> *Mais l'être impur paraît! ce frêle révolté*
> *De la sainte Maïa déchire les beaux voiles*
> *Et le sanglot des temps jaillit vers les étoiles. . .*

> But the infirm creature appears, the feeble rebel
> Snatching away the veils of holy Maya.
> The dirge of ages rises toward the stars.

The Middle Ages are evoked in Romantic terms. The fifth stanza is a series of exclamations, a list of things to be lost with earth—invention, music, arts and science—and although the formal interest is slight, the twentieth-century reader thinks of another vision of the eclipse of culture, Paul Valéry's, in 'A Thousand Despairing Hamlets.' After the musings on Buddha and Jesus already quoted, the poem reaches its highest degree of concreteness in the penultimate stanza:

> *Et plus rien! ô Vénus de marbre! eaux-fortes vaines!*
> *Cerveau fou de Hegel! doux refrains consolants!*
> *Clochers brodés à jour et consumés d'élans.*
> *Livres où l'homme mit d'inutiles victoires!*
> *Tout ce qu'a la fureur de tes fils enfanté,*

Tout ce qui fut ta fange et ta splendeur si brève,
O Terre, est maintenant comme un rêve, un grand rêve. . .

Then nothing more! O marble Venus! vain designs!
Mad brain of Hegel! Mild consoling songs!
Lace-light steeples spent with man's aspirings.
Books wherein man his futile gains inscribed!
All that the fury of your sons engendered,
All of your mire and momentary splendor,
O earth, is now like a dream, a great dream.

This is oratorical verse, eloquence of a kind whose neck Laforgue
would be at pains to wring a little later on. But as the poem ends
slipping into the Schopenhauerian dark, 'sans nom dans le noir
sans mémoire,' we cannot fail to admire the poet for the amount
of intellectual history he has compressed into a poem and a collection.

V

The Great Dream

A SURE instinct led Laforgue to introduce himself to Paul Bourget. The elder by eight years, Bourget had by 1880 published only two books, both of them verse: *La Vie inquiète*—clear accounts of feelings rather than lyrics; and *Edel*—a novel in spite of its fluid alexandrines, and for that reason the better of the two. During Laforgue's lifetime, Bourget was to publish more verse, tales, a sound unambitious novel, and the fine *Essais de psychologie contemporaine*. A sharp distinction must be drawn between 'l'aîné des jeunes,' as young Bourget was called by his younger admirers, and the later author of increasingly desiccated novels. Bourget's natural clarity had not yet degenerated into dry demonstration. Even his verse is far from negligible—slight, but with a crystalline quality refreshing after the turbid effusions of a naturalist such as Jean Richepin.

Laforgue called Bourget 'Lord Buddha,' partly because his language was already tinged with irony in his twentieth year, but mostly because he respected the older man immensely. He owed Bourget an ideal of literary elegance and personal dandyism, encouragement to study English, and the realization that his own poetry left something to be desired.

'I remember the time,' Jules wrote to Emile from Germany several years later, 'when I used to take Bourget plays, chapters of novels, and whole heaps of verses, thinking to myself surely this time he'd be bowled over. And the next Sunday he would say, "You have learned neither the French language nor the poet's craft, and you are still incapable of thinking for yourself." When I read over such of those old things as are still around I feel unmistakably how right he was and I congratulate myself on my stay here in so far as this remoteness from Paris has kept me from publishing nonsense that would have made me fret and fume the rest of my days.' [1]

Probably not much of the 'heaps of verses' survives in *Le Sanglot de la terre*, on which Laforgue worked till late in 1882 before giving it up in disgust. We have no record of what Bourget thought of this collection, but it is safe to assume that he liked it little better than he had the earlier apprentice work. To write, in the year of 1880, about the birth and death of the planet must certainly have struck him as amusing. The grave, high-sounding, fateful words, the kind of words that occur to lonely young men in libraries, would have made him reflect, as such diction made his friend Henry James reflect, on how much more difficult it is to write by oneself than as a member of a literary group. And in a way Bourget would have been right: the ordinary poetic moods do not come off in *Le Sanglot de la terre;* only the extraordinary ones do. Along with plain unmetaphorical platitudes in the vein of Sully-Prudhomme there are reminiscences not only of the writer's poetic grandfathers and great-grandfathers (fit subjects for imitation, according to Mr. Eliot [2]) but of his literary sires as well. The impact of 'Eclair de gouffre' would be greater if it were not so patently Hugoesque:

> *J'étais sur une tour au milieu des étoiles.*

> *Soudain, coup de vertige! un éclair où, sans voiles,*
> *Je sondais, grelottant d'effarement, de peur,*
> *L'énigme du Cosmos dans toute sa stupeur! . . .*

> I was on a tower with the stars around.

> Suddenly, dizziness! an unveiling flash
> In which I penetrated, shuddering,
> The enigma of the cosmos in its vastness.

'Spleen des nuits de juillet' lets off sexual steam in the manner of Jean Richepin. There are infantile stammerings straight out of

Verlaine and series of disjointed substantives that can be described only as Rimbaldian. Naturally the influence of Baudelaire is pervasive. And these reminiscences are not always decently distributed in separate poems, but occur one after another on the same page. Thus, the Rimbaud-Baudelaire-Verlaine sequence, in 'Sieste éternelle' [3]:

Le blanc soleil de juin amollit les trottoirs.
Sur mon lit, seul, prostré comme en ma sépulture
(Close de rideaux blancs, oeuvre d'une main pure),
Je râle doucement aux extases des soirs.

Un relent énervant expire d'un mouchoir
Et promène sur mes lèvres sa chevelure
Et, comme un piano voisin rêve en mesure,
Je tournoie au concert rythmé des encensoirs.

Tout est un songe. Oh! viens, corps soyeux que j'adore,
Fondons-nous, et sans but, plus oublieux encore;
Et tiédis longuement ainsi mes yeux fermés.

Depuis l'éternité, croyez-le bien, Madame,
L'Archet qui sur nos nerfs pince ces tristes gammes
Appelait pour ce jour nos atomes charmés.

The white June sun disintegrates the streets.
Upon my bed, alone, prostrate as in my tomb
(Closed with white curtains, work of a pure hand),
I gently gasp at evening's ecstasies.

A weakening breath stirs from a handkerchief
And touches to my very lips her hair.
A neighboring piano dreams in measure.
I whirl with the censers' rhythmic arc.

All is a dream. Come, cherished silken body,
Let us love, aimlessly, ever more forgetful,
And for a long time warm my closed eyes, so.

From the beginning, mark it well, Madame,
The bow that scrapes sad tunes upon our nerves
Ordered for this day our enchanted atoms.

The line 'comme un piano voisin qui rêve en mesure' gives no
hint of subsequent Laforguian pianos, just as another poem,
'Crépuscule de dimanche d'été,' offers small reason to suppose
that this poet will capture the bleakness of Sunday afternoons for
several generations of readers.

In 'Rosace en vitrail' we have some color symbolism, far from
original. The white in the stained-glass window stands for childhood, purity, simplicity. 'Bleus francs, verts des juillets, écarlates
superbes' are interesting only in view of what will happen to them
later; and it is noteworthy that this, a line of poetry, is commonplace, whereas the 'violet assez grand-deuil' of the early prose
fragment is not.

Le Sanglot de la terre is important, then, for its exposition, in
conventional verse of excellent texture, of ideas unusual in modern poetry. They are ideas such as might arise in the mind of an
intellectually curious young man of 1880, one without much
experience of the ordinary emotions that furnish the material for
most poetry, who, venturing into such realms, is likely to emerge
with hard-won commonplaces. Occasionally he will produce a
simple poem of great beauty, such as 'Noël sceptique,' which
succeeds where many have failed, since the poem of single impulse
seldom achieves such concentration and when it does gives only
a one-sided rendering of a mood. The best poems of *Le Sanglot
de la terre* are either like 'Noël sceptique,' touching but oversim-
plified, or like 'Pour la Mort de la terre,' philosophic efforts whose
interest derives mainly from the subject matter. They would not
have made a poet's reputation, and we can understand Laforgue's
frame of mind when he wrote to Ephrussi one day from Germany: 'I have become aware that my volume of verse is a ragbag
of worn-out trash, and I am busy doing it over with a kind of
cold fury.' [4]

This salutary spirit of self-criticism was due for the most part
to Bourget, to whom Laforgue was to stand in debt on another
score. The Empress Augusta of Germany, who had literary

pretensions and a cult for things Gallic, had already maintained two French readers at her court.⁵ In 1881 the second of these came into an inheritance and resigned. Bourget and Ephrussi, but chiefly the former, undertook to secure the position for Laforgue. 'I thought of him at once for the post,' the novelist was to recall later. 'He had good manners, a mild and correct way, a bit fragile and secret. I thought that in Germany he would be able to work as he saw fit, sheltered from need.' ⁶

By 20 November Jules knew of his appointment; and on that day came news of his father's death at Tarbes. He had not known how ill his father was. Two months before he had been urging him, through Marie, to see a doctor, to take treatment, adding, 'He's a good father now, even if he did read too much Jean-Jacques Rousseau.' ⁷ Charles Laforgue died, of tuberculosis and misfortune, on a day when his son went to Ephrussi's as usual in the morning, to the library in the afternoon. Whether the father had taken Rousseau's pedagogy too seriously and treated his children with mingled neglect and overseverity is a question that will never be answered. He had sent his eldest sons to school in France, and eventually in Paris, had tried to make Emile a painter and Jules a *bachelier*. Before he died he had taken his remaining children back to the place that was, more than any other, their home. Yet in letters of 20 and 22 November we find Jules asking insistently whether his father had not some 'good word' ⁸ for him before his death; and there seems to have been none. Jean Pérès, the psychologist who knew Jules longer than anyone else outside his family, and wrote about him with a penetration that has never been surpassed, thought that he had his father in mind when he wrote the following to the meter of an old French folk song: *

LE VAISSEAU FANTÔME

Il était un petit navire
Où Ugolin mena ses fils,
Sous prétexte, le vieux vampire!
De les fair' voyager gratis.

* 'Il était un petit navire qui n'avait jamais navigué.'

Au bout de cinq à six semaines,
Les vivres vinrent à manquer,
Il dit: 'Vous mettez pas en peine;
Mes fils n' m'ont jamais dégoûté!'

On tira z'à la courte paille,
Formalité! raffinement!
Car cet homme, il n'avait d'entrailles
Qu' pour en calmer les tiraill'ments.

Et donc, stoïque et légendaire,
Ugolin mangea ses enfants,
Afin d'leur conserver un père . . .
Oh! quand j'y song', mon coeur se fend!

Si cette histoire vous embête,
C'est que vous êtes un sans-coeur!
Ah! j'ai du coeur par d'ssus la tête,
Oh! rien partout que rir's moqueurs!

THE FLYING DUTCHMAN

Once there was a little boat
Ugolino boarded with his sons,
Making believe, the sly old goat,
It was for sailing lessons.

When five or six weeks out of port
Supplies were dwindling sadly,
He said, 'My friends, do not lose heart!
My offspring won't do badly!'

There was a show of drawing straws.
Formality! Too soon belied!
For Ugolino's ravening jaws
Existed to be satisfied.

And so, stoic and mythical,
That honest man his sons devoured—
Ah! at the thought my senses fail—
So their poor father might be spared.

If such a tale wearies you,
You are indeed a hardened sort!
But I have heart enough for two—
Ah, mocking laughter, bitter sport!

If Jules Laforgue confounded in his imagination the long
voyage of his seventh year with the futile course of the Flying
Dutchman, if he saw his father as a sort of Ugolino sacrificing
his offspring while he lived on unencumbered in Montevideo, he
was too charitable to mention it except in the ambiguous medium
of verse. And if his father was harsh, the son understood why:

> *Mon père (un dur par timidité)*
> *Est mort avec un profil sévère. . .*
>
> My father (shyness hardened him)
> Died with a stiff and frowning air. . .

Jules did not go to Tarbes for his father's funeral, explaining
that he had to wait in Paris for instructions from Germany. Instead, he wrote two long letters to Marie, trying to console her
a little with thoughts of the nine thousand francs a year he was
going to earn, living in a palace, waited on by a private servant,
watched over by a court physician. He promises to support two
of his younger brothers, Charles and Adrien. 'If it's just a matter
of making money, I'll do that, you'll see,' [9] he writes bravely, and
one can hardly blame him for bragging a little. Nine thousand
francs was the salary of a Senator or member of the Chambre des
Députés at that time, the equivalent of 1,800,000 francs at present.
On the other hand, Jules confesses himself totally unable to take
stock of the family finances.

For some time Jules had been planning, if he got the position
in Germany, to pay a visit to Tarbes. And now it would seem that
he could have managed to attend his father's funeral, especially
since he did not leave France for another ten days. One suspects
that he was appalled at the thought of facing the kind of task
that he knew to be most foreign to him.

Early on the morning of 29 November he left from the Gare

de l'Est to journey into his 'great dream,' as he called the German adventure in a farewell note to Ephrussi. He departed with his Buddhistic sense of fatality. 'My heart may beat a little faster. But all said and done I let myself go; for I believe that all is written, that everything is marked out in advance. It was written that I should meet you in this life, it was written that I should go to Coblenz; and how I will do in all this has been decided from all eternity.' [10]

He had lunch at the Belgian frontier, dinner at Cologne. At eleven o'clock that night he reached Coblenz. A carriage and coachman, a brisk footman were waiting. In the castle park the paths seemed endless, and gaslights, closely spaced, gleamed on the points of steel helmets. The carriage set Jules down before a flight of steps. A big fellow in a uniform bowed and opened a door. This was his manservant, who had a wife likewise delegated to look after the French reader. The servants moved about lighting a fire and setting out a supper on a silver tray, while Jules noticed that his apartment included an antechamber, a vast high-ceilinged study with two broad windows, a desk with writing materials in readiness, and other furnishings (including a spittoon and a foot-muff). Left alone, Jules warmed himself and sat down to eat sparingly, because, as he confided in a letter to his sister, this kind of dinner seemed so insipid to a stomach that had digested so much *vache enragée*.[11]

'Everything is quiet,' he wrote to Marie on the night of his second day in Germany. 'I ask myself whether it isn't all a dream. I pull my curtains aside and see the long façade of the castle all lighted up, and the solemn sentinels pacing back and forth with rifles over their shoulders.' Then he went into his bedroom, where another fire had been lit, and fell asleep in sheets 'as fine as silk.'

The ceremonious introduction to the Empress had taken place that morning, Jules answering questions simply, satisfactorily. At 8:30 in the evening he had read for the first time to the seventy-year-old monarch, who meanwhile did water colors in the midst of her retinue, two princes leafing through albums, four young princesses embroidering, the first lady-in-waiting keeping a sharp eye on the proceedings. He read, he reported, 'as

in a dream,' was less timid than he had been many times in
Ephrussi's office, and skipped nimbly over a passage in the *Revue
des deux mondes* which alluded vaguely to illicit passion. After
the reading the Empress asked more questions, this time about a
Paris art exhibition, and once more he answered with presence of
mind. Bourget and Ephrussi had judged their man well. He was
off to a good start and dashed back to his apartment to write to
Charles Henry, Ephrussi, and at great length to Marie. He told
Henry and Ephrussi about the principal events and the dazzling
expanses of white staircase. But he told Marie everything, and
finished exultantly: 'Oh, my dear Marie, the worst is over! I'm
saved! I'm going to blossom out in all this opulence. I'm going
to get used to it, loosen up, pamper my stomach, take care of
my appearance, and grind away at my books, my beloved books
—my only ambition after all!' [12]

The next day, 1 December, following the normal court schedule, Augusta and her household left Coblenz for the winter palace
at Berlin. The train traveled all day through mountains densely
bristling with dark fir trees; through idyllic valleys and dis-
couraged-looking market towns, which were, nonetheless, flag-
bedecked for the Empress; through nineteen tunnels—Jules
counted them, riding in the same compartment with the Grand
Master of the court and the Empress' physician, with whom
he had dined at Coblenz, telling about some of the medical books
he had pored over in Paris libraries.

In Berlin Jules moved into quarters even larger than those at
Coblenz, in the Prinzessinnen-Palais, Unter den Linden. He had
only three rooms, but the study was large enough to hold six
tables and much miscellaneous furniture without crowding. Five
windows looked out on the parade ground of the Platz am Zeug-
haus with its leveled canon, on the University and the Museum,
not to mention the tall, muscular soldiery of Wilhelm I and officers with pale monocles thrust in their eyes. And the young
Frenchman who had had his share of provincial frugality and
Parisian parsimony observed with satisfaction that the three
porcelain stoves in his apartment were tended hourly.

By 5 December, when he wrote to both Henry and Ephrussi
again, he was settled in his schedule. Every morning at nine

o'clock three newspapers were delivered to him: *L'Indépendance Belge*, the *Journal des Débats*, and *Figaro*. He marked the 'interesting' articles for reading, and others, 'political bulletins and book reviews,' for summarizing. He also ran through numbers of the *Revue des deux mondes* for articles that the Empress might have missed. Dreary as this occupation must have been, it was not quite fruitless: one day in an old *Revue* he stumbled on an article about Walt Whitman—bad, scolding, but nevertheless an introduction to the American poet that had a far-reaching effect on his verse technique. Ordinarily Jules read to the Empress and a single lady-in-waiting at eleven in the morning in a little room hung with engravings. But sometimes the reading took place in the evening. Then there would be more ceremony and Jules would go half an hour early to be with the Countess Hacke.

From the start this first lady-in-waiting showed a tendency to mother the young reader. Jules was quite ready to return her good will. He never referred to her except as a sort of good angel smoothing his path through the intricacies of court etiquette. 'Oh the good and charming lady, how she takes me under her wing!' [13] he writes to Ephrussi. Countess Hacke may have had another side, revealed to less innocent observers. Auguste Gérard, the first of the Empress' French readers, helped compose a book of memoirs about Berlin in which the first lady-in-waiting is described as follows: 'Countess Adelaide Hacke is a hunchback, and though she lacks the intelligence that ordinarily distinguishes that breed of the human species she has all of its characteristic meanness. Her influence over the Empress, whom she often maltreats, is considerable. She is the Empress' *alter ego*, replacing her on every possible occasion. She likes intrigue, excitement, commotion. Her mild voice has affected intonations. She calls everybody "my dear," assumes madonna-like airs which swear with her features, and secretly, indirectly, she undermines the reputation of this person, speaks ill of that, gives discreetly to understand the shortcomings of Mme X. . . . hints at the weaknesses of M A. . . . spreads her treacherous insinuations right and left. She is evil without suspecting it and injures others not out of malice but by simple prompting of her nature, which, being ugly, cannot tolerate any trace of nobility in her neighbor.' [14]

With this lioness, if such she was, Jules lay down like a lamb, trusting and unexploited except in minor ways. True, Countess Hacke made him correct her French pronunciation for half an hour before the evening readings began, for she spoke French, she admitted, 'comme un cochon.' But Jules took this with good grace and went driving with her past guards who presented arms to the carriage bearing the great lady and Ephrussi's one-time assistant.

Even unfriendly critics found less acid things to say about the Empress Augusta. She was, they said, less intelligent than she wished to appear (an uncommon trait, indeed), insisted 'on playing a part, taking infinite pains to seem highly educated, well read, well informed about everything going on in the world of science and the arts.' She sought to make herself popular, and surrounded herself with 'favorites who were the first to speak evil of their protector.' [15] But there is something distinctly ready-made about these detractions. They could be applied without alteration to so many of the great.

Marie Louise Catherine of Saxe-Weimar, the Empress Augusta, a princess of Russian origin brought up at Weimar in Goethe's circle, prided herself on being as little German as possible. Like some other German sovereigns, she was only distantly interested in her subjects. She spoke French almost without accent and insisted that only French be spoken around her. Like another well-known German of these years, Friedrich Nietzsche, she detested Wagner and doted on *Carmen*. Immensely proud, elaborately artificial in her dress, with disconcerting gray eyes that jarred with her forced smile, affectedly plaintive voice, and languid movements, Augusta seems to have been less deserving of criticism than most rulers and easily the most interesting person in official Berlin. Though she suffered from an improperly treated injury and had great difficulty in standing, she managed to do so on occasion. 'As for the Empress,' Laforgue wrote after having been her reader for two months and a half, 'she is the perfect type of great lady, the kind admired by those who look back longingly to the drawing rooms of the seventeenth and eighteenth centuries.' [16]

No doubt we are prejudiced in Augusta's favor because of the liking she took to Laforgue. Of course, she could hardly have failed to appreciate such a paragon. He was a model cutter-out and summer-up of articles, keeping his eye open for fashion hints that might interest the ladies-in-waiting; he could outline a book by James von Rothschild or choose appropriate passages from Metternich's *Memoirs* and dextrously introduce small doses of poetry. But the Empress' good will was to outlast Jules' early zeal, pursue him during years when he was thoroughly bored and not very conscientious about his duties, right down to the time when he would leave Germany with the fiancée she did not want him to have. Something like the attraction of opposites was at work. Augusta had heroic qualities that Laforgue lacked, and he possessed, or developed during the German years, when he matured very rapidly, a flexibility of mind of which the Empress was quite incapable.

At first the court routine left Laforgue little time to stray from the narrow path of his preparations, his readings, his conversations with Countess Hacke. He finally visited the art gallery because of the Empress' persistent urgings. But he knew very little German—his sentences were formed, he said, with ridiculous slowness at the beginning and unseemly haste toward the end—his conversations with the servants were mainly pantomime, and he was afraid to enter shops even to make small necessary purchases. Meanwhile he was beginning to appreciate the full ugliness of the Berlin scene. The working girls who scurried along beneath his windows had thick ankles and red noses. The palaces, though spacious, were awkward and none too comfortable: we are told, for instance, that there was not a single bathroom to be found anywhere. The corridors were cluttered with clumsy plaster figures and the sitting rooms lacked any suggestion of coziness. There was a cramped greenhouse where china parrots could be swung out creakily over shaggy palm trees. Inside the palace as outside, the women were ill-dressed, poorly groomed. On afternoon walks he missed the wrought ironwork of Paris balconies, and the houses were all one monotonous dull tan color. He did not admire the town hall, despite its celebrated pinkish tower. Unter den Linden had struck him at first as a miniature Boulevard des Italiens, but as he became familiar with it the buildings looked more and more like barracks. His first impression of the River Spree had been 'Quel ruisseau ignoble!' [17] and that did not change.

First and second impressions had been formed and he was in a curious state of outer calm and inner bewilderment when he made the acquaintance of a French journalist stationed in Berlin. Jean-Aubry has quoted at length from the recollections of Théodore Lindenlaub. But certain passages from Lindenlaub's original letter to Jean-Aubry are worth quoting again, for the journalist was something of a literary critic besides being a practiced writer.

Lindenlaub had been in Berlin long enough to know both of the previous French readers, and one day early in December he rang the bell at the Prinzessinnen-Palais expecting the second of these, one Amédée Pigeon, to appear. Instead he was confronted with 'an unfamiliar face, extremely curious, all fine shades of expression . . . an almost childish face, yet so serious, and (now and then) with such aged wrinkles, the Breton eyes, sea-colored, looking beyond or within.' The face was meticulously clean-shaven and its owner was dressed in a tight-fitting black frock coat. Lindenlaub could not imagine what kind of person he had before him. His first thought was that the Empress, with her well-known fondness for Catholics, had taken a little Rhenish priest for her reader. 'No,' he decided, 'not with those eyes!'

Lindenlaub found Laforgue in a semi-somnambulistic state. 'I have never met,' he said, 'a being more completely lost than Laforgue during his first days in Germany, or one filled with a more intense phobia for creatures and for things. . . That impenetrable mask, that calm and level voice, hid an almost morbid state of timidity and uncertainty . . . I wonder by what extraordinary effort of will he managed, from one day to another, to go about his duties, to keep up the appearances of court life, to get dressed, remember his hours of work, make an entrance, utter a greeting, to speak—answer, that is to say—without anyone noticing in the least his palpitating distress.'

It turned out that Lindenlaub knew Bourget and Charles Henry, and at the mention of these familiar names Laforgue said, 'How strange! How remarkable!' but without excitement, as though he knew that some pre-established harmony had ordained this meeting at just this moment. The young men talked for a long time, and Laforgue told Lindenlaub more about his family, his early experience then than he ever did again, apparently driven by a deep need to fasten onto someone from the world he knew.[18]

The journalist ran small practical errands for the newcomer, did chores of the kind that Laforgue seemed helpless to perform for himself. Lindenlaub, as much attracted as Gustave Kahn had been a year and a half before by the combination of qualities, the clerical air, the artistic tastes, the enthusiastic talk about books, called again without delay, bringing two music-student friends with him. These were the Ysaÿe brothers, Eugène, who was to become one of the greatest of violinists, and Théo, a pianist. The Ysaÿes were much sought after by musical Berliners, and before long Jules was accompanying them on social evenings, as did Lindenlaub and another French-speaking attendant at the court, the Empress' Belgian dentist. Taken in by the little band, Laforgue could not complain of being left alone, though he mentioned his loneliness often enough in letters to Paris.

He never became a close friend of Eugène Ysaÿe, the more vigorous and extroverted of the brothers, and Lindenlaub was kept busier by his newspaper than Laforgue by the court. But from the first Jules hit it off with Théo, who was only sixteen and if possible even dreamier and more inexperienced than Laforgue himself. Jules was anything but a solitary worker, in spite of the timidity that biographers have overstressed. As he became more accustomed to his duties and accumulated reading matter for a month and more ahead, he would spend whole days in the pianist's room, reading or making notes to the sound of the practicing. He did not have a deep feeling for music, his imagination being primarily visual, but he found in music liberation, forgetfulness, contact with what he was coming to call the Unconscious. He liked Théo's student room, so comfortable after the stiff ornateness of the palace, and after the courtly exchange of formalities he liked the broken snatches of student talk. Between conversations, while Théo was playing, and at night in the Prinzessinnen-Palais after his tasks were done, he read widely in works that were, as his friends confessed, quite foreign to their understanding. They nicknamed him 'Colline,' after the out-at-elbows philosopher in a book they read together, Henry Murger's *Scènes de la vie de Bohème*. They had no way of knowing that this pale, round-faced comrade with the carefully brushed hair, the forward-tilting head, the dark, formal garb demanded by his position, 'the look beyond or within,' had the widest-ranging mind among writers of his time, a mind quite independent of his still childish feelings, one that delighted in going out to meet philosophers on their own ground. It was Laforgue's destiny, typical of the intellectual, that his reflective capacities matured more rapidly than his artistic talent. His novel, *Un Raté*, which he rose at five every morning to write—in spite of the motherly cautionings of Countess Hacke—has disappeared and is probably no great loss. But almost all his notes toward an aesthetics, jottings inspired by his readings in the history of ideas, are of interest, so meaningful and fruitful was his dissatisfaction with the materialistic doctrines he had left behind him in France.

VI

Aesthetic Ideas

'YESTERDAY,' Jules had written from Paris early in 1881, 'Taine (whose course I follow regularly in spite of the Ingres fresco staring down from the wall) was truly astonishing on the subject of Angelico.' [1]

The course was at the Ecole des Beaux-Arts, where Emile was a student and Jules, in 1880-81, an auditor. The lectures were those that Taine was shortly to turn into the completed form of his *Philosophie de l'art*. Laforgue was one of those most deeply influenced by this historian-aesthetician; those who could hear him speak, meanwhile meditating on how old-fashioned, how non-Impressionist, how lifeless in spite of the beautiful drawing, was *Romulus vainqueur d'Acron remporte les dépouilles opimes*, the Ingres fresco on the wall of the hemicycle behind the speaker's stand. Laforgue left a picturesque note, unpublished till now, on one of these lectures: 'Taine's course.—His ridiculous trousers, too short, with a marked bagging at the knees.—Rich in facts. For an hour one is transported to the multifarious Italy of the sixteenth century. I look at the bent skulls of the attentive auditors, on which light falls from above, without nuance, February-pale. These people are chewing marshmallow creams, they have neckerchiefs, rubbers on their feet, flannels, umbrellas. They are listening to the memoirs of Cellini, the lives of the Borgias (see Taine, *Philo. d'A. en Italie*).' [2]

A dialogue with Taine, consisting of expostulation against this point, grudging agreement with that, stirrings of obscure dissent, runs from one end of Laforgue's notebooks to the other. He was

74

one of several to rattle the chains that Taine had forged between the external fact and the work of art. Sainte-Beuve, Gautier, Flaubert, and the Goncourts had all protested against Taine's determinism, his insensitiveness to the spark that makes each work of art unique, distinct from every other product of the same race, environment, and historical moment. So, indirectly, had Bourget, a Tainean in some respects, by the quality of the insight and the extent of the analysis introduced into his critical essays.

Any artist of that time or since would have felt something deeply amiss in Taine's Beaux-Arts lectures, 'astonishing' though they were. Nowhere is the formula of determination by race, milieu, and moment applied quite so mechanically (not even in the *Histoire de la littérature anglaise*) as in the lectures on Italian and Dutch art. Nowhere are the criteria of artistic merit set forth quite so rigidly as in the series of lectures entitled *De l'Idéal dans l'art*. And this last work is in fundamental disaccord with the other Beaux-Arts lectures. It would seem that a thoroughgoing determinist should recognize the authenticity of many kinds of art, products of an indefinite number of combinations of race, environment, and historical moment. Taine, however, imposes a narrowly exclusive, Hellenic ideal, and not the Greek ideal as it was understood by more searching students of antiquity even in his time—the resolution of tragic conflicts, constantly imperiled, continually renewed, but as the 'natural' outgrowth of 'stable and beneficent' qualities: Winckelmann's neoclassic conception of antiquity turned to the taste of a nineteenth-century lecture audience. One of the worst features of this work is its unfairness to Taine himself, who understood his own time, if not antiquity, much better than this would indicate. In *De l'Idéal dans l'art* he is more than once trapped by his own principles, as when he interrupts one of his tirades against realism to say that Rembrandt did not really produce art at all, but a kind of poetry.

Taine is thus reduced to maintaining that Rembrandt was not exactly an artist, and that poetry is not precisely an art, because he began by saying that art is meritorious to the extent that it expresses 'the most elementary, intimate and general characteristics,' which characteristics are also the most 'important,' 'stable,' and, more gratuitously still, the most 'healthy and simple.' There is a whole hierarchy of artistic worth according to the generality, importance, stability, health, and simplicity of traits represented. Pictures in which considerable attention is paid to dress only suggest the fashion plate. Studies of manners, of the effect of an environment, a trade, occupational deformations, are comparatively superficial (this from the author of an epoch-making study of Balzac and one of the chief inspirers of Zola's naturalism). The most universal, stable, important characteristics are those of the nude human figure in its simple health and perfection.

If the first section of *De l'Idéal dans l'art* is arbitrary, the second is even more so. What is universal, stable, and so on, is said to possess 'beneficence' in proportion. Taine has his own definition of this new term. The beneficence of an individual or a society is to be judged by the extent to which it 'prospers, increases its power.' Beneficence begins at home. True, Taine mentions duties to one's neighbor, even says that the highest faculty is that of loving. However, he assumes without explanation that the qualities that enable an individual to be just toward himself are also those that promote social justice. And he sets up another scale of merit parallel to the first. Flatly realistic art—for example, that of Henry Monnier, portrayer of the vapid bourgeois of the 1830's and '40's —shows us only the limited, twisted, and mean creatures of every day. Even the characters of Shakespeare and Balzac are lacking in nobility because they are distorted. The heroic Greek nude is more important, more beneficent. Taine should have stopped here, since there is no place for the saint in a system defining beneficence as his does. But at this point he leaves room to imagine that loftier souls build more stately mansions.

With the full force of his artistic instincts Laforgue rebelled against Taine's serene, stoically moral ideal of art, 'which leads to the classically beautiful, to the Greek nude . . . wherein moral nobility is the consummation of physical perfection, and which is inadequate when confronted by anything not of Greek or Renaissance inspiration' (as Laforgue writes in an unpublished draft of his essay 'L'Art moderne en Allemagne').[3] How can anyone maintain that such an ideal is elementary, universal, in view of the masterpieces of Chinese and Japanese art . . . or a Persian rug?[4] And since he disapproves of Taine's habit of assigning to every work its place on a ladder, he suggests whimsically that the ladder be kicked aside.[5] Having looked long at the Egyptian collections in Berlin, he writes on the spiritual, death-denying qualities of this art, enhanced by stylization by no means universal, as foreign to Taine's materialism as the works of the Christian Middle Ages.

Laforgue launches into enthusiastic appreciation of the least stable form of aesthetic expression, dress. It is, he says, as important to the painter as the mental world is to the psychologist. 'Even in our submerged time, paralyzed by the ready-made,' minute differences in dress distinguish one person from another, reveal character and occupation. Clothing is no less important than that other kind of toilette imposed upon the person, 'the cut of the beard and hair, care of the nails and skin, manners, bearing.' [6] In this defense of artifice, this extension of the very meaning of 'costume,' we feel the influential presence of Baudelaire.

As a champion of the Impressionists, Laforgue attaches much importance to significant bodily deformations as well as to costume. 'Isn't the nude figure of a working girl twisted by her trade, or one of Donatello's frail nudes, just as interesting as Diana Huntress? And aren't the busts of the Caesars [whose modern tormented look, lack of classical equilibrium, Taine had noted], close to us as they are, fully as interesting as the heads of the Niobides?' [7] The caricaturist occupied a lowly rung on Taine's ladder. Laforgue proclaims his devotion to caricaturists in general and to Charles Keene in particular. He liked the 'deep, harsh, compact' sketches of this English designer of Master Punch; and he wrote about Keene's work in a way that helps us to understand Laforgue's own aims. 'The pen is coarse, not a bit elegant or airy. One might take it to be timid and fumbling. But look a little closer and see how supple and knowing it is. . . These geniuses of the inelegant pen, subtle without seeming to be . . . The pen is coarse, it blots, is inept at pretty penmanlike hatchings, at rendering a profile by a single feature . . . yes, it is coarse and it blots, but how it bears down at *just, just* the right place, and with an apparently careless and accidental stroke catches astonishing varieties of expression.' [8] He imagines that Jean-François Raffaelli, a painter of Paris suburbs, must have learned from Keene.

From 1882 till the end of his life, Laforgue was interested in the possibilities of polychrome sculpture, statuary relieved of its monotony, restored to the variegated complexity of Greek times. His chief consolation, returning to Baden-Baden in the fall of 1883, was a polychrome head modeled in wax by Henry Cros. We are not told much about how it looked, 'this wax by Cros that smiles at me in sickly fashion, its back to the lamp.' [9] But he was delighted with it, sickly smile and all, mentioning it gratefully in letters [10] and in his diary.[11] What was more, he tried to stir up enthusiasm for polychrome sculpture, to find buyers for Cros' work. Although he does not seem to have been particularly successful as an agent, such wax figures helped him to formulate his polychrome ideal: 'Just as I prefer to a scene reproduced in an engraving the original with all its vibrancy of tone and atmospheric values, so do I prefer to marble or bronze this bust modeled out of wax, with blue eyes or black, with the hair and necklace and all the rest.' [12] This much is from the *Mélanges posthumes*. In an unpublished continuation of this thought Laforgue goes on to say that if there were only more such polychrome busts Taine and Renan would not be obliged to speak of sculpture 'with such a funereal air.' Men who refer to evolution so often should be more aware of the self-renewing potentialities of art.

As we might suspect, the poet has no patience with any standard of beneficence. Sometimes his opinions are superbly unsupported by argument. 'No, that is simply not the way things are in art. Nero, an anti-social creature, a sort of deadly germ, was right when he said, "Qualis artifex pereo!" ' [13] He does not say why, except that 'art is a matter of being interesting.' [14] In Laforgue's best-known story, Hamlet dies with the same last words of Nero on his lips, and there they are distinctly appropriate because Hamlet is a notorious aesthete. But here, if Laforgue really means to take up the good fight against 'didactic heresy,' moral message in art, we should like to see the steps of the argument. Failing that, we tend to regret just a little the earlier notion of art as a form of moral discipline.

By way of opposition to Taine's view that great art expresses 'stable' characteristics, Laforgue proposes an 'ephemeral' ideal, the term probably being lifted from *De l'Idéal dans l'art*, where

Taine uses it repeatedly. 'Ephemeral creature that I am, the creature of a day interests me more than the perfect hero, just as a human being in everyday garb appeals to me more strongly than a sculptor's nude model. . . A Paris working girl, a young lady in a drawing room, a Burne-Jones head, a Parisian as seen by Nittis, Orpheus' maiden as conceived by Gustave Moreau—these are the figures that touch our hearts, because they are the true sisters of our mortality, with their air of being of our own day, their coiffure, their toilette, their modern look!' [15] In the same way Baudelaire had insisted on the artist's obligation to show us 'how great and poetic we are in our neckties and patent-leather shoes'—had urged the artist to draw from the humblest details of the contemporary scene a sense of the heroism of modern life. Laforgue is demonstrating here his sympathy for the very great aestheticians, those who do not tie the protesting body of art to a Procrustean bed of preconceptions, but who win their way from the work of art toward the values it reluctantly reveals. We remember how the Reverend James Bowyer urged the young Coleridge to write not about the Pierian Spring but about the cloister pump; and how faithfully Coleridge's criticism teaches that poetry must assimilate the familiar, the near-at-hand. Laforgue's terms for the near-at-hand are the 'ephemeral,' the 'quotidian.' He would not have made his clear call for modernity without Baudelaire's example, nor would Joris-Karl Huysmans, although this is not to diminish the importance of either of these 'Decadents.'

Laforgue admired Huysmans sincerely, in spite of the 'heavy-jointed style' ('style aux lourdes attaches') that he was heard to deplore in Berlin [16]; and Huysmans, for his part, considered Laforgue the most gifted among the Symbolists.[17] The poet's second published piece of writing was a brief appreciative review of Huysmans' *En Ménage*, in a German periodical, *Magazin für die Literatur*, and several times we find him urging this novel upon his friends. *En Ménage* is basically a simple tale about two friends, a lymphatic writer who can live neither with nor without his dull wife, and a choleric, brilliant painter. It is not a particularly well-sustained work. But the fifth chapter is of considerable interest because Cyprien, the painter, makes a spirited brief exposition of a working aesthetics of *c.*1880—beliefs, tendencies, prejudices of the artistic as opposed to the Tainean mind—which Laforgue approved wholeheartedly. Cyprien propounds, according to Laforgue in his review, 'artistic theories as valid, in our opinion, as they are remarkable, concerning what is nowadays called "modernity." ' [18]

The tone of a landscape was, according to Cyprien, 'lent by factory chimneys rising above the treetops, spewing flakes of soot into the clouds.' [19] (Laforgue was to call himself 'the poet of factory chimneys.') The painter confesses to exultant bursts of joy when, seated on the talus of the old walls of Paris, his gaze plunges far into the distance, taking in 'the gasometers rearing up into the sky, their dark skeletons shot through with light, like blue-walled amphitheaters borne up by black columns . . .' and all the other beautiful monstrosities of the industrial landscape. Like Dostoevskyan heroes, like Baudelaire and Corbière, he sings the beauties of the morning twilight, the city streets disgorging at dawn the delights that few have eyes to see, certainly not the 'old charlatans who come up with ready-made enthusiasms about ancient basilicas or those chalets of rough-hewn stone they call the marvels of Greek art! May they all go to the devil with their Parthenon, one tied on in front and another behind! Or let them set up shop in front of the Bourse and they'll see another Parthenon, this one a bit livened up though, because someone has had the good sense to put up a big clock in front and plant a few chimneys on top, all of which breaks the harmony of those grand stupid lines.' Cyprien regrets that people seem destined to admire the Venus de' Medici for some time yet. He exclaims, and the words undoubtedly were at the back of Laforgue's mind when he wrote the passage quoted above: 'The Venus that I, for one, admire, the Venus I worship on my knees as the type of modern beauty, is the girl who scampers along the street, the factory girl just as she is in her coat and dress, the milliner with her sallow complexion, her mischievous eyes full of pearly glimmers, the errand girl with her pale little face, her breasts that shake and hips that sway!'

Underlying Cyprien's enthusiasms and condemnations is a sense of communion with those who bear the heat and brunt of creation, those who are not only exiled from society but actively at odds with it. The artist of 1880 is beginning to regard himself as a transvaluer of values. The position implicit in Cyprien's words is explicit in Laforgue's, who speaks of 'poets too feline, too debile to be criminals . . . anarchists, nihilists nourished in the critical school but who have abandoned it and cast themselves out into life . . . the only beings who no longer acknowledge any discipline whether imposed by conscience or by society.' [20]

If we pursue Huysmans' and Laforgue's conceptions of the value of what is novel, if we reflect on the implications of Laforgue's belief that 'every individual is a keyboard played on by the Unconscious,' [21] that what each human being says is important, we may decide that the poet was more Tainean than he acknowledged, that he was only carrying out to its logical conclusion a determinism of race, milieu, and moment and preserving Tainean doctrine from its own negation of itself in *De l'Idéal dans l'art*. He was, moreover, indebted to the philosopher-historian for a critical method into which he lapsed involuntarily, as when he wrote, in a so far uncollected article, of the 'faculté-maîtresse' of the German painter Adolph Menzel.[22] Though he was persuaded that the work of art was neither stable nor beneficent, he judged it as Taine did by the 'convergence of effects'—different effects. Finally, the emphasis placed on the 'nerves,' especially in the notes on Baudelaire, is traceable to *De l'Intelligence*.

One conclusion from the Beaux-Arts lectures is sure: the lecturer emerged from his investigations of Buddhism and Christianity untouched by either. There is no place for spirit in these sweeping condemnations of medieval art, this praise for the healthful works of peoples 'bien portants et contents de vivre.' Taine attached sufficient importance to the unconscious human mind, the slumbering force in each man; he could not have been deeply interested in the kind of Unconscious that came to preoccupy Laforgue more and more during his years in Germany. Jules had been an orthodox Catholic child, a convinced Buddhist in his teens; the anti-religious revulsions of his twenties are those of a religious temperament. The aggressive materialism of the Beaux-Arts lectures must have irritated him quite as much as the pigeonholing. During the winter of 1880-81 he had already begun to read a work that was to satisfy his need for metaphysical explanation without offending his cult for science, and to provide optimistic solutions to pessimistic problems. This remarkably versatile work was called (if we translate its German title into English) *The Philosophy of the Unconscious: Speculative Results according to the Inductive Method of Physical Science.* Written by a one-time German army officer of twenty-seven, Eduard von Hartmann, and published in 1869, it was translated into French eight years later. By December 1880 Laforgue was sufficiently familiar with it to be planning an epic based on the three stages of illusion described in the work.[23] During his first year in Germany he was in the habit of carrying the *Philosophy* with him to Théo Ysaÿe's room, to cafés, everywhere—no small tribute, considering its eleven hundred pages—and had the hero of his unfinished novel, *Un Raté*, dreaming about another nineteenth-century epic.[24] Hartmann's work did much to shape Laforgue's aesthetic ideas, and the Hartmannian Unconscious became a key term in his writings.

Nowadays we are used to understanding by the term 'unconscious' the submerged part of the human mind. Hartmann and Laforgue were incidentally concerned with the unconscious in this sense as well as with the subconscious, the transition zone between unconscious and conscious. *Die Philosophie des Unbewussten* and Laforgue's many references to the Unconscious reflect conjectures made concerning the nature of the human mind ever since Descartes had grounded his long chain of reasoning on ideas somehow and somewhere 'innate,' since Leibniz, upholding the existence of such ideas, had argued that the unconscious mind is formed from a multitude of 'petites perceptions' and had declared that unconscious ideas are the bond uniting each being to the rest of the universe. Kant had devoted part of his *Anthropology* to 'the ideas which we have without being conscious of them,' and had remarked on the paucity of 'the illuminated spots on the great chart of our minds.' Schopenhauer had spoken of the mind's 'unconscious rumination,' and of the consciousness of subordinate nerve centers in the human body. Hartmann was pursuing a line of inquiry already well marked out when he brought bulky evidence to show that the mind is more than rational. His language was metaphorical, to be sure, but the unconscious could not then have been written about in any other terms. His thoughts on the dividedness of so-called individuality are especially interesting. His conception of wit as a 'flash,' something given, attracted the attention of Freud. *The Philosophy of the Unconscious* is a valuable pioneering work in the field of psychology.

Hartmann was chiefly concerned, however, with the unconscious human mind in so far as it gives access to something quite different, an Unconscious—a divine understanding, a primordial being, what philosophers call an Absolute. Kant had not attributed unconsciousness to the Absolute, within which, he said, the distinction between perceiver and perceived is lost. But his follower Fichte had said that the Absolute works its way toward consciousness in the minds of individuals. Hartmann stated what Fichte had implied; he called the Absolute unconscious. And he reverted to Fichte's definition of the Absolute as both Reason and Will in opposition to Schopenhauer's view that it was Will alone.

Hartmann maintained that he was raising up Reason from the 'false and subordinate' position accorded it by Schopenhauer. He was, however, only a little less concerned than the sage of Frankfurt with demonstrating the unreasonableness of volition and the misery of existence. It was this pessimism, this prolongation of Romantic melancholy, that first drew the attention of the late Romantic poet that was Jules Laforgue. Like other Romantic philosophers, Hartmann leans heavily on Christian terminology, and he is as disturbed as any other idealist by the contrast between things seen and unseen. For Hartmann the blessed state—wholeness of the Unconscious as both Will and Reason—is reserved for a time before the Fall and after a final Revelation. At the Fall the two elements of the Unconscious became separated, Reason was cut off from Will. The latter rules the world as we know it. In order to encourage men to perpetuate themselves, to obstruct progress toward nirvana, Will fosters three illusions: (a) that happiness is actually attainable at a given stage of the world's development, is within the grasp of the individual during his earthly life; (b) that men will be happy in a hereafter; (c) that the race will some day be happy in this world. The first of these illusions was cherished by the ancients and is entertained by every man during his childhood; the second was characteristic of the Middle Ages and is typical of the young man; the third is peculiar to modern times and the individual grown old. And the world will die just as the individual dies. Reason, gradually dispelling the three illusions one after another, will so far enlighten mankind, bring it to such a degree of consciousness, that all men will simultaneously thwart the activity of Will, deny the will to live, and attain nirvana by a kind of race suicide.

The dénouement of Hartmann's 'History of the Unconscious in the World,' as he calls a section of his book, is grotesque and has provoked merriment in widely scattered camps. Nietzsche called Hartmann's system a 'philosophical joke,' and in our day Frederick Copleston, S.J.,[25] one of the best historians of pessimism, writes as though he agreed with Nietzsche on this point at least. The *Philosophy of the Unconscious* has considerable historical importance, however, as eight editions and a translation within a decade of publication testify. It evidently satisfied a popular demand for a work equally sensitive to pessimistic attitudes and to Darwin's *Origin of Species*. Pessimists of every description were legion. Almost equally numerous were those who based an optimistic faith on the power of organisms to *become*. Hartmann's system holds two conflicting points of view in uneasy suspension. Yet the third part is an interesting melioristic document: awaiting nirvana, men go about improving the lot of their fellows. And Hartmann's book is a necessary background for understanding what Laforgue meant by the Unconscious, a world principle working by diverse means, 'loves, religions, languages, sciences, arts, social apostolates, mysticisms,'[26] to regain an original unity that philosophers and artists had glimpsed within the Absolute. Laforgue's Unconscious is, obviously, only a remote forebear of the unconscious of the surrealists, for the unconscious invoked by André Breton and his group is the unconscious human mind investigated by Freud. More closely related to the Collective Unconscious of Jung, it is even beyond and above that.

Of course, like Hartmann and many a philosopher and poet before him, Laforgue was fascinated by the unconscious human mind, its mystery and its vastness. In Hartmann's book he found a sentence from the German Romantic poet Johann Richter: 'Our measurements of the rich territory of the Me are far too small or narrow when we omit the immense realm of the *Unconscious*, this real interior Africa in every sense.' Laforgue's imagination runs riot as he quotes this phrase and invents inhabitants of the inner realm: 'The fury of wanting to know oneself, of desiring to plunge beneath one's conscious culture toward "the interior Africa" of our unconscious domain. And there were reconnoiterings step by step, pushing aside the branches, the undergrowth of the coppices, noiselessly, so as not to frighten the rabbits that play by moonlight, imagining themselves alone. I feel so meager, so overfamiliar, I, Laforgue, in relation to the outside world. And yet I possess rich mines, veins, submarine worlds that ferment unknown. There it is that I would be, there would I die. Strange flowers that turn slowly like wax hairdressers' heads upon their stalks, fairy jewels where Moreau's Galatea slumbers watched over by Polyphemus, happy dreamless corals, ruby creepers, subtle flowerings which the eye of consciousness has not ravaged with axe and fire. Whole days spent spying within oneself, motionless as the monks of Mount Athos. . . *Observe the instincts with all possible absence of calculation, denial of will, for fear of making them deviate from their natural course, for fear of influencing them.'* [27] Laforgue sought and found in a philosophy of the Unconscious deliverance from intellectual constraints, freedom for exploration of a domain relatively new to imaginative writing. And as his sense of discovery recalls that of Johann Richter before him, so does it suggest that of the surrealists to follow. Passages such as that quoted above are part of a current that runs from the German Romantics to Apollinaire and a considerable body of writing done in the 'twenties and 'thirties. The image of the 'wax hairdressers' heads upon their stalks' is particularly prophetic, not only of Breton's prose but of verse written on the fringe of surrealism by Jules Supervielle, Henri Michaux, and Léon-Paul Fargue.

But Laforgue's Unconscious is only incidentally 'a domain which has recently revealed to science the virgin forests of life.' [28] Primarily it is the world-essence, essentially perfect, self-sufficient: 'the last divinity, the mystic universal principle revealed in

Hartmann's *Philosophy of the Unconscious*, the only divinity minutely present and everywhere watchful, alone infallible—because of its unconsciousness—the only divinity truly and serenely infinite, the only one that man has not created in his own image.' [29] Accidentally, the Unconscious is incomplete, 'objectifying itself in exploratory worlds toward consciousness.' [30] Manifesting itself in artistic production, one of its means of fulfillment, the Unconscious finds its own way: 'I bestir myself too! But the Unconscious leads me,' as Laforgue succinctly puts it. 'The genius has no direction of his own; he is the immediate priest of the Unconscious,' [31] he says elsewhere. Or, as we find in unpublished notes on Schelling, 'Genius is the mystical manifestation, sign of the immediate elect of the Unconscious, able to speak directly in its name.' [32] The genius is merely the instrument of the Unconscious that 'bloweth where it listeth.' [33]

The Unconscious that chooses its vessels in this manner is overwhelming. In his chapter on aesthetic judgment and artistic production Hartmann quotes the letter in which Mozart describes his heaven-sent creative impulse. He cites the passage from the *Phaedrus* in praise of frenzy, Cicero on *furor poeticus*, Shaftesbury on enthusiasm, making it clear that all these thinkers were really writing about the Unconscious. Similarly Laforgue speaks of 'the transcendent force that impels Beethoven to sing, Delacroix to exert himself to find tonal combinations, Baudelaire to ransack his language, Hugo to be prodigious.' [34] And as Hartmann disdains minor artists, or conscious craftsmen, so does Laforgue dismiss the minor painters of the Low Countries whom Taine had admired as expressive of a race, environment, and moment in history. 'Taine admires the Dutch painters because they are bourgeois satisfied with life, not eccentric, not hypertrophic. Well, those Dutchmen did the literary painting of mediocre bourgeois, devoid of genius (genius, elect of the Unconscious).' Taine excepts the Low Country painters from his general stricture of realism because they are 'healthy.' With equal inconsistency Laforgue wanders from the main argument of his aesthetics—'all keyboards are legitimate'—because of a Romantic insistence that the artist be possessed by enthusiasm.

Free and uncontrolled as genuine artistic expression is with reference to the artist, it is not purposeless, because the Unconscious moves toward an end. The arts are 'enfeoffed' to the improvement of the race. The arts have only a secondary, but marvelously necessary, importance for the divine ends: 'their function is to develop indefinitely the respective organs they exploit and to contribute thereby to a ceaseless refining of the whole organism, to a divinatory intoxication of the brain . . . in a word to the purification of the mirror wherein the Unconscious seeks itself.' The 'optic arts' have a special province, 'development to the utmost of the exploited organ, the Eye. Is there any need to recall the already familiar truth, that like every vital force, the eye, color-blind at first, learned only gradually to perceive the waves, more and more rapid and less and less long, from red to violet, and continues its evolution toward perception of the ultraviolet . . . that the eye learned only little by little to search into the complication of lines and perspectives, mingled and conflicting in rich vibrations.' [35] At this point we must interrupt Laforgue's most sustained presentation of his aesthetic ideas, the opening section of his essay, 'L'Art moderne en Allemagne,' to protest that though a single pair of eyes can acquire traits, it cannot transmit them. Like many who have been seduced by one form or another of evolutionary theory—one thinks especially of Diderot—Laforgue fell into the Lamarckian error. He believed that in the course of time eyes organically superior to earlier ones had developed: 'In short, the Impressionist eye is, in human evolution, the most advanced eye, the organ which up till now has perceived and registered the most complicated known combinations of shadings.' [36] Needless to say, no grounds exist for such a belief.

There are not many aesthetic systems, Laforgue says in this same essay; 'there are exactly two, and these so mutually intolerant that ten lines from a book suffice to show with which camp sympathies lie: that which classifies and judges schools in the name of some ideal or other; and that which, naturalistic and deterministic, professes only to arrange documents.' Neither the scientific nor the traditionally idealist approach is the right one, he tells us. The determinists are able to describe the 'how' of genius and its works but unable to explain the 'why' or the essence, and have to accept works of art as so many 'legitimate

phenomena.' Meanwhile the idealists, with an explanation for inspiration and genius, have always been forced to judge by the
standard of a fixed ideal. Laforgue takes issue with the determinists
on the grounds that 'thought is identical with its object . . . and
that metaphysical knowledge is in accord with transcendental
reality,' and then proceeds to offer his own kind of ideal, one
that will change mysteriously with the times, evolved by the
Unconscious 'in an indefinite becoming.' [37]

There is considerable obligation to Friedrich Schelling in this
argument, that philosopher of Romanticism having recognized
two fundamental directions of inquiry, the scientific and the
traditionally idealist, having found fault with both, and having
offered his own kind of idealism, taking as the basis of knowledge
identity between the thinking subject and the object. At many
points in his discussion of the Unconscious and its activities,
Hartmann acknowledges his debt to Schelling, as well he might,
since it is a short step from the 'universal activity' of Schelling's
system to Hartmann's dynamic Unconscious. If Hartmann is a
secondary figure, a derivative philosopher, Schelling, in whose
thought Coleridge found 'genial coincidences' with his own, is a
major one. Laforgue's obligation to Hartmann has long been
taken for granted. About the relationship with Schelling little or
nothing has been said, partly because it has been difficult to gauge
how much Laforgue knew about him directly and to what extent
he encountered him second-hand through Hartmann. Fourteen
pages of notes for an essay on Schelling among the poet's unpublished papers make us reasonably certain that he had studied and
profited from the *Transcendental Idealism* itself.

This essay on Schelling would probably have had as an epigraph an unwieldy sentence from Hartmann: 'Philosophy, as
the ultimate expression of ideas dominant at a given period of
civilization, as the conscious flower in which blossoms spon-
taneously the unconscious virtue of history, can alone express in
a few concise and convenient formulas the spirit of that period.' [38]
Laforgue writes this sentence boldly across the first page of his
notes, indicating that it comes from the first book of Hartmann's
work and that the translation into French is his own. There is a
certain justice in this salute to philosophy by a poet, Schelling

being of all philosophers the one who held poetry in highest esteem. Beginning as a disciple of Fichte, he soon came to feel, like Coleridge, that the thought of that subjective idealist did not allow enough importance to nature. As befitted a man who was to become the chief of Romantic philosophers, Schelling sought in nature the 'hieroglyphs of the soul,' expressions of spiritual meaning such as the poet Novalis was also seeking—at the same time and in the same place—at Jena on the eve of the nineteenth century. The *System of Transcendental Idealism,* published in 1800, represents the attempt of a powerful poetic imagination to find in the outer world equivalents for inner realities, one reality in particular: the confrontation of a reflecting mind with something not quite itself, its 'unconscious.' Like a great Symbolist poem, Schelling's transcendental idealism projects this drama, this polarity within the human mind, across nature. At every level, matter possesses some degree of consciousness. And however obvious the poetic analogy may be, at least it allowed poets to recover the primitive sense of a universe where nothing is quite inanimate, in which man can lose himself the more readily because its life differs from his only in intensity. These manifestations of consciousness, weakening but distinct, might be compared to ripples on a pool, except that the movement is all in the other direction. Consciousness is forever striving to break free from its inert part. 'All beings have one thing in common,' Laforgue writes, 'discontent with the stagnation of their present state, passion for ascent, et cetera. The plasma dreams vaguely of that unknown world: two hinged halves of an oyster shell that open and shut. . . Man is tormented by the idea of progress. . . The point in common is possession by the demon of the infinite. This point is their inmost nature. All these souls are not only of the same family but have a single soul. And the universal flower is the indefinite torment of the ideal.' [39]

With regard to aesthetic intuition, the highest power of spirit according to *Transcendental Idealism,* Laforgue's most significant pronouncement is probably one collected in the *Mélanges posthumes:* 'Object and subject are irremediably in motion. . . The lightning flashes of identity between subject and object—that is the attribute of genius.' [40] Thus Heine had spoken of the lightning flashes of artistic intuition. Thus Coleridge, inspired by Schelling, had called the artist the 'shaper into one,' the 'esemplast.'

Like other creative artists of his century, Laforgue drew from Schelling a conception of the unique power of aesthetic intuition. More than most other poets, he had felt the weight of the positivistic argument, the importance of the sciences. Yet in the notes on Schelling he could write as follows on the restricted role of science: 'True philosophy, in spite of the autonomous emancipation of the sciences (a God is above beavers), must forever remain the first, universal, and last science. . .' And further on: 'None of the cathedral of Herbert Spencer. We must have poets. The sciences in their limited anarchy must remain the *ancillae diligentes* of philosophy, of metaphysics. All these poor sciences are based on common sense, the arbitrary. They don't have to trouble themselves about first principles. Besides, theirs is only the sort of fling that urchins make when they sow their oats. The progress of specialized sciences can only, in the long run, bring them back to the first and last science, to metaphysics. The radical vice of the sciences is that they are impersonal, whereas a metaphysics springs from a soul.' [41]

Laforgue's most considerable debt to Schelling, after all, was contracted indirectly through the derivative philosophy of Hartmann. After having refuted the positivists, as he thinks, by the argument that a transcendental reality must exist because we can conceive one, Laforgue proposes an aesthetic ideal 'placed in an indefinite becoming and in such a category—unconsciousness . . . that the subject can only conceive it within the limit of his capacities conditioned by an ephemeral stage of an indefinite evolution.' By situating the ideal where human beings can perceive it only imperfectly, and with different eyes at each epoch, Laforgue believes that he can be both an idealist and a guardian of claims of the 'ephemeral.' During the rest of these notes he is really concerned with two ideals, the one within the Unconscious and another which the Creative Unconscious presents to the artistic consciousness of each epoch. This is somewhat confusing, because Laforgue is an aesthetic idealist only in a special, not to say transcendental, sense. He is above all a relativist, anxious to prove what he reproaches the positivists for believing, that all works of art are so many legitimate phenomena, that all keyboards are legitimate.

He may play on the meaning of the word 'ideal,' but the statement of his aesthetic faith is not ambiguous: 'My sentiment at this moment before works of art of any given genre, epoch, or latitude has no more sufficient authority than that which I possessed at other moments of my individual evolution. But from the total of these sentiments, at the conclusion of my evolution, can be drawn my sentiment of the beautiful. My sentiment of the beautiful will have no more sufficient authority than those of my contemporaries. But our epoch will be summed up by a certain formula of aesthetic sensibility.' In this longest statement of his aesthetic position, 'L'Art moderne en Allemagne,' Laforgue justifies in his own mind the significance of the 'ephemeral.' The outworn concepts of which he has made use, his inconsistencies along the way, are less important than the fact that he has prepared the groundwork for his criticism and his poetry.

VII

Literary Criticism

LIKE Coleridge, Laforgue would have traced his poetry and his aesthetics to the same profound 'stirrings of power,' and would have acknowledged no difference between the springs of truth and of poetry. He is one of the authentic amateur philosophers of literature. However, the cogitations of such poet-thinkers derive much of their importance from the poetry, which should be tested, whenever possible, by the quality of the poet's reaction to other writers. As it happens, Laforgue's literary criticism is always stimulating and sometimes so important as to lend weight to all the rest of his work. That most penetrating and ineluctable of literary historians, Gustave Lanson, could hardly be accused of overindulgence for Laforgue or for any other writer chronologically too close to him. He described the *Moralites légendaires* equivocally as 'the inspired hoaxes of a young man in whom there begins to burgeon an artist and a genius.' [1] Of the notes on Baudelaire, on the other hand, he declared that they showed 'an extraordinary openness of mind,' [2] and he had read only the small fraction that appeared in the edition of 1903.

Laforgue's literary criticism exists only in fragmentary state, in telegraphic style, as jottings toward essays never pulled together. However, four sheaves of such notes give ample evidence of his critical capacity.

His remarks on Hugo are brief, barely more than a review of one of the last volumes, *La Fin de Satan;* yet a good deal of substance is compressed into two pages of workshop criticism. The tribute to Hugo's breadth and stature is more generous than might have been expected from a young writer only a year after the great man's death. We are told of 'the ennui of these periodical paving stones rolled down from the customary Sinai, these three hundred and fifty pages of heavy paper, large print,' and that 'there seems to be no reason for this ever to stop.' But Laforgue is duly appreciative of the disciplined, easy rhymes and the technical virtuosity which make the reader overlook the parasitic adjectives.[3] Hugo seating himself at his organ every morning is like the great Bach heaping score on score without bothering himself about the consequences. He has his Bastille Day aspect,[4] but pieces such as 'Cantique de Bephthagé' will last as long as poetry itself.

One of the interesting passages is the comparison of Hugo with Flaubert, though it is hardly necessary to say which writer is favored by a critic leaning so heavily toward Unconscious abundance. Set the poems on Biblical subjects beside 'Hérodias,' 'Saint Julien,' *Saint-Antoine*, he tells us, and see how laborious Flaubert is in comparison. The tales are 'passable because they are prose, and Flaubert's prose, and because they are still alone of their kind. But imagine them put into verse by a poet equivalent to the prose-writer Flaubert. They would be decidedly meager.'[5] There is something wrong with the reasoning here, for a poet equivalent to the prose-writer Flaubert could only be a great poet. Laforgue is right, however, about the heavy going in the exotic tales; and he points to the comparative lifelessness of these works only to do more honor to *L'Education sentimentale*, which he places among the very great novels.[6]

The remarks on Mallarmé make up the least satisfying page of Laforgue's criticism. He had been reading the author of 'Toast funèbre' ever since 1881, had spoken of him in enthusiastic though general terms in letters. When it came to taking notes toward an essay, probably in 1885, he lapsed too readily into the everlasting arms of the Unconscious. He identifies Mallarmé with 'the Unconscious, the principle (after effort, the apotheosis of the Parnassian artistic conscience consoling itself with Buddhistic protestations) the principle of stammering, of withdrawal in poetry.'[7] What Buddhistic protestations, we wonder, and what kind of stammering? What has the Unconscious to do with one of the most deliberate of all literary artists, the one who most thoroughly rejected all forms of enthusiasm? 'Not the stammering of the child in pain,' Laforgue adds, 'but that of the Sage divagating—never a divagation of images as in dream and unconscious ecstasy, but *reasoning* divagation. His technique is equally *reasoned*, conscious, and one perceives that there is nothing of the first jet about it.' [8] This is more like it; but one remark pretty well cancels out the other.

Laforgue acknowledged too handsomely his poetic debt to Mallarmé. 'After having favored eloquent developments,' he wrote to Henry, 'then Coppée, then Sully's *Justice*, then Baudelaire, I am becoming, as far as form is concerned, Kahnesque and Mallarméan.' [9] Actually the resemblances to Mallarmé are slight, occasional reproductions of caesura patterns. The aims and techniques of the two poets were radically different.

When the *Complaintes* appeared, Mallarmé transmitted his good opinion of the book through Gustave Kahn, one of the faithful in the rue de Rome. Laforgue's reply is valuable for its frank avowal of difficulties encountered. The same day he wrote to Kahn saying just how many of Mallarmé's then uncollected poems he had read. Important omissions are partly explained by his absence from France. He was given further opportunity to judge Mallarmé when three prose poems were published in the first number of *La Vogue*.[10] Of one, 'Frisson d'hiver,' he wrote appreciatively, quoting two memorable sentences: the evocation of a Saxon clock—'Pense qu'elle est venue de Saxe par les longues diligences d'autrefois'—and the delicate recreation of a season—'Il n'y a plus de champs et les rues sont vides, je te parlerais de nos meubles.' The two other prose poems, based on farfetched conceits, he disapproved. The close reading is revealing even on Mallarmé. It was too early for a general estimate of the most abstruse of the Symbolists.

Rimbaud is unmentioned until 1885, after Verlaine's *Poètes maudits* had lifted him above the literary horizon, and it was only after reading the 'Illuminations' in *La Vogue* that Laforgue called Rimbaud 'the precocious absolute flower without before or after, the *only isomer* of Baudelaire.' [11] Apropos of Rimbaud, there is arresting reflection on the word as father of the idea. 'A poem is not the utterance of a preconceived sentiment. Let's admit the importance of the drift of the rhyme, the deviations for lucky finds, the unexpected symphony arising to accompany a motif, just as a painter is led to this pearl-gray tone for no particular reason, or to that gratuitous geranium, or as the musician is shown the way to the apparently parasitic harmony.'[12]

The remarks on Tristan Corbière are several times as extensive as those on any of the other poets so far mentioned and correspondingly more important. For Laforgue, who had the interest any newcomer was bound to have in Hugo, Mallarmé, and Rimbaud, had special reasons for scrutinizing the Breton poet closely. The most thoughtful reviewer of the *Complaintes* labeled its author a Decadent of the school of Corbière; so, in effect, did Rémy de Gourmont later on. The poet protested, but a glance at his letters is enough to show that he had time, and his first book proves that he took occasion, to profit from the novel idiom that Corbière brought into French verse.

'Corbière has style and I have humor,' Laforgue wrote. 'Corbière flutters and I purr; I live by an absolute philosophy and not by nervous twitchings; I am a plain blunt man, not too spirited to lay a finger on; love, for me, is not yellow but white and deep-mourning violet. Finally, Corbière troubles his head about neither stanzas nor rhymes (except as a springboard to conceits) and never about rhythms, and I am sufficiently preoccupied with all three to have devised new stanzas, rhymes, and rhythms; I aim for symphony and melody, and Corbière saws away on that one everlasting fiddle of his.'[13] He is willing to admit only 'a grain of cousinship' with Corbière, the 'Breton nuance.' Laforgue's Breton origins are open to question; but the cousinship, at least a gram of it, is not. Laforgue's Gascon wit only goes to show that he is on the defensive, and the study of Corbière that he told his reviewer he had in mind is the sort of criticism in which the critic has much at stake.

'Bohemian of the ocean . . . picaro and crackpot,' the notes for that essay begin; and Laforgue recalls that Edouard-Joachim Corbière, for so he was christened, adopted the name of an earlier Breton knight-errant of sorrowful countenance. He sees Corbière as a sort of lean satyr, libidinous, droll, unkempt, tied to a mast with his hands behind him, staring off to sea, soaked by the sea-rain, his felt hat flung down beside him. The poet is as strident as the gulls and as tireless. The wind of the Breton coast inspires him to invent and savor the word 'plangorer.' And at the same time he is always warning his readers not to take him seriously: 'All this is for effect; I'm posing; I'll even let you in on how it's done!' [14] Was the sailor-satyr obscene? Huysmans in a famous passage of *A Rebours* had said that he was, that the strange congeries that is Corbière's verse included traveling-salesman pleasantries. Laforgue finds no obscenity. He admits that Corbière is guilty of a 'léger priapisme de barrière'—a slight water-front excess of desire. Yet his verse is wholly free from provocative picturings; and despite his own disappointing experiences, he reserved for womankind the term 'Madame,' the reverent word of the medieval courts of love. Laforgue is, incidentally, right. A fresh salt breeze disinfects Corbière's pages.

The Breton is given due credit for his vivid language, his aversion for padding, his avoidance of rhetorical bluff. But Laforgue finds little else to praise in the poems, which he divides into two kinds: those that spin a yarn in straightforward verse that would disintegrate without the whiplash of the language; the others 'more intimate, subjective, withdrawn into the self, either in Paris or upon the water.' [15] Just where the boundary between these two groups would come is none too clear. The first would undoubtedly include the great poem about the hunch-back Bitor, the sailors' mascot and sacrificial victim, and the equally great 'Rapsodie foraine et le pardon de Sainte-Anne.' Here, too, we would probably have to put a number of dramatic lyrics, of which 'Steam-Boat' is a good example. But what would we do with certain poems partaking of the essay in verse, vastly energetic, rambling mixtures of metaphor and abstraction, neither narrative nor meditative? Under the second heading would certainly fall the handful of poems in which Paris is half stage setting, half dramatic personage, among them the autobiographical piece beginning 'Bâtard de créole et Breton,' a few of the Breton poems, and the lovely 'Rondels pour après.'

Since the merit of this verse resides in its sting, its spirit, its 'Romantic staccato,' it lacks what Laforgue calls 'plastic interest,' shapeliness. No line can be singled out as beautiful. The technique is 'stupid,' the stanzas lacking in individuality. The frequency of eleven-syllable lines meant to be alexandrines indicates an incurable indelicacy of ear. Habitual failure to alternate masculine and feminine rhymes betrays an inherent carelessness corrected, occasionally, with a laboriousness painful to observe. Citing rhymes 'neither rich nor poor, merely insufficient and haphazard'—*prêter* and *rimer, cousu* and *décousu, maison* and *non, jour* and *jour*—Laforgue digresses to deliver a hundred-word history of rhyme. In the seventeenth century, rhymes were mostly stereotyped, the word that counted coming within the line. The reaction against classical technique centered on its weak point, the rhyming, till the time came when Hugo 'really wrote for the sole pleasure of turning up out-of-the-way rhymes.' [16] Corbière's rare original rhymes are too original, outlandish, and always poured into the same mold, a low-down word being rhymed with a high-toned one. We are confronted by two virtual homonyms that are far from being synonyms, by combinations like *coquelicot* and *calicot, pastille du serail* and *ail, paradis* and *radis* [17] . . . The trouble is that for each such pair of rhymes culled from Corbière, such shotgun weddings of 'red poppy' with 'calico,' 'harem pastille' and 'garlic,' 'paradise' and 'radish,' the reader of Laforgue can readily counter with *elégiaques* and *claques, veulent* and *s'engueulent, demoiselles* and *vaisselles*—'elegiac' and 'opera-hats,' 'desire' and 'mud-sling,' 'young ladies' and 'dishes.' With a certain self-righteousness, Laforgue is protesting against a use of paradox that is definitely a part of his own procedure, especially in the *Complaintes*.

Corbière's 'gongorisms of antithesis' can be accounted for psychologically. He is a man who declares his love without wanting to be listened to, who flees society and complains about being left alone—the spoiled child who refuses his soup and then blubbers when it is taken away. [18]

The least literary of poets, in Laforgue's opinion, influenced neither by Romantics nor by Parnassians, Corbière admired most of all the customs-house coast guard who strides along the shore with his pipe between his teeth, too full of genuinely poetic feelings to bother with false poetry. He was so wary of all the pitfalls that beset the lyric poet—the apocalyptic, fatal, tubercular, lunar, and upright-citizen postures—that he ended by having no lyric quality to speak of, except, on Breton subjects, an over-simplified ballad music. 'The most delicate, the most tenuous, the purest' part of his work is the 'Rondels pour après,' poems such as 'Biographie':

> Mais il fut flottant, mon berceau,
> Fait comme le nid de l'oiseau
> Qui couve ses oeufs sur la houle. . .
> Mon lit d'amour fut un hamac;
> Et, pour tantôt, j'espère un sac
> Lesté d'un bon caillou qui roule.

> A floating thing, my cradle was,
> Wrought like the nest of the bird
> That broods her eggs on the wave. . .
> My bed of love was a hammock;
> And, for anon, I hope for a sack
> Weighted with a fine rolling stone.

Despite a certain haste on the part of Laforgue to flog Corbière for his own faults and laud him for his own qualities, we are confronted here with acute criticism of one of the great initiators of modern poetry, indeed the best criticism that has so far been written on this extremely difficult subject. Laforgue knows quite well that all the blemishes to which he points are concomitant to Corbière's singular power, that the Breton had performed a remarkable feat in shattering beyond all possibility of real repair a tradition of eloquence, the 'epic national guard' stop in the Hugoesque organ. He was insufficiently aware that Corbière had pondered well all the rules he broke, that not the least important aspect of his poetry is its implicit criticism not only of Hugo but of other predecessors, his negative opinion of Lamartine and his appreciative view of Musset. But he says that all of Corbière's shortcomings as an artist must be forgiven for the sake of 'perfect and immortal plaints like Le Poète contumace' (in which, incidentally, Corbière proves that he was steeped in the literature of

'UN CIEL DU SOIR PLUVIEUX'
Unpublished verse, 1886

82441

Romanticism). Laforgue saves for the end the sample given above of the ballad music that he had pretended to condemn, which happens to be some of the author's best. A similar sort of simplified music constitutes some of Laforgue's best verse. And if he clutches too eagerly at straws of difference between Corbière and himself, observes that the earlier poet is not gripped by 'modern cosmologies, dead stars, unechoing stellar deserts,' [19] and notices deficiencies in musical qualities in which Laforgue himself did not abound, these remarks are of interest for what they reveal about his own aspirations.

There is no such overinvolvement in the notes on Baudelaire. 'To understand him better,' Laforgue writes toward the beginning of the notes, 'think for a moment of the opposite pole, of the sick and Christ-like child, no Creole, who really did plumb the depths of human philosophy, who gave way to his crises, without pose—Heine.' [20] It is impossible to say whether years of development, filling in youthfully spare outlines, would have given to Laforgue's works the substance of Heine's; but at least he was of the same race of poets. Laforgue writes of Baudelaire with the perspective afforded by his radical difference from the author of *Les Fleurs du mal*.

Presumably these notes are that 'contribution to the cult of Baudelaire' which Laforgue mentioned in a letter of February 1885 to Kahn. To this day they can be read complete only in the *Entretiens politiques et littéraires* for April 1891, for the 1903 editors of Laforgue were too much concerned with form and left out whatever was unpolished. Some, but by no means all, of the remaining notes were published in the Connaissance edition of 1920. In their entirety, the notes filled nineteen pages.

They begin where most studies of Baudelaire have begun and too many have ended—with the poet's temperament. Particularly interesting at a time when the Russian novel was only beginning to be known in France is the comparison of Baudelaire with Marmeladov of *Crime and Punishment*. Early in 1885 Laforgue had read the first French translation of this inquisition into the nature of guilt, confessing to spiritual perturbations as he did so. He found in the creator of *Les Fleurs du mal* and in Dostoevsky's passive witness of evil the same pleasure in self-defilement. Baudelaire was, moreover, 'terrified by the discouraging and diabolical revelations of modern medicine, seeing only neurosis and finally being overwhelmed by it.'

Of modern poets in general Laforgue writes: 'Since they are idle and childlike they have time to be afraid of death and are frightened by all its calls, the winds of autumn nights, twilights, the whistles of express trains—they need to be pitied, comforted, and are sad for everything and for nothing—life passes for them as for a grave and curious child who turns through fine colored pictures and finds among them friends, and traitors, and beautiful forlorn ladies whom he consoles.' Of Baudelaire in particular: 'He is enthusiastic about his toys, then breaks them—cries for the moon on a silver platter and sulks when it is offered to him. . . A poet. An eternal grown-up child, saddened by the circus and the tireless refrains of balls—in love with glory and the crown of thorns for himself and those he loves . . . forever pubescent, in spite of having overtaxed his senses early. . . He sees each season come and go with the joy and sadness of a girl.' And like a child he seeks to make himself interesting to grown-ups.

The learned pose, the passion for ironbound folios, is merely a manifestation of this desire to be interesting. It is the more misleading because Baudelaire, according to Laforgue, neither reasons nor learns. He is fundamentally credulous, living with bowed head. But he does pillage scraps of erudition far and wide, and assumes a Benedictine air for the benefit of the deistic bourgeois. It may be difficult for the American reader to see how Baudelaire's disgust for democracy could have been appreciably strengthened by Poe's 'Monos and Una'; but Laforgue thinks that it was. Venturing toward the more disturbing motives for Baudelaire's actions—and it is not wholly clear how the child fell so ill—he quotes from 'Bénédiction':

> *Tous ceux qu'il veut aimer l'observent avec crainte,*
> *Ou bien, s'enhardissant de sa tranquillité,*
> *Cherchent à qui saura lui tirer une plainte,*
> *Et font sur lui l'essai de leur férocité.*

All those whom he would love view him with fear
Or else made bold by his passivity
See which can be the first to make him whimper,
Trying on him their own ferocity.

Laforgue discovers 'four abysses of psychology' in these four verses:

> *Lis-moi pour apprendre à m'aimer;*
>
> *Ame curieuse qui souffres*
> *Et vas cherchant ton paradis,*
> *Plains-moi! . . . sinon, je te maudis!*

> Read me that you may learn to love me
>
> Curious soul that suffereth
> And go seeking your paradise
> Pity me! Or else I curse you!

Of the four abysses, or needs—for love, suffering, heaven, and pity—the second, that of the soul that caresses its suffering, is apparently considered the most profound. In the lines

> *Soyez béni, mon Dieu, qui donnez la souffrance*
> *Comme un divin remède à nos impuretés*

> Be blest, my God, that grantest suffering,
> Refining fire for our impurities

Laforgue sees only masochism, a vicious cycle of self-punishment and debauchery toward further self-punishment. At this point, with Laforgue's refusal to see any purpose in suffering, we begin to glimpse the limits to his view of Baudelaire's mind.

This criticism oscillates between discussion of Baudelaire as man and as artist. It is continually endowing the poetry with the traits of a poet whose fundamental ambition, according to the critic, is to astonish. Just as the religious imagery and its refinement, the satanic, are meant to shock bourgeois hearts, so are poems of the kind that would nowadays be called 'pure,' poems on the slenderest of subjects, airy as the beat of a fan, meant to make the uninitiate inquire when they are over, 'and then? . . .' Inasmuch as readers are used to thinking of their poets as inspired, Baudelaire 'proclaims the necessity of work, patience, calculation, charlatanism.' His originality is 'shrewdly willed and wrought.' If his verse has in it the sense of steel, the mineral, the sterile, that is because the bourgeois are accustomed to finding their humane sentiments reflected in lush, humanized landscapes. Baudelaire was the first poet to break conclusively with the public he systematically insulted, the first to write for the happy few a book that would be the bible of a cult—a single book, a quintessential book into which he had distilled all his passion, 'and as a result, Laforgue notes, 'devotion of the faithful and outside these precincts no salvation.'

Laforgue's presentation of Baudelaire as the infantile anti-bourgeois is not very satisfying. He would have had trouble, if pressed, explaining what he meant by the bourgeois of Baudelaire's time, whose lack of heroism did not deprive them of complexity or variety. 'It is well known,' Laforgue writes, 'that the anti-Christian or atheistic pieces are a game for the benefit of the simpletons who call themselves materialists, the Voltairians of the age.' Well, were the Voltairians materialists or were they not? The Homais of the epoch, people like the pharmacist in *Madame Bovary*, were materialists who would have had no reason to be offended by anti-Christianity or atheism. But Laforgue thinks that there are some others who would have been offended; and in this he is perfectly right. There were the materialist and the non-materialist bourgeois, and it does not illumine Baudelaire greatly to say that he was defying people whose points of view remain so ill defined. Neither honestly religious nor honestly intellectual, the Baudelaire of Jules Laforgue tends to be too little the grave and curious child and too much the posturing adolescent.

It is in his close reading of Baudelaire's verse that Laforgue reveals his capacities, his potentialities as a critic. After the 'chaste and fatalistic' Vigny, the 'apotheotic, bucolic, and ridiculously gallant' Hugo, 'the worldling and declamatory schoolboy,' Musset, after the lachrymose Lamartine, came Baudelaire, 'the *first* to write in a moderate, confessional manner,' leaving off the inspired air:

> les maisons, dont la brume allonge la hauteur
>
> un brouillard sale et jaune

le faubourg secoué par les lourds tombereaux

houses, to which the haziness lends height

the dirty yellow fog

the suburb jolted by the ponderous carts. . .

Laforgue is aware of the importance of Sainte-Beuve's poetry, uninspired but expertly pitched, in preparing the way for Baudelaire. Through his friend Paul Bourget, a student of the English Lake poets, Laforgue probably knew that Wordsworth had exercised an influence on Sainte-Beuve. Yet among French poets it was Baudelaire who had the genius to write at once moderately and poetically.

The verse form that came most naturally to Baudelaire was neither moderate nor confessional. It was the rhymed couplet, 'unquestionably the period of the preacher,' Laforgue says, the longish poem in rhymed couplets, sustained and tending to be unctuous. The characteristic rhythms are ample, grandiose, Biblical: 'Ta peau miroite, ta démarche—un serpent au bout d'un bâton, ta chevelure un océan, ta tête se balance avec la mollesse d'un jeune éléphant, ton corps se penche comme un fin vaisseau qui plonge ses vergues dans l'eau, ta salive remonte à tes dents comme un flot grossi par la fonte des glaciers grondants.' Yet there is in these descriptions of woman as Baudelaire sees her— Delilah, sphinx in spite of herself, 'déshabillable . . . vil animal ou du moins avilissable'—a new note, something that Laforgue calls 'Americanism applied to the Song of Songs.'

So it is that Baudelaire never prolongs his Biblical rhythms unduly, or yields to the temptation of eloquence. He never 'beats his breast, never insists or charges.' Indeed, at vital points his poetry stands opposed to a whole tradition of eloquence:

La nuit s'épaississait ainsi . . . qu'une cloison . . .

The final word lets us tumble almost as far from the high plane of that admirable love poem, 'Le Balcon,' as its English equivalent, 'partition,' would have done. Here, where the traditional poet would have found some oratorical image, Baudelaire makes a

'Yankee comparison.' Suddenly, in the midst of a harmonious period, he 'plants his foot in the plate.'

Not unnaturally, Baudelaire was the first poet to write of Paris as one of its daily galley slaves, to tell of its gas lights wavering in the wind, the prostitutes, the restaurants and their air vents, the hospitals, gambling dens, cats, beds, stockings, perfumes of modern manufacture. In short, Baudelaire was the first to write what critics after Laforgue have learned to call urban poetry. But as Baudelaire is never overeloquent, somehow he is never over-familiar either. All of these everyday objects are described in a way that is somehow lofty, superior. 'Baudelaire is well-behaved. He is courteous to the ugly.' Sometimes he redeems by means of the classical reference inserted with the utmost naturalness. 'Andromaque, je pense à vous!' he exclaims, having described the hurly-burly of the city streets in which the swan is wandering. And he adds, 'Veuve d'Hector, hélas!'—the interjection being neither a bit of classical pomp nor padding, but having 'great and touching subtlety.' Sometimes the instrument of his trans-forming power is more mysterious, as in the memorable lines:

> à l'heure où sous les cieux
> Froids et clairs le Travail s'éveille, où la voirie
> Pousse un sombre ouragan dans l'air silencieux . . .

> at that cold clear hour
> When Labor rouses, when the scavengers
> Fracture the silence with their somber dust-storm . . .

But always the 'courtesy' is there, and that is what distinguishes Baudelaire from his disciples, 'who have set Paris out on display like provincials dazzled by a turn on the boulevards and weary of the tyranny of their brasseries.'

Laforgue misses much of Baudelaire, partly because he is writing in 1885. The *Ecrits intimes* had not yet been published. If Laforgue had read them he might not have been able to dismiss the religious question with a few casual references and the remark, 'metaphysical anguish could not touch him; the epidermis of his soul was of different stuff.' The whole question of Baude-

laire's possible conversion to the Christian religion aside, the
problem of belief was of the greatest urgency for him. The
private notebooks make this especially clear; but then some of
the *Fleurs du mal* are almost as revealing. The emancipated Laforgue was simply not a good judge on such matters. He is, unfortunately, little better on the subject of Baudelaire's intellectual
powers. At one point he declares, 'Neither a great heart, nor a
great mind, but what plaintive nerves, what nostrils open to
everything, what a magic voice.' Baudelaire's superb criticism,
his aesthetics that has kept most other poets going ever since, the
architectural design to which the poems of *Les Fleurs du mal*
were firmly subjected, almost any of the jottings in his journals,
is enough to confound such a statement.

Yet in one way or another, Laforgue manages to touch on
several of the discoveries of that mind as well as to acknowledge
many of the qualities of that voice. Here, in the poems 'airy as the
beating of a wing,' is the prophecy of 'pure poetry,' poetry detached from events, concerned with essences, the kind developed
by Mallarmé and Valéry. Here is the conception of the poem as
a work painstakingly constructed rather than inspired, a theory
for which Poe was responsible and which Baudelaire welcomed
with enthusiasm and passed on to Mallarmé and Valéry. Here,
most certainly, is appreciation of the conversational note struck
by Baudelaire—not the first, since poets of antiquity had had their
satires and epistles, imitated over the centuries, and before the
Lake poets there had been Matthew Prior and, for that matter,
several intimate French poets among the classicists—yet a note
that Baudelaire could strike with the sureness of genius. By im-
plication, recognizing Baudelaire's power to transform mire into
gold, Laforgue does a general sort of justice to Baudelaire's idealism. Until Valéry no poet of consequence was to write so well on
Baudelaire.

As in any criticism, we must look for the image of the critic,
and we find it in that of the 'grave and curious child.' We are
told of both Corbière and Baudelaire that they were children
who asked only for the pain of having wishes granted or the
pleasure of having them refused. We cannot help noticing that
this description fits Corbière rather ill, Baudelaire somewhat bet-

ter, but Laforgue (until the last year of his life) admirably. As in any criticism of a poet by a poet, we must look for the element of the manifesto, the thinly veiled announcement of what he plans to do himself. The emphasis Laforgue places on Baudelaire's 'Yankee,' anti-eloquent traits will help us materially to understand the progress of his own verse.

VIII

Many Voices

THE Empress' schedule was varied only once during Laforgue's years in Germany. In 1884, when her health was bad, she stayed on longer than usual in Berlin. Otherwise she left on the nineteenth of April for Baden-Baden—the watering place that Jules hated most of all and upon which he finally took his revenge in one of his stories, 'Le Miracle des roses.' Coblenz, where the court spent June and July, had more in its favor; the way the Moselle cast itself into the Rhine was 'a sight for sad eyes.' The first three weeks of August were passed in Potsdam at the Castle of Babelsberg—many details of which were to crop up in 'Hamlet'; and it was usually from there that Jules left on his generous vacations, two months and a half on the average, which from 1882 till 1885 he spent in France. The first of November he would rejoin the court at Coblenz, in time for the journey back to the winter palace in Berlin.

This was the order of events, maintained with a regularity befitting the Empress' age and temperament, that shortly had Jules 'tearing in shreds the bitter fern of spleen.' [1] Yet the country holidays furnished the unforgettable landscapes of Laforgue's poetry: casinos by the water in season and out of season, valleys with horns and hunting calls in autumn. And even the dull inevitability of the round had its advantages. It would be a simplification to say that Jules detested the vegetating kind of life he saw about him. He was simultaneously attracted by it, especially at Baden-Baden, where he never could get down to work—there were too many 'tentations de promenades.' [2] He knew that he must try hard to keep in touch with poetry as it was understood in Paris. 'The placidity of Berlin exasperates and frightens me,' he remarked in a letter. 'I never write a phrase, a line of verse, without trying for the *suraigu*, just to prove to myself that I am not going into a decline. But no doubt the brandy of Berlin is herb tea in Paris.' [3] If the *Complaintes* have the savor of honest *alcool*, and they do, the distilling flame was fed by miscellaneous fuel: the art criticism that the editors of the *Gazette des Beaux-Arts* patched up almost beyond recognition, the oddly assorted readings for the Empress, the atmosphere of the resort towns with their usual boredom and distractions.

By May 1882 Laforgue was conclusively dissatisfied with *Le Sanglot de la terre* and its eloquence. Six months later, writing from Coblenz in front of his window overlooking the Rhine, he confides to Charles Henry that he has in mind a volume of 'entirely new poems which will be called *Complaintes de la vie* or the *Livre des Complaintes*, deplorable poems rhymed any old way . . . including the Complaintes du Soleil, du petit hypertrophique, des quatre saisons, de la Vieille Fille, du Foetus, du Pharmacien, du Père éternel, de Pan, et cetera.' [4] Obviously, the tone of the volume is set. A year and a half later, the book finished except for corrections, he writes to his sister about his new poems: 'They will perhaps seem strange to you, but I have abandoned my ideal of the rue Berthollet, my philosophical poems. It seems stupid to me now to assume a solemn air, to play the stops of eloquence. Nowadays, being on the one hand more skeptical, less easily carried away, and on the other hand possessing my language in a more minute, clown-like fashion, I compose whimsical little poems with only one purpose in mind, originality at any cost.' [5]

In November 1882 he had only five *Complaintes* in hand. By the following August he was able to write in the Agenda he used for a diary during 1883 that he had finished his book of forty poems (later increased to fifty). The burst of activity is startling, the more so since he had brought few projects to completion during his first year in Germany. We must look beyond mere clarification of poetic purpose for the explanation.

We do not know much about 'R.,' the woman referred to by

that initial a score of times in the Agenda. Evidently she was attached to the court, going to Baden-Baden along with the official
retinue. Théodore Lindenlaub could remember only one occasion
when Laforgue had mentioned her (not a surprising fact, considering the poet's talent for secrecy) and he cautiously identified 'R.' as the daughter of a burgomaster of either Cologne or
Coblenz, 'an intellectual, analytical, extremely sensitive woman of
almost stormy disposition.' [6] Entries in the Agenda bear out the
storminess, at any rate. On 16 April: 'Reading—then at R.'s—interminable scene—iceberg and firebrand.' Two days after arriving at Baden-Baden, 'Mad walk with R. Lamentations of an
ambitious slave.' On 23 May: 'Scene with R.! Schemes of fortune,
market for pictures and sketches. Impressionism and wax sculpture!' 27 May: 'Big scene with R. . . She was born to be a
mother.' 30 May: 'Done in.—Tenderness at R.'s. Explosion.' On
5 June, after an eventful night spent with others: 'R., when she
saw my sorry appearance—.' 8 June: 'Scene of the unworthy' [7]
('. . . to be loved by so pure a creature,' according to the exe-
gesis of Théodore Lindenlaub, who puzzled over the passage
later). On 19 July there is the record of another clash, and that
is the last we hear of R. in the Agenda. This does not mean her
disappearance from Laforgue's life, however, but simply that he
left on his vacation. He continued to see her until some undetermined later date.

Several prose fragments, including the following unpublished
one, deal with the adventure with R.: 'The rendezvous to which
she did not come. An hour after the time agreed on he is still
wandering about, eyes streaming, teeth clenched. He comes back
from the street corner to look at the clock—on the sign before
the watchmaker's shop. It's a good ten o'clock. He keeps going.
He wants to hoard up all the grief there is, to the point of bursting, to the point of tears, before going home. He walks along
imagining word by word the scene he will make tomorrow, and
his face acts out the words. What will she find to say? The second
time this week she has failed him! He will be implacable! Though
the heavens had fallen *he* wouldn't have missed a rendezvous,
would have let her know, et cetera. . . On the way home he
realized that he loved her madly. He swore to himself to make an

end of all this. The very next day he would propose, or carry her off. She loved him. There would be nothing to it. He had hesitated too long as it was, had no doubt allowed her passion to cool. He imagined the scene of tears and eternal vows tomorrow.

Je t'en avais comblé, je t'en veux accabler. . .' [8]

From such jottings and transpositions it is easy enough to reconstruct the situation: a man of twenty-three, with no resources beyond those provided by his somewhat humiliating post, in full tilt after the impossible. That young man does not cut an admirable figure. Two years later, when he writes sourly to Charles Henry, 'I am beginning to think that it was my whole person which displeased the illustrious R.,' [9] we find it in ourselves to agree with him. An ambitious slave in more ways than one, moving with deep-seated uneasiness in bored and boring society, girding himself with defensive bravado, the Laforgue of 1883 is far from having found himself.

Amid adventures intellectual and emotional, composition of the *Complaintes* proceeded, sometimes on a day directly following a quarrel with R. Under date of 2 August we find the words, 'Fermé mes Complaintes.' At once Laforgue began casting about in his mind for a likely publisher.[10] He would have liked his poems to appear in the Kistemaeckers editions, along with the work of Huysmans, Catulle Mendès and Maupassant. But inquiries by letter and in person during his vacation in France were equally unfruitful, and it was not until March that he came to terms with Léon Vanier, [11] Verlaine's publisher. He promised to pay Vanier two hundred francs in July (by this time he was living as a matter of course on his salary for the next quarter). Lengthy delays ensued. The poems lay in manuscript at the publisher's shop on the Quai Saint-Michel until July 1885, while their author raged and despaired and gave Vanier the nickname of Fabius Cunctator. The manuscript was not neglected, however, since Laforgue charged both Vanier and Henry to make corrections for him, and made some himself while in Paris in 1884. At least once he confessed that he was glad of the chance to revise. During the spring and early summer of 1885 seven of the poems came out in the review *Lutèce*, provoking a slashing attack from

Edmond Haraucourt.[12] At length, in July, *Les Complaintes de Jules Laforgue* appeared in a sky-blue binding with the epigraph, 'Au petit bonheur de la fatalité,' expressive of the author's aesthetics and of his sense of fatality.

'I am very particular about the empirical aesthetics of the Complainte,'[13] he wrote to Charles Henry. We have mentioned that 'empirical' origin in an earlier chapter. During the carnival after the dedication of the Lion de Belfort in September 1880, he had conceived the idea of writing songs a shade more literary than those sung by organ grinders on the streets, by entertainers in the public squares. Like the popular singers, he would count his line lengths on the basis of syllables actually pronounced, disregarding the mute 'e's' when he did not throw them out entirely. He would make liberal use of lines of eight syllables or less, because the caesura is mobile in short lines. He would employ ballad measures and refrains. And he would keep his verse close to the candidly sentimental and satirical feelings of the people.

The outrageously sentimental 'Chanson du petit hypertrophique,' mentioned in letters of February and November 1882, is pretty certainly the first *Complainte* written, even though Laforgue left it out of the volume and his editors eventually placed it in *Le Sanglot de la terre*. It might almost have been sung by an organ grinder on that carnival night of September 1880. The boy's mother, we are told in the first stanza, has died of heart disease:

> On rit d' moi dans les rues,
> De mes min's incongrues
>   La-i-tou!
>   D'enfant saoul;
> Ah! Dieu! C'est qu'à chaqu' pas
> J'étouff', moi, je chancelle!
> J'entends mon coeur qui bat,
> C'est maman qui m'appelle!
>
>   . . .
>
> Non, tout le monde est méchant,
> Hors le coeur des couchants,

Tir-lan-laire!
Et ma mère,
Et j' veux aller là-bas
Fair' dodo z'avec elle. . .
Mon coeur bat, bat, bat, bat. . .*
Dis, Maman, tu m'appelles?

The popular singer would slur the mute 'e's' in just this way, and plug the gaps between vowels with such a 'z' sound. Another rejected experiment, the 'Complainte de l'organiste de Notre-Dame de Nice,' has stanzas of more merit that point toward both earlier and later work.

Voici que les corbeaux hivernaux
Ont psalmodié parmi nos cloches,
Les averses d'automne sont proches,
Adieu les bosquets des casinos. . .

Le jour qu'elle quittera ce monde,
Je vais jouer un Miserere
Si cosmiquement désespéré
Qu'il faudra bien que Dieu me réponde!

Non, je resterai seul, ici-bas,
Tout à la chère morte phtisique,
Berçant mon coeur trop hypertrophique
Aux éternelles fugues de Bach. . .

Now that the flights of winter crows
Have psalmodized upon our eaves
The autumn downpours menace us,
Goodbye to groves of casinos.

The day she leaves this world behind,
I will intone a *Have mercy on us*

* In all editions of *Le Sanglot de la terre* this verse reads: 'Mon coeur bat, bat, bat. . .' Léon Guichard pointed out, in a letter of 5 September 1949 to G. Jean-Aubry, that another syllable is needed to make the line fit the pattern of the poem.

Full of such cosmic hopelessness
That God cannot but make a sign!

Yet though the time be out of joint
I'll linger on, vowed to the dear departed,
Lulling my hypertrophic heart
With Bach's eternal counterpoint.

Some of the best and most spirited of the *Complaintes* are only
one remove from the popular source, beaten out to the rhythms
of popular ditties:

COMPLAINTE DU PAUVRE JEUNE HOMME

Sur l'air populaire:
'Quand le bonhomm' revint du bois'

Quand ce jeune homm' rentra chez lui,
Quand ce jeune homm' rentra chez lui;
Il prit à deux mains son vieux crâne,
Qui de science était un puits!
Crâne,
Riche crâne,
Entends-tu la Folie qui plane?
Et qui demande le cordon,
Digue dondaine, digue dondaine,
Et qui demande le cordon,
Digue dondaine, digue dondon?

To the popular air:
'When the good man came back from the wood'

When the young man went back to his room,
When the young man went back to his room,
In his two hands he grasped his skull
Which of high knowledge was so full!
Skull,
Rich skull,
Do you hear Madness' hovering call?
Asking for the rope or knife

As big as life, as big as life,
Asking for the rope or knife, as big as life?

There are five more stanzas of similar form. The poor young man hears scales being practiced on a neighboring piano, as Laforguian heroes are wont to do. He laments that *her* husband has closed the house to his visits and remarks:

> *Ame,*
> *Ma belle âme,*
> *Leur huile est trop sal' pour ta flamme!*

> Soul,
> O my rare soul,
> Your flame's too fine for their crude oil!

He further notes that his wife has left him, having first taken the trouble to disconnect the gas so that he could not asphyxiate himself. He finally has recourse to a razor.

> *Quand les croq'morts vinrent chez lui,*
> *Quand les croq'morts vinrent chez lui;*
> *Ils virent que c'était une belle âme,*
> *Comme on n'en fait plus aujourd'hui. . .*

> When the howlers hied themselves upstairs,
> When the howlers hied themselves upstairs,
> They saw this soul was of a superior kind
> Now discontinued by the manufacturers. . .

The 'Complainte de l'époux outragé,' in which the offending wife stubbornly maintains that the officer with whom she was speaking in a corner of the church was Christ, is in about the same vein, of about the same vintage, and similarly fitted to the rhythmical pattern of a popular tune. So is the 'Complainte-Variations sur le mot *falot, falotte,*' one of the poems most generally appreciated during Laforgue's lifetime.

The quality of the *Complaintes* that impressed contemporaries, that eventually moved even Gustave Lanson, uncompre-

hending at first, to admit that they were 'une date dans l'histoire
poétique de la fin du XIXe,' was the bold appropriation of popular speech. Most significant, no doubt, was the use of it in traditionally elevated poetic contexts, so that Laforgue unmistakably
does what he credited Baudelaire with doing: 'puts his foot in the
plate,' expresses high thoughts in low language, lights upon
'Yankee' comparisons instead of lofty, harmonious ones. Due
importance, however, must be attached to the simplest kind of
Complainte, where Laforgue's vigorous diction appears in all its
impure purity.

Of the fifty titles, all but five begin with 'Complainte de . . .'
We are turned loose in a wilderness of genitives. But if we cannot
quite agree with James Joyce that the subjective and objective
genitives explain the world, we at least find them very serviceable
in clearing up the microcosm of the *Complaintes*. There are, in the
first place, the songs put in the mouths of someone or something
on the order of the 'Petit hypertrophique,' though usually far
different from it in tone: the 'Complainte du foetus du poète,'
'Complainte de Lord Pierrot,' 'Complainte du Roi de Thulé,' and
so on. In the same class come the poems spoken by two or more
figures: the 'Complainte des voix sous le figuier bouddhique,'
'Complainte de cette bonne lune,' 'Complainte de l'orgue de Bar-
barie,' and the like. All these are titles in which the genitive is
subjective: the foetus's, Lord Pierrot's, the King of Thulé's, the
Voices' complaints. In the second place we have the Complaintes
on a given theme: 'de la bonne défunte,' 'd'un certain dimanche,'
'de la fin des journées,' and so on. Here the genitives are objective: 'Complaint concerning the Good Deceased,' 'Complaint
concerning a Certain Sunday.' Finally we have the five titles in
which the stated theme is the object of a preposition other than
'de': 'Complainte propitiatoire à l'Inconscient,' 'Complainte sur
certains ennuis,' and three others.

In these titles, incidentally, Laforgue deployed all of his considerable ingenuity. We find such rubrics as the 'Complainte
des pubertés difficiles,' 'Complainte des nostalgies préhistoriques,'
'Complainte du pauvre chevalier-errant,' 'Complainte des formalités nuptiales,' 'Complainte des noces de Pierrot,' 'Complainte

du vent qui s'ennuie la nuit,' 'Complainte-Litanies de mon sacré-coeur,' and others no less colorful.

The poems of the second kind just named are lyrical expansions of personal emotion; they are called 'complaintes' to preserve the unity of the collection, but might almost equally well have been entitled 'elegies,' or simply 'La Bonne Défunte,' 'Un Certain Dimanche,' 'La Fin des journées.' In the gray loneliness that is the subject of the 'Complainte de la fin des journées' we rediscover

> *l'enfant qui vit de ce nom, poète!*
> *Il se rêvait, seul, pansant Philoctète*
> *Aux nuits de Lemnos; ou, loin, grêle ascète.*

> the child who answered to this name, poetic,
> Dreamed of himself, alone, tending Philoctetes
> In Lemnos' nights; or, far off, frail ascetic.

The child is none other than Stéphane Vassiliew, who in the desolate *lycée* of Tarbes dreamed of tending Philoctetes. A poem of protest such as the 'Complainte de la lune en province' is even more revelatory of personal mood, the mood of late summers when Laforgue vegetated at Tarbes. The 'Complainte d'un certain dimanche' is a graceful elegy, a farewell to R., with interesting 'liberated' alexandrines:

> *L'homme n'est pas méchant, ni la femme éphémère.*
> *Ah! fous dont au casino battent les talons,*
> *Tout homme pleure un jour et toute femme est mère,*
> *Nous sommes tous filials, allons!*

> Man is not wicked nor is woman ephemeral.
> Madmen whose loitering heels pound at the casino,
> Each man weeps one day, each woman's maternal,
> We are all filial, come now!

The classical caesura after the sixth syllable could not be more marked than in the first line, and it is sufficiently clear in the third. But the second line is divided with unusual effect after the second and seventh syllables.

Laforgue's mind, which was forever disintegrating the traditional verse line, time-hallowed sequences of imagery, the conception of the work of art as 'the expression of a dominant characteristic,' could not remain satisfied with the kind of poetry that gives direct expression to personal emotion. What, to begin with, is the 'individual'—etymologically 'one'? From Hartmann, Laforgue had learned to think of the human individual as an aggregate, a sum of many individuals. He had noted Hartmann's quotation from Spinoza, 'the human body consists of several individuals of various nature, each of which is very complex.' [14] He had pondered Hartmann's enlargement on this idea in the second part of his work. The poet who wrote, satirically,

> Quand j'organise une descente en Moi,
> J'en conviens, je trouve là, attablée,
> Une société un peu bien mêlée,
> Et que je n'ai point vue à mes octrois
>   —'Ballade,' Fleurs de bonne volonté

> Whenever I make bold to turn my gaze within
> I find there, I admit, drawn up at table
> Such a heterogeneous band of people
> As makes me wonder how they ever got in

was aware of the diversity within the individual, the complexity of the subconscious mind. Since he also believed in the Unconscious as a spiritual principle, a superior force driving the individual toward self-fulfillment in a swift succession of impulses, he felt moved to write about an individual divided in time as well as in space. We have, for instance, the emotion and its negation in the same poem, 'La Complainte de la bonne défunte,' beginning as ingenuously as Yeats' 'Song of the Wandering Aengus,' and ending with a Heine-like disavowal. Laforgue's irony, which springs from these psychological depths, will be discussed later.

Closely related to the drama of the irony is the dramatic form of the most characteristic Complaintes. In the earliest of these the poet did as he had done nowhere in his 'philosophical' verse. He assumed a role, a mask: 'Le Petit hypertrophique,' 'L'Organiste de

Notre-Dame de Nice.' These lyrical monologues led naturally to dialogues, still on the popular level; the 'Complainte de l'époux outragé' is a conversation between man and wife. The popular accent is preserved in poems where we can see the poet working his way back toward distinctive themes. In the 'Complainte de cette bonne lune' we hear from a chorus of stars as well as from Our Lady the Moon, and the accent of both parties is *faubourien*. Certain dialogues, however, and very important ones (the 'Complainte des voix sous le figuier bouddhique,' for example), turn about problems close to the poet's heart, and are couched in quite un-Naturalistic language. The dramatic design of this group of Complaintes is retained even when a fundamental intention, reproduction of popular spech, is abandoned. This is not, of course, to say that Laforgue always succeeds in finding words and sentiments suitable to dramatic personages and detached from himself. Some paradoxical titles simply conceal the unburdening of private emotions. From bottom to top of this first and most numerous group of the Complaintes, however, there is a movement toward dramatization, a tendency, having its origin in self-awareness and self-defense, to exteriorize the lyric emotion. This movement was ultimately to occasion 'Le Concile féerique,' a verse drama. Meanwhile it is felt in dramatic verse. And it is by the diversity and interest of this drama that Laforgue distinguishes himself from another poet, Tristan Corbière, whose starting point was also the *chanson populaire*.

None of these poems is better known, or deserves to be, than 'Autre Complainte de Lord Pierrot,' a conversation between ingenuous female and meditative male, which will be mentioned later as an example of the poet's irony. There are equally interesting dialogues of differing voices, some of them more sustained and furnished with a prologue and conclusion, which this Pierrot poem does not have. Three such poems are the 'Complainte des grands pins dans une villa abandonnée,' the 'Complainte des pianos dans les quartiers aisés,' and the 'Complainte du soir des comices agricoles.'

Sometimes the voices emerge hesitantly, uncertainly, as though from sleep, so that we are not always certain to whom they belong. They suggest, as they are meant to do, the mind looking into its own depths, given over to reverie, or awakening. The voices are thus blurred in the 'Complainte des grands pins,' but the contrast between them is certain. The introduction is in alexandrines:

> *Tout hier, le soleil a boudé dans ses brumes,*
> *Le vent jusqu'au matin n'a pas décoléré,*
> *Mais, nous point des coteaux là-bas, un oeil sacré*
> *Qui va vous bousculer ces paquets de bitume!*

> All day long yesterday the sun stayed hidden;
> Until daybreak the wind did not relent,
> But now dawns on the hills an eye intent
> On breaking up those masses of bitumen!

Except for the failure to rhyme a plural in 's' with a word ending in 's' (a commandment of the old prosody which Laforgue learned to break early in his career) the alexandrines are conventional. The middle caesura of the third line is weakened, which increases its rhythmic interest.

The first voice now speaks in octosyllables:

> *—Ah! vous m'avez trop, trop vanné,*
> *Bals de diamants, hanches roses;*
> *Et, bien sûr, je n'étais pas né*
> > *Pour ces choses.*

> —Oh you have done for me but right, but right,
> Glittering dances, rosy hips;
> One thing is certain, I was never meant
> > For things like this.

The second voice comments in classically divided alexandrines:

> *—Le vent jusqu'au matin n'a pas décoléré.*
> *Oh! ces quintes de toux d'un chaos bien posthume.*

> —Until daybreak the wind did not relent.
> Oh these coughing fits of a posthumous chaos.

For the 'posthumous chaos' we are referred to the end of the poem, where we learn that the storyteller's parents are dead; or, to the next to last quatrain, where we are told that he is ill of tuberculosis. The Gaspard Hauser-like story continues:

> —*Elles, coudes nus dans les fruits,*
> *Riant, changeant de doigts leurs bagues;*
> *Comme nos plages et nos nuits*
>   *Leur sont vagues!*

> —They, with bare elbows plunged in fruits,
> Laughing and toying with their rings,
> To them our beaches and our nights
>   Must seem such far-off things!

Then comes the exclamation

> *Oh! ces quintes de toux d'un chaos bien posthume,*
> *Chantons comme Memnon, le soleil a filtré.*

> Oh these coughing fits of a posthumous chaos,
> Now sing like Memnon! The sun's broken through.

For once, a Laforguian speaker is glad to see the sun; there is none of the anti-solar invective so conspicuous elsewhere. The mythological reference, like this one to the statue that bursts into song at the touch of the sun's rays, will become more and more frequent as a means of reconciling images. The parts of the 'Complainte des grands pins,' the narrative interrupted by a kind of choral commentary, were in danger of dispersion. Laforgue met the difficulty, partly, by using the rhymes of the first pair of alexandrines throughout:

> —*Et moi, je suis dans ce lit cru*
> *De chambre d'hôtel, fade chambre,*
> *Seul, battu dans les vents bourrus*
>   *De novembre.*

> —*Qui, consolant des vents les noirs Misérérés,*
> *Des nuages en fuite éponge au loin l'écume.*

—Berthe aux sages yeux de lilas,
Qui priais Dieu que je revinsse,
Que fais-tu, mariée là-bas,
    En province?

—And here I am in this bare bed,
This hotel room with rattling blinds,
Alone and shaken by the rude
    November winds.

—Which, comforting the black Misereres of the winds,
 Sponges away the foam of flying clouds.

—Bertha of the violet gaze
Who prayed God for my homecoming,
What are you doing, married, far away
    From everything?

The last two pairs of alexandrines have more rhythmical variety
than the early ones:

—Memnons, ventriloquons! le cher astre a filtré
Et le voilà qui tout authentique s'exhume!

—Il rompt ses digues! vers les grands labours qui fument!
Saint Sacrement! et Labarum *des* Nox irae!

—Ventriloquize like Memnon! the dear star's broken through
And in good earnest comes to life again!

—Breaking its dikes toward the broad smoking plowlands!
Blessed Sacrament! and *Labarum* of *Nox irae!*

The last verse is Romantic trimeter dividing evenly into three
parts, with a strong accent on the last syllable of each, and the
first of these lines is classically divided in two. But lines two and
three are 'liberated' verses, divisible into three parts according
to the once revolutionary patterns of 4-5-3 and 4-6-2. The unac-
cented sixth syllable in both lines disappoints classical expectations, allowing the long middle parts of the lines to convey the

sensation of great breaths of wind. The poem ends with these quatrains, interrupted by a last choral comment:

> *—Oh! quel vent! adieu tout sommeil;*
> *Mon Dieu, que je suis bien malade!*
> *Oh! notre croisée au soleil*
> > *Bon, à Bade.*

> *—Et bientôt, seul, je m'en irai,*
> *A Montmartre, en cinquième classe,*
> *Loin de père et mère, enterrés*
> > *En Alsace.*

> —Oh! What wind! and so farewell
> To any sleep. How sick I am!
> And oh our window in the gentle
> > Sunshine at Baden.

> —And soon, alone, I will be going
> Off to Montmartre in baggage class,
> Far from father and mother sleeping
> > In Alsace.

Alliteration, as in the fourth of these lines, is frequent in the poetry of Laforgue, who needed a formal element to strengthen purposely broken rhythms. The rareness in the poem of *rimes riches*, or rhymes with three similar sounds instead of the 'sufficient' two, is equally typical of the later verse.

The 'Complainte des grands pins' is dated from Baden-Baden, October 1882, in the copy of the *Complaintes* that Jules gave to his sister Marie. Reconstructing the circumstances that led up to its composition, we may suppose that the poet, walking one day in the outskirts of the town, came upon an empty villa. To the sound of the autumn wind in the pines, he imagines how it might have come to be empty, because of the dreaminess of someone like Gaspard Hauser—the wistful and unfortunate grandnephew of the Empress Josephine, about whom Verlaine wrote one of his memorable poems—someone who 'was not born for these things,' who was sickly and unsure of himself and allowed himself to be ruined. Such a story could have been told by the quatrains alone, and the poet may have written it that way first, as he wrote a similar poem in quatrains in a later collection, before inserting verses of choral commentary. But the comment, conceived on one level as the voice of the pine trees that have been witnesses to these things, permits a different tone, a saving irony, which keeps us from imagining that the poet himself is Gaspard Hauser, even though he may be lying 'in a bare bed' waiting for daylight.

The design of the 'Complainte des pianos qu'on entend dans les quartiers aisés' is the same as that of the 'Grands Pins'; and it happens to be well known in this country because it was one of the poems published by Ezra Pound in an influential number of the *Little Review* (February 1918). The introduction is, again, four lines long. A literary young man is shown strolling down the rue Madame in the springtime, and in the sound of the practicing coming from the windows he hears the plaint of miserable imprisoned souls:

> *Menez l'âme que les Lettres ont bien nourrie,*
> *Les pianos, les pianos, dans les quartiers aisés.*
> *Premiers soirs, sans pardessus, chaste flânerie,*
> *Aux complaintes des nerfs incompris ou brisés.*

> Conduct the soul well versed in literature,
> Pianos, pianos, in the prosperous quarters.
> First evenings, coatless, innocent adventure,
> To the complaints of nerves misunderstood or shattered.

He wonders:

> *Ces enfants, à quoi rêvent-elles,*
> *Dans les ennuis des ritournelles?*

> Tell me, what do they dream of, tell,
> In the ennuis of ritournelles?

and the voice of the pianos replies:

—'Préaux des soirs,
Christs des dortoirs!

'Tu t'en vas et tu nous laisses,
Tu nous laiss's et tu t'en vas,
Défaire et refaire ses tresses,
Broder d'éternels canevas.'

—'Schoolyards at nightfall,
Carved Christs upon the wall!

'You go away, we stay behind,
We stay behind, you go away,
We bind our tresses and unbind,
Embroider everlasting frames.'

Once more the poet has borrowed a rhythm, even a line, quoted exactly further on, from a popular song of the day: 'Tu t'en vas et tu nous quittes.' The poem continues thus, a quatrain of commentary succeeded by the two voices. Many details are memorable; for example, the beautiful Baudelairian third line in the following:

Fatales clés de l'être un beau jour apparues;
Psitt! aux hérédités en ponctuels fermonts,
Dans le bal incessant de nos étranges rues;
Ah! pensionnats, théâtres, journaux, romans!

Keys of all being one day bursting out
In punctual ferment to heredities,
In the incessant ball of our strange streets,
Ah! schools, playhouses, daily papers, stories!

The following brief couplet has imagery of interest to Freudian psychologists, while the quatrain suggests the medieval image of the rose as woman:

—'Rideaux tirés,
Peut-on entrer?

'Tu t'en vas et tu nous laisses,
Tu nous laiss's et tu t'en vas,
La source des frais rosiers baisse,
Vraiment! Et lui qui ne vient pas . . .'

—'Curtains drawn,
May one come in?

'You go away, we stay behind,
We stay behind, you go away,
The rose tree spring is running dry,
Truly! And he who doth delay . . .'

The power of observation and the humor are equally acerb:

Allez, stériles ritournelles,
La vie est vraie et criminelle.

Il viendra! Vous serez les pauvres coeurs en faute,
Fiancés au remords comme aux essais sans fond,
Et les suffisants coeurs cossus, n'ayant d'autre hôte
Qu'un train-train pavoisé d'estime et de chiffons.

Mourir? peut-être brodent-elles,
Pour un oncle à dot, des bretelles?

The devil, sterile ritournelles,
Life is real and criminal!

He'll come all right! You'll be the timid souls at fault,
Pledged to remorse as to unending trial,
And the stout bustling souls boasting no other thought
But the gay round of prestige and apparel.

Dying? Or maybe she embroiders
For some rich uncle, bright suspenders?

Few poems of sixty lines run so wide a gamut of perceptions.
    One of Laforgue's earliest prose fragments, we remember,
dealt with a girls' boarding school. The motif turns up again

here and the girl of the gray convent school is equated with the
Shulamite, the bride in the *Song of Songs.*

> —'*Coeurs en prison,*
> *Lentes saisons!*

> '*Tu t'en vas et tu nous quittes,*
> *Tu nous quitt's et tu t'en vas!*
> *Couvents gris, choeurs de Sulamites,*
> *Sur nos seins nuls croisons nos bras.*'

> —'Hearts in prison,
> Sluggish seasons!

> 'You go away, we stay behind,
> We stay behind, you go away!
> Gray convents, choirs of Shulamites,
> On our flat breasts press our arms tightly.'

The file or chorus of girls appears and reappears in Laforgue's
poetry after *Le Sanglot de la terre,* a symbol with several meanings. Sometimes the 'keys of being' are viewed pessimistically indeed, as a 'faithful vegetable' ('Complainte de l'orgue de Bar-
barie'). Woman is the 'little beast with a hank of hair . . . bone
of she-cat, body of ivy, futile masterpiece' ('Complainte des
voix sous le figuier bouddhique'). But more often the poet seems
inclined to absolve her, as he does in another part of the 'Complainte des voix.' Certainly in the 'Complainte des pianos' the
feeling is one of sympathy for fellow victims of the big houses,
the drawn curtains, the other images of bourgeois obtuseness.
Often the girls are shown going off to church, prayer books
clasped firmly in gloved hands, their appearance suggesting souls
stiffly starched; and then, with morning or evening churchbells
ringing above, they are symbols of the faith that Laforgue had
abandoned. The churchgoers are not invariably stiff: 'Yesterday
I wept, right in my prayer book!' ('Figurez-vous un peu,' *Des
Fleurs de bonne volonté*). But most often, and in one of Laforgue's last and best poems, 'Dimanches,' beginning

Le ciel pleut sans but, sans que rien l'émeuve,
Il pleut, il pleut, bergère! sur le fleuve . . .

The sky rains purposeless and unperturbed,
It rains, it rains, shepherdess, on the flood . . .

we find the girls of the boarding schools as Laforgue first noticed them, herded along on Thursdays and Sundays in double file. In this last poem one of the girls breaks out of line, runs to the bank of the still, rained-on river and throws herself in. At the end of the 'Complainte des pianos' the second voice ends the poem by saying,

'Tu t'en vas et tu nous laisses,
Tu nous laiss's et tu t'en vas.
Que ne suis-je morte à la messe!
O mois, ô linges, ô repas!'

'You go away, we stay behind,
We stay behind, you go away.
I would to God that I had died!
O months, O three meals a day!'

The 'Complainte du soir des comices agricoles' (dated from Baden-Baden in Marie's copy) is another poem in which two voices discourse on different levels after a brief introduction.

Deux royaux cors de chasse ont encore un duo
Aux échos,
Quelques fusées reniflent s'étouffer là-haut!

Two royal hunting horns make up a duo
To the echoes,
A few stray rockets gutter and out they go.

These opening lines are noteworthy for several reasons. They show Laforgue ill at ease in the alexandrine. Trying more and more to shape each line to its emotive idea, according to its own logic, he found that it sometimes turned out longer, sometimes shorter than the prescribed twelve syllables. What he really had in mind here was a fifteen-syllable line. A little later he would be writing out such verses as they occurred to him, having freed himself from the constraint of the traditional measure.

Line three of this introduction contains one of Laforgue's rare experiments in syntax. He was by no means an innovator in this domain, as Mallarmé was, and his experimentation was almost exclusively with rhyme, rhythm, and vocabulary. Here, however, to the vast subsequent indignation of M. Brunot, a venerable historian of the French language, he uses the verb 'renifler' somewhat as though it were 'aller' or 'venir.' The result is at once pyrotechnical and untranslatable, something like: 'A few rockets snuff (and) go out up there.' It is of some interest, too, that the beat of the popular voice,

> *Allez, allez, gens de la noce,*
> *Qu'on s'en donne une fière bosse!*

> Come along, come along, men of the party,
> Let's get wild as wild can be!

had been used by Gérard de Nerval in his satirical farewell to the parliamentarians: 'Nos adieux à la chambre des députés de l'an 1830, ou, Allez-vous-en vieux mandataires.' Finally we encounter here, in circumstances that can be described only as sordid and in a situation that must be termed ironical, those hunting horns that even Laforgue usually reserves for romantically poignant situations ('La Complainte des formalités nuptiales,' 'La Légende des trois cors,' in *Derniers Vers*, and so on). The disgust for human vulgarity manifest in this poem is all but Swiftian.

The best way to take leave of the *Complaintes* and this stage of Laforgue's poetic development is to look at his own valediction to his philosophical ideal. The 'Préludes autobiographiques' of the *Complaintes* is dated '1880, 5, rue Berthollet,'—by which notation Laforgue is probably only reminding himself of his most troubled period. The greater part of the poem seems to have been written on 22 March 1883, when he mentions 'Prologue à mes Complaintes' in his Agenda. He attached considerable importance to this poem, arguing against Kahn,[15] Henry, and Vanier for its inclusion. The publisher having urged that it be omitted, Laforgue wrote in an unpublished paragraph of a letter (April 1885), 'It remains my firm conviction that to take away the first piece would be to leave out what is morally half of the volume.' [16]

> *Ah! dérisoire créature!*
> *Fleuve à reflets, où les deuils d'Unique ne durent*
> *Pas plus que d'autres! L'ai-je rêvé, ce Noël*
> *Où je brûlais de pleurs noirs un mouchoir réel,*
> *Parce que, débordant des chagrins de la Terre*
> *Et des frères Soleils, et ne pouvant me faire*
> *Aux monstruosités sans but et sans témoin*
> *Du cher Tout, et bien las de me meurtrir les poings*
> *Aux steppes du cobalt sourd, ivre-mort de doute*
> *Je vivotais, altéré de* Nihil *de toutes*
> *Les citernes de mon Amour?*

> Ah! derisory creature!
> River with shadows, where grief for the Unique
> Survives no others. Did I dream that Christmas
> When I burned with dire tears a handkerchief,
> Choking with sorrow for the griefs of Earth
> And brother Suns, not to be reconciled
> To the pointless unwitnessed outrages
> Of the great Whole, weary of bruising my fists
> On steppes of deaf cobalt, drunken with doubt
> Barely alive, thirsting for Nothingness
> With all the cisterns of my Love?

This Christmas is 'gras,' as Laforgue has told us; it is just the opposite of his 'Noël sceptique.' He is aware now of the stubborn insensitivity of created things, himself among them, for he has not continued to mourn the death of incarnate charity. The sorrows of the earth and suns now seem far away. The word 'vivoter' ('to live sparely') had fitted him then, for it was so that he had lived, mortifying himself in his search for the Absolute, drunk with doubt, thirsting for the Buddhistic void.

Seul, pur, songeur,
Me croyant hypertrophique! comme un plongeur
Aux mouvants bosquets des savanes sous-marines,
J'avais roulé par les livres, bon misogyne.

Alone, pure, dreambound,
Dreaming myself hypertrophic! like a diver
In moving groves of submarine savannahs,
I roved through many books, misogynist.

Here is a specimen of the new and interesting imagery that comes
after *Le Sanglot:* underwater life representing in Laforgue's mind
the profound, obscure life of the Unconscious, and in our mind
standing for his struggling adolescence. One after another the
poet dismisses the themes of his earlier verse:

Cathédrale anonyme! en ce Paris, jardin
Obtus et chic, avec son bourgeois de Jourdain
A rêveurs, ses vitraux fardés, ses vieux dimanches . . .

Nameless cathedral! in this Paris, obtuse
And stylish garden, with its bourgeois Jordan
Haunted by dreamers, primped windows, stodgy Sundays . . .

This refers to the color symbolism of his long poem about the
stained-glass window of Notre-Dame de Paris. Laforgue speaks
of the mother-nebula in more offhand style than he had done
in 'Crépuscule de dimanche d'été,' and he recalls ironically his
solemn questionings of death and destiny in 'Eclair de gouffre.'
He wonders how he could ever have supposed that his cry toward
other worlds might find an echo:

. . . *mon Cri me jaillissant des moelles,*
On verrait, mon Dieu, des signaux dans les étoiles?

. . . my Cry arising from my very marrow,
Would signals, Lord, be sighted in the stars?

He explicitly disclaims whatever ambitions he may once have
entertained to save the world:

Puis, fou devant ce ciel qui toujours nous bouda,
Je rêvais de prêcher la fin, nom d'un Bouddha!
Oh! pâle mutilé, d'un: qui m'aime me suive!
Faisant de leurs cités une unique Ninive,
Mener ces chers bourgeois, fouettés d'alléluias,
Au Saint-Sépulcre maternel du Nirvâna!

Maintenant, je m'en lave les mains (concurrence
Vitale, l'argent, l'art, puis les lois de la France . . .)

Half crazed beneath the ever-frowning sky
I dreamed, in Buddha's name! of preaching the last days,
Pale, stricken, crying, 'Let whoso loves me follow!'
Turning their cities to one Nineveh,
Leading these bourgeois lashed with alleluias
To the maternal Sepulchre of Nirvana.

But now I wash my hands of it (the struggle
For survival—money, art—besides the laws of France . . .)

The penultimate line—which the unelided mute 'e' following
the caesura virtually divides into two parts, one of six and one
of five syllables—is only one of many boldly conceived verses in
a poem that requires throughout new rhythms to fit new substance.

The diversity of voices in the *Complaintes*, the sometimes uneasy originality of rhythms and imagery, and the systematic
reversal of former sentiments bring us to the problem of the
poet's irony.

IX

Ironic Equilibrium

Today . . . the European Hamlet stares at millions of ghosts. But he is an intellectual Hamlet. He meditates on the life and death of truths. For phantoms he has all the subjects of our controversies; for regrets he has all our titles to glory; he bows under the weight of discoveries and learning, unable to renounce and unable to resume this limitless activity. He reflects on the boredom of recommencing the past, on the folly of always striving to be original. He wavers between one abyss and the other, for two dangers still threaten the world: order and disorder.

PAUL VALÉRY

THE first of January 1886, Laforgue, still reader to the Empress but growing more and more restless in that post, visited Elsinore. 'The whole heartbreaking irony,' he wrote to Kahn, 'of being in these rockbound, windswept islands on the first day of '86 (the year when we'll check out, perhaps) . . .' He erred by only a few months in his prediction, and he was entirely right and true to his own vein when he went on to say, 'in any case we shall have spoken into the wind a respectable number of relatively immortal words.' [1]

He mentions, among other events of that wind-tormented day, the composition of some 'literature.' By this he did not mean 'Hamlet, ou les Conséquences de la piété filiale,' though he was then in the process of writing that tale, and it was certainly on its account that he had ventured beyond the picture galleries of Copenhagen and exposed himself to the seven-hour boat trip between Kiel and Korsör. Nor did he mean his little sketch, 'A propos de Hamlet,' which eventually appeared in the magazine *Le Symboliste*. He was referring to a poem that apparently surprised him on the journey, the spare and confessional 'Avertissement,' in which many of the emotions of 'Hamlet' are brought to a poetic point. 'Avertissement' is interesting throughout, with its nine unsettled syllables to the line and the colloquial slurrings by which that number is often obtained; with its incisive details— 'My father, a timid man, hence hard, Died with a stiff and frowning air'; with its establishment of this Hamlet as a literary man.

> *Alors, j'ai fait d'la littérature,*
> *Mais le Démon de la Vérité*
> *Sifflotait tout l'temps à mes côtés:*
> *'Pauvre! as-tu fini tes écritures? . . .'*

> So then I determined to be a writer,
> But the Demon of Truth at my elbow
> Had a way of murmuring soft and low,
> 'Well, lad, have you spoiled enough paper?'

The poem ends:

> *C'est pourquoi je vivotte, vivotte,*
> *Bonne girouette aux trent'-six saisons,*
> *Trop nombreux pour dire oui ou non . . .*
> *—Jeunes gens! que je vous serv' d'Ilote!*

> And that is why I struggle and veer
> Like a weathercock with the winds that blow,
> Too various to say yes or no.
> Young men! There's a moral here!

Of course, 'Avertissement' might never have been written without Verlaine's poem on Gaspard Hauser. But whereas 'Je suis venu, calme orphelin' was a sort of happy accident ('travail de manoeuvre,' as Baudelaire might have called it), Laforgue realizes Baudelaire's desire that the poet be thoroughly aware of what he is doing. Undoubtedly Laforgue had read Corbière's autobiographical 'Bâtard de créole et Breton,' and perhaps taken suggestions from it. But if we compare Corbière's quatrains with Laforgue's we see that the latter are distinguished by more complexity, more salutary irony. 'Avertissement' is conspicuously ironical. It was unexpected that a poet should make such deprecations with such intonations. And beneath the irony of expression lie profounder ironies of situation. This Hamlet is the first to notice the disparity between what he is able to do and all that ought to come out of what he should be doing. He is like Marlow in Conrad's *Lord Jim*, the observer wise to the world's ways, who cannot help the victim; and he is also like Jim, the actor who cannot act. He is the slayer and the slain. To present this kind of irony not many words are necessary, only enough to cover the given segment of the human situation. In *Des Fleurs de bonne volonté* and in *Derniers Vers*, Laforgue's last two collections, we have come a long way from the verbal self-indulgences of the young poet exulting in his instrument and in his newly discovered manner of using it—the 'logopoetic' ironies of some of the lesser Complaintes.

Having looked at some of the themes and images that are treated straightforwardly in Laforgue's early work, we might do well to indicate what is meant by irony susceptible to 'equilibrium.' We must proceed warily, of course, for irony is like Syrinx, the nymph restored to life in the most purely delightful of Laforgue's tales—a figure that flees before the pursuer and vanishes when pressed, leaving only the syrinx, a somewhat pathetic reed instrument, in overanxious hands. We are grateful for every indirect, light-footed approach to the subject of irony. Ezra Pound wrote, out of his enthusiasm for Laforgue, that 'the ironist is one who suggests that the reader should think,' and 'this process being unnatural to the majority of mankind, the way of the ironist is beset by snares and furze-bushes.' [2] This, while it does not define, illumines. So does another critic's description of Laforgue's irony as a magnesium spark struck out between the halves of a divided personality.[3] Even a definition of irony as 'the fragile inheritance of ancient French wisdom' [4] has its tenuous element of truth. François Ruchon characterizes Laforgue's irony as an attitude of detachment from emotions, ideas, life itself.[5] Irony does involve detachment. None of the pursuits of the evanescent essential quality of Laforgue's work has been quite fruitless.

The essence of ironic utterance is oppositeness. Not the expected, but the unexpected, and even the contrary of the expected thing, is said. Of course, unexpectedness in some degree is characteristic of most witty remarks, of wit in general. Laforgue's irony is always verging on the melancholy pleasantry, as when he writes in a love poem wordily entitled 'Autre Complainte de Lord Pierrot,'

> *Celle qui doit me mettre au courant de la Femme!*
> *Nous lui dirons d'abord, de mon air le moins froid:*
> *'La somme des angles d'un triangle, chère âme,*
>   *Est égale à deux droits.'*

> She who on womankind must be my mentor,
> We shall tell her at once, in my least chilling tones,
> 'The angles of a triangle, my dear,
>   Equal, all told, two right ones.'

The reader is surprised by such lines in a poem of putatively amorous intent. He is probably taken aback by the contrast, within the lines, between the theorem and the ceremonious 'chère âme.' 'Celle qui doit me mettre au courant de la femme' is not exactly a Romantic formula for the beloved, and the plural 'nous' is more in the style of the prefect of a French département than that of a proper poet. Within the title itself there is a collision between the terms 'Lord' and 'Pierrot.' The surprise occasioned by these and other differences between the reader's expectation and the poet's statement is evidence of the irony. If the early I. A. Richards was right, if the differences between reader and poet are slight, if the poet is only a person somewhat more proficient than the reader at channeling his impulses, the poet himself must be astonished by the contrarieties proceeding from the divided 'individual,' by the chorus of mixed voices arising from that 'compagnie un peu bien mêlée' within the self.

In matter-of-fact discourse, the understanding of the ironic remark as the opposite of the expected one is sufficient. But in

the further reaches of connotative language it becomes clear that
what is opposite on one level of signification may be apposite on
another. In a poem a word or group of words may have more
than one meaning. In the quatrain just quoted, for example, the
remark that contrasts so sharply with the expected Romantic
protestation is also, on another plane of meaning, in dead earnest:
this geometrical theorem is one of the symbols of Laforgue's sense
of fatality. The speaker of the poem is, among other things, telling the lady that what will be is bound to be. In poetry, oppositeness between expectation and fulfillment can exist only along
with other relationships between the thing said and the thing
anticipated. But the fact that this irony, this oppositeness, exists
on one level is at once a revelation and a safeguard of the multi-
fariousness of experience. The flash of irony illumines for an instant, if not the chaos, at least the complexity of the reader's
mind—'the equilibrium of opposed impulses,' as I. A. Richards calls
it, existing there. That equilibrium, says Richards, 'which we
suspect to be the ground-plan of the most valuable aesthetic responses brings into play far more of our personality than is possible in experiences of a more defined emotion. We cease to be
oriented in one definite direction; more facets of the mind are
exposed.' [6] A flash born of ironic utterance illuminates the complexity, the 'equilibrium' within the reader's mind, which he then
surmises to exist within the poet's. In any case, ironic poetry, a
poetry of inclusion rather than exclusion, which puts several
kinds of poetic force to work upon the page, satisfies that need
for light on his own mind which the reader learns to expect
from poetry.

A procedure of Laforgue's wit closely related to the ironic
consists in the unexpected confrontation of ideas in mixed words.
Sometimes the invention is as amusing as that of Heine's poor
lottery agent, who bragged that the great Baron Rothschild had
treated him as an equal, quite 'famillionaire.' In the 'Complainte
des nostalgies préhistoriques,' the cry of someone 'violupté à vif'
is heard from the bushes. Elsewhere 'volupté' is wedded to
'nuptial' in 'voluptial.' We read of the 'spleenuosités' instead of
the 'sinuosités' of cities. The prelude to the *Complaintes* has one
of the most ambitious of these combinations:

Mondes vivotant, vaguement étiquetés
De livres, sous la céleste Eternullité.

Worlds jogging along, identified obscurely
By books, beneath the celestial Eternullity.

'Sangsuelles' is untranslatable, since there is no way of fitting
'blood' into a word sounding exactly like 'sensual.'

Mais, fausse soeur, fausse humaine, fausse mortelle,
Nous t'écartèlerons de hontes sangsuelles. . .
　　　　　　　—'Complainte des voix sous le figuier bouddhique'

But, false sister, false human, false mortal,
We will draw and quarter you with disgrace *sangsuelles* . . .

Nor can we do much with 'crucifiger,' where the word ends in
the equivalent for 'clot.' But no reader familiar with Baudelaire's
'Harmonie du soir,' where 'Le soleil s'est noyé dans son sang qui
se fige,' could fail to be struck by

　　　　Soleil qui, saignant son quadrige,
　　Cabre, s'y crucifige! [7]

Not all of these combinations are instantly plausible. 'Omni-
vers' [8] and 'omniversel,' for instance, fall rather flat. But the passion for verbal invention, sometimes successful, sometimes not,
was enduring. 'Love me over a slow fire, inventory me, massacre
me, massacrilege me,' [9] Elsa appeals to Lohengrin in the tale bearing that hero's name. And we read of 'elephantastic' [10] jokes in
'The Two Pigeons,' one of the last stories.

Like the examples of Laforgue's irony, these mixed words are
unexpected. But whereas the ironic utterance depends on the
degree of difference between what is expected and what is said,
here success seems to be in proportion to the closeness with
which the new invention fits an anticipated syllable-pattern, the
nearness with which it misses a mark.

The Latinisms that Laforgue relished—'alacre' [11] from 'alacer,'
'albe' [12] from 'alba,' 'errabundes' [13] from 'errabundus'—are regularly pressed into ironic service, and clash with colloquial vocables

in the same or proximate lines. Words lifted or derived from the rich and fine sixteenth-century language—'arbrillon' [14] meaning 'little tree,' 'pigrite' [15] for 'idleness'—are ironically erudite. Equally so are the scientific terms. We read in 'Lohengrin': 'The golden valves of the Tabernacle dehisce,'—the verb ordinarily being reserved for ripe pods that open to release their seeds. When Lohengrin appears in the nick of time to save Elsa from the executioners, the latter inquire, 'Who is this fine knight advancing over the seas, melodious with gallantry, his forehead carunculated with fidelity?' 'Carunculated,' like 'aptère' [16] (wingless) and 'fongosité,' [17] is a biological term. So is the adjective in the description of Pierrot, 'hydrocephalic asparagus.' [18] Naturally, in poetry with strong popular ties, the colloquial word is likely to let down the lyric mood. 'C'est le printemps qui s'amène,' we read in the 'Complainte des printemps,' and the word 's'amener' is one with which a workingman might urge along his laggard wife on a Sunday outing. Puns such as 'dies irraemissibles' [19] and 's'in-Pan-filtrer' [20] reflect the same satiric intent.

Rimbaud had already made free use of scientific and popular words in poetry. Romantic verse, especially Hugo's, had enriched the poetic vocabulary on a massive scale. The Decadents of the Left Bank coteries into which Laforgue had ventured as a very young man were addicted to neologisms, and the Symbolists who followed them coined rare and mysterious vocables for musical effect. It is, however, accurate to state that no young writer of the last hundred years has experimented with a more varied vocabulary than Laforgue's. In none has the 'life of words' been more ebullient. No other nineteenth-century writer anticipates so clearly the intense word-consciousness, the linguistic innovations of Léon-Paul Fargue and James Joyce.

After the uneven *Complaintes*, where the verbal inventions are not uniformly happy, and where the arrangement of lines of varied length in novel stanza-forms is often arbitrary, Laforgue moved toward delicately balanced poetic discourse in two quite different collections. The first is the volume of forty-one poems, most of them brief, which appeared early in 1886, dedicated 'to Gustave Kahn and also to the memory of little Salammbô, priestess of Tanit': *L'Imitation de Notre-Dame la Lune*.

The most limited tonally of Laforgue's collections, this is the one in which he most consistently attains that *suraigu* for which he strove during his years in Germany. The moon is exalted at the expense of the sun: the elaborate anti-solar invective opening the book shows a poetry of praise yielding to one of recrimination. The poet who now calls the sun 'old trooper plastered all over with decorations and crosses,' and who fills another line with miscellaneous abuse—'fop, pimp, ruffian, low adventurer'—had once invoked the 'picturesque star,' like any docile disciple of the Romantics, and had written the conventional sunset passages of *Stéphane Vassiliew*.

There have been a number of attempts to seize the symbolic significance of Our Lady the Moon. Jean Pérès remarked on the sterility, the death-like attributes of the planet in his friend's verse.[21] François Ruchon finds the Laforguian moon to be 'queen of Silence and of Sterility.' [22] Marc Eigeldinger sees in it a symbol of Buddhistic renunciation: 'the moon is raised to the dignity of a symbol, representing a world empty of all intellectual content, escape into nirvana, aspiration to death in nothingness.' [23] This applies at least as well to Laforgue's aquarium symbol as to Our Lady of the Evenings. Associating the moon with an irrational Unconscious and pointing to its non-temporal connections, Anna Balakian considers it a symbol of dehumanization.[24] But what Mallarmé's symbols illustrate very well, Laforgue's hardly exemplify. Our Lady the Moon should have a meaning that would not rob a notoriously human poet of his humanity. Of Kant's *History of Nature and Theory of the Heavens* Laforgue knew at least the passage in which the philosopher makes the fineness of bodies and faculties in his series of inhabited worlds depend on distance from the sun. For Laforgue as for Kant, the sun was a source of grossness; it is a short step to make the moon source and symbol of the opposite quality. Of course, Our Lady the Moon has a perfect right to change her meaning, and she does, standing, like any frequently recurring poetic image, for a number of things: for sterility, for evasion by suicide, for unrealizable Romantic aspiration. She also represents, frequently and simply, finesse.

Framed by half a dozen prefatory poems and a dozen concluding ones, twenty-three poems presenting Pierrot or expounding his ideas form the lunar center of the volume. For Pierrot is first and last the creature of Our Lady the Moon, despite a family tree springing directly from the *commedia dell' arte*. Before the first Pierrot (or Pedrolino) there had been Pagliacco, who differed from other buffoons of Italian farce in that he wore no mask but had his face whitened with flour. He was a butt, an unsuccessful lover, a lackey. At the end of the sixteenth century came Pedrolino (or Piero). Slightly more complex than his predecessor, he rather resembled the butts in Molière's farces; he was a vainglorious coward, a cuckold on occasion, but not invariably victimized, and was endowed with a rough, comforting common sense. The give and take between comic characters was such, moreover, that for a while Piero lost his identity to his hated rival, Arlecchino, who had a fanciful twist to his humor; and Harlequin was the first Pierrot-type to appear in France, when companies of Italian players began to perform for Paris audiences about the beginning of the seventeenth century. He speedily became naturalized, assuming the sentiments along with the accents of popular songs, hesitating delicately between comic and pathetic, for Harlequin-Pierrot—and this is his distinguishing quality—lost his buffoon-like traits to take on the profounder nature of the clown.

Laforgue and some of his elders were devoted to eighteenth-century prints and paintings, among them Watteau's picture of Gilles, a close cousin of Pierrot. But it remained for an actor at the celebrated Théâtre des Funambules to give Pierrot the costume that we recognize in Laforgue's word-portraits, the black silk skullcap and ample blouse. At the Théâtre des Funambules, Pierrot earned the right to say things that people would tolerate from no one otherwise attired, because what he had to say was too much like their shamefast thoughts. Thanks to the genius of a mime named Deburau he became once for all a clown rather than a figure of farce. Baudelaire remarked that what distinguished the French from the English Pierrot was his melancholy, moon-pale air.

French writers who flourished a decade or two before Laforgue thus had a familiar clown-like figure at hand, and they interpreted him according to individual lights. Gautier wrote enthusiastically

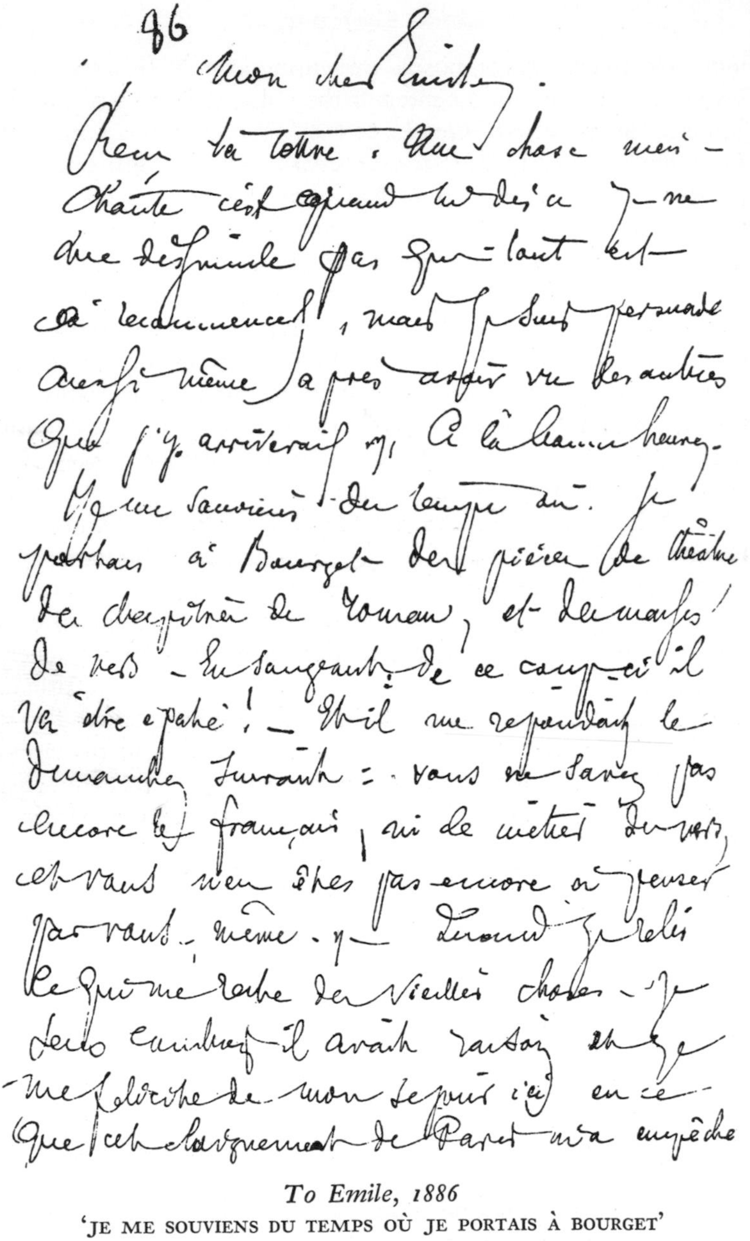

86

Mon cher Emile,

Reçu ta lettre. Une chose méchante c'est quand tu dis que je ne me désespère pas que tout est à recommencer, mais je suis persuadé aussi même après avoir vu les autres que j'y arriverai à la bonne heure.

Je me souviens du temps où je portais à Bourget des pièces de théâtre des chapitres de roman, et des masses de vers — en songeant de ce coup-ci il va être épaté! — et il me répondait le dimanche suivant : vous ne savez pas encore le français, ni le métier du vers, et vous n'en êtes pas encore à penser par vous-même — je [illegible] relis ce qui me reste des vieilles choses — je [illegible] il avait raison et je me félicite de mon séjour ici en ce que cet éloignement de Paris m'a empêché

To Emile, 1886

'JE ME SOUVIENS DU TEMPS OÙ JE PORTAIS À BOURGET'

about Deburau and composed *L'Esquisse d'un Pierrot posthume*.
Théodore de Banville was concerned for the most part with
lighter aspects of the figure; but he also wrote the 'Saut du
Tremplin,' in which the circus clown prays for a loftier spring,
a mightier bound, and vaults into eternity. And his *Promenade
galante* has wraith-like figures surprisingly like those that Verlaine fitted into his better known *Fêtes galantes*. Verlaine, in a
later sonnet, reflected a change that had been wrought in the
character of Pierrot, while others, including Joris-Karl Huysmans
and Léon Hennique, authors of that *Pierrot sceptique* [25] which
Laforgue urged upon Charles Henry in 1881, were exploiting
Pierrot's appeal to theater audiences.

Once we have traced Pierrot's long lineage and glanced at
treatments that attracted Laforgue's attention, we are struck more
than ever by the originality of this young poet's clown, by the
vibrancy of the life Laforgue is able to instill in a figure that
another might have regarded as quite literally played out. He
was without rival when he turned the venerable flour-faced creature into one subject to all the hesitations and interior debate
characterizing an impressionable man of the time.

His Pierrots (for Laforgue often used the plural, thereby gain-
ing a greater degree of ironic detachment) are white-faced, in
obedience to tradition. In fact, everything about them is white
except the black skullcap and the scarlet mouth.

> *C'est, sur un cou qui, raide, émerge*
> *D'une fraise empesée idem*
> *Une face imberbe au cold-cream,*
> *Un air d'hydrocéphale asperge.*
>
> *Les yeux sont noyés de l'opium*
> *De l'indulgence universelle,*
> *La bouche clownesque ensorcèle*
> *Comme un singulier géranium.*
>
> *Bouche qui va du trou sans bonde*
> *Glacialement désopilé,*
> *Au transcendental en-allé*
> *Du souris vain de la Joconde.*
>
> —'Pierrots'

You see a neck that, stiff, emerges
From a ruff starched tight as a drum,
A beardless face smeared with cold cream
Like a hydrocephalic asparagus.

The eyes are blurred with the opium
Of universal tolerance,
The scarlet clown-like mouth enchants
Like a singular geranium.

Mouth supremely flexible,
From the hole gaping glacially
To the transcendental fadeaway
Of Mona Lisa's futile smile.

When they dine as Laforgue dined in his Paris days, their food
is white, or at least appropriate to pilgrims of the Absolute.

Ils vont, se sustentant d'azur,
Et parfois aussi de légumes,
De riz plus blanc que leur costume,
De mandarines et d'oeufs durs.

Ils sont de la secte du Blême. . .
                                    —'Pierrots'

They dine upon the absolute
And occasionally on vegetables,
On rice bleached whiter than their dress,
On hard-boiled eggs and a little fruit.

They are of the pallid sect. . .

They have

Le coeur blanc tatoué
De sentences lunaires,

Their white hearts tattooed
With lunar sentences,

these 'blancs parias,' these 'purs pierrots,' for they are as white inside as they are out, abstaining archly from such consolations as other men seek. The Pierrots

> . . . *n'ont personne*
> *Chez eux, qui les frictionne*
> *D'un conjugal onguent.*

> . . . have nobody at home,
> No one to rub them down
> With conjugal balm.

But then they do not want anyone, or profess not to.

Of course, it is all a joke, given away in the fifth and sixth of this set of 'Pierrots' and in nearly all the 'Locutions des Pierrots' that follow. Laforgue really believes in this world and

> *Qu'il faut pas le traiter d'hôtel*
> *Garni vers un plus immortel,*
> *Car nous sommes faits l'un pour l'autre.*

> That it shouldn't be treated like a hotel
> Toward some less mortal lodging place,
> For we're by nature complementary.

Some of his finest verse is to be found in these poems in which the human fragility pierces through the irony. And yet, paradoxically, Laforgue was possessed by an ideal of intactness, of purity. It is, to say the least, ironical that Pierrot, for centuries the disappointed or deceived lover, should become the disappointer and gay deceiver, the ostentatiously chilly creature of the poems and the little play, *Pierrot fumiste*, who subjects his lawful wife Columbine to the harshest kind of indignity before overwhelming her with affection one night and then abandoning her utterly. We think of Lohengrin, an extension of the Pierrot figure, hard pressed by Elsa on the marriage bed, gripping his pillow so hard, so imploringly that it turns into the swan that lifts him safely away from the Will to Live. We think of Andromeda and Salomé, furiously self-possessed in their different ways, and of

Syrinx, who ran away. Never was there a Pierrot, or a gallery of Pierrotic characters, like this. Even Verlaine's Pierrot allowed Columbine to lead him by the nose. But if the Swiss Amiel, another witness to the hesitations of the late nineteenth-century intellectual, had written smilingly ironic verse instead of tormented diaries, it might have been something like Laforgue's.

If the voice of the Pierrots is sharper, keener than that of any speakers in Laforgue's early verse, that of his feminine interlocutor (the human one, not the Moon) is correspondingly graver and more ingenuous. Out of this calculated dramatic opposition the poet drew one of his best brief dialogues, 'Pierrot: on a des principes,' compactly plotted, melodious, with two final quatrains abstaining nicely on the point of eloquence:

> *Mais voici qu'un beau soir, infortunée à point,*
> *Elle meurt!—Oh! là, là; bon, changement de thème!*
> *On sait que tu dois ressusciter le troisième*
> *Jour, sinon en personne, du moins*

> *Dans l'odeur, les verdures, les eaux des beaux mois!*
> *Et tu iras, levant encore bien plus de dupes*
> *Vers le Zaïmph de la Joconde, vers la Jupe!*
> *Il se pourra même que j'en sois.*

But now suppose that some fine evening
She died! aha! Now there's a change of tune!
You will, needless to say, be resurrecting
On the third day, if not in person, then

In summer's fragrance, in the leaves and waters.
And you'll go on collecting innocents
Toward Mona Lisa's veil, toward the skirt!
I do not say I won't be one of them.

This clear definition of the parties to the dialogue was accompanied by a general whetting of tools. The *Imitation* contains Laforgue's most polished verse. Getting away from the involved stanza divisions of the *Complaintes,* so often artificial and confusing, he makes excellent use of alexandrines rhyming in couplets, of octosyllables in quatrains with the usual *abab* or *abba* schemes, and writes some of the most vigorous decasyllables since the sixteenth century.

> *Voilà le Néant dans sa pâle gangue,*
> *Voilà notre Hostie et sa Sainte-Table,*
> *Le seul bras d'ami par l'Inconnaissable,*
> *Le seul mot solvable en nos folles langues!*

> *Au delà des cris choisis des époques,*
> *Au delà des sens, des larmes, des vierges,*
> *Voilà quel astre indiscutable émerge,*
> *Voilà l'immortel et seul soliloque!*

> There is the ore of Nothing unrefined,
> There is our sacrament and its holy board,
> The only arm outstretched through the Unknown,
> In our mad tongues the single solvent word.

> Beyond the senses, beyond tears and virgins,
> Beyond the chosen utterances of history,
> There the unchallengeable star emerges,
> There the immortal lone soliloquy.

The metaphors stand for the moon in its whiteness; and the originality of three of them, together with the ironic 'solvable' and 'discutable,' lends the quality of Laforgue's later verse to lines possessing the rhythmic vitality of his earlier. Such metrical and rhythmical experimentation as there is succeeds. The first of the 'Locutions des Pierrots' has an unprecedented combination of ten- and seven-syllable lines. There is an interesting pattern of sevens and threes in 'Stérilités.' The tenth of the 'Locutions' is in those five-syllable lines that have more movement than any other verse in French; and the fourteenth poem of the same group, which by a certain heartiness of manner recalls Corbière, also has five-syllable lines. 'Jeux' is a skillful exercise in nines. Altogether, the uneven, the *impair* recommended by Verlaine, receives its share of attention.

As far as rhyming is concerned, Laforgue is not quite so perversely intent as before on upsetting the Malherbian applecart. But the *rimes riches* are decidedly in the minority (about one in seven), and often these rhymes are far from 'unexpected,' as sound tradition prescribed, but associate too obviously similar words. No attempt is made to satisfy the capricious rules 'for the eye': singulars rhyme regularly with plurals. In the absence of rhyme, words are linked by assonance or by similar consonants. What might have been rich or sufficient rhymes or true assonances are often rendered 'false' by differing vowel quality.

From Laforgue's production up to and including *L'Imitation* we might conclude that he wrote verse either appreciably less free than that of the Decadents or perceptibly more so; he is not at ease with a Verlainian technique of guarded liberties. He can write strong-membered Parnassian alexandrines having neither more nor less musical timbre than the traditional French measure usually has in capable hands. It is as though he sometimes consented that his verse should sing, and sing bravely, using the firmest accentual patterns the language afforded. This means, fundamentally, the binary alexandrine:

> *Sache que les Pierrots, phalènes des dolmens*
> *Et des nymphéas blancs des lacs où dort Gomorrhe,*
> *Et tous les bienheureux qui pâturent l'Eden*
> *Toujours printanier des renoncements,—t'abhorrent.*

It means, incidentally, the ringing decasyllables of 'Au Large,' with their pauses after the fourth syllable. In this lyrical verse there are no innovations to speak of. Meanwhile the other and principal current, the conversational monologue, is straining the dikes and dams of traditional versification.

In the third and fourth lines of 'Pierrot: on a des principes' cited above, for instance, the overflow of 'jour' is awkward. Line three was crying to be written thus:

> *On sait que tu dois ressusciter le troisième jour*

except that the poet would then have had a line of at least four-teen syllables, fifteen if 'siè' were counted as two, as it should have been all the time.

L'Imitation offers many examples of ill-poised conventional measures. The most striking examples of lines dragging their anchors, however, are to be found in *Des Fleurs de bonne volonté*, a collection on which Laforgue worked at intervals between 1883 and 1886.

> *Un Soir, je crus en Moi! J'en faillis me fiancer!*
> *Est-ce possible . . . Où donc tout ça est-il passé! . . .*
> *Chez moi, c'est Galathée aveuglant Pygmalion!*
> *Ah! faudrait modifier cette situation. . .*

Laforgue had good reasons to abandon these lines except as raw material for the fine passage in *Dernier Vers:*

> *Bref, j'allais me donner d'un 'Je vous aime'*
> *Quand je m'avisai non sans peine*
> *Que d'abord je ne me possédais pas bien moi-même.*
>
> *(Mon Moi, c'est Galathée aveuglant Pygmalion!*
> *Impossible de modifier cette situation.)*

The earlier lines are manageable as alexandrines only by difficult synaereses, and even so are unconscionably broken up. The same ideas and images find inevitable form in five verses of uneven length. The following passage is likewise subject to transforma-tion:

> *Oh! qu'une, d'Elle-même, un beau soir, sût venir,*
> *Ne voyant que boire à Mes Lèvres! ou mourir. . .*
>
> *Je m'enlève rien que d'y penser! Quel baptême*
> *De gloire intrinsèque, attirer un 'Je vous aime'!*
>
> *L'attirer à travers la société, de loin,*
> *Comme l'aimant la foudre; un', deux! ni plus, ni moins.*

> *Je t'aime! comprend-on? Pour moi tu n'es pas comme*
> *Les autres; jusqu'ici c'était des messieurs, l'Homme . . .*

This becomes:

> *Oh! qu'une, d'Elle-même, un beau soir, sût venir*
> *Ne voyant plus que boire à mes lèvres, ou mourir! . . .*
>
> *Oh! Baptême!*
> *Oh! baptême de ma Raison d'être!*
> *Faire naître un 'Je t'aime!'*
> *Et qu'il vienne à travers les hommes et les dieux,*
> *Sous ma fenêtre,*
> *Baissant les yeux!*
>
> *Qu'il vienne, comme à l'aimant la foudre,*
> *Et dans mon ciel d'orage qui craque et qui s'ouvre. . .*

The ejaculations obviously gain vividness with brevity, and the contrasting sixth line has its hint of grandeur, albeit ironic. Why should not the ideas, 'under my windows' and 'lowering his eyes,' be expressed in four syllables each?

Sometimes the poet deliberately adds a word that disrupts the neat rhythmic pattern of an earlier effort:

> *Nous nous aimions comme deux fous;*
> *On s'est quittés sans en parler.*
> *(Un spleen me tenait exilé*
> *Et ce spleen me venait de tout.)*

remains the same except for the loss of the 's' on 'quittés' and the last line, which becomes

> *Et ce spleen me venait de tout. Bon.*

These are examples of the free verse that Laforgue began to compose early in 1886—ten poems published in *La Vogue* between August and December of that year, which his editors eventually assembled in the volume they called *Derniers Vers*. There have been numerous attempts to say what free verse is; there have even been some denials that it ever was, on the not wholly unreasonable grounds that verse is never free but always has its own laws. However, to deny the existence of free verse is to assume a superbly paradoxical, unhistorical position. For there is no doubt whatever that Rimbaud included in his *Illuminations* two poems free as poetry had never been before; that Gustave Kahn theorized at length on the nature of free verse and did what he could toward providing examples to fit his theories; that Jules Laforgue theorized very little but wrote a substantial volume of a kind of verse that represents a logical final step in the evolution of nineteenth-century poetry. Critics of the time perceived that a new form had developed and felt called upon to define it. 'True free verse,' said Rémy de Gourmont, 'is conceived as such, that is to say as a fragment designed on the model of its emotive idea and no longer determined by the law of number.' [26] A line of free verse is ordinarily a unit unto itself, obedient to a law of its own, what Gourmont called its 'emotive idea.' There is no overflow; the line finds its own length, longer or shorter, and a stanza usually forms a sentence.

The question of who first used it (after Rimbaud) has been much vexed, and none too profitably. One claimant for the honor was a certain Marie Krysinska, familiarly known in literary circles of the time as 'The Queen of Poland.' After reading 'L'Oiseau crucifié,' which verges on *vers libre*, Laforgue commented, 'Marie Krysinska does have an original artistic sensibility, but one pretty well submerged in fashionable rhetoric.' [27] The judgment is a fair one and could be applied to most other free versifiers writing in France during the nineteenth century, Rimbaud and Laforgue excepted. However fine the artistic sensibilities of the other *vers-libristes*, however praiseworthy their attempts to parcel the poem into portions corresponding to the broken lines of Impressionist painting, their gifts were not up to their aspirations. Gustave Kahn, theorist of the movement, prescribed better than he was able to perform. As Jules Supervielle, himself a *vers-libriste* at one time, has written: 'There has been much conjecture as to whether Laforgue or Gustave Kahn was the first to use free verse in France. For me the question does not arise. I don't know whether Kahn is a poet so far as other people are concerned; for me he is not. Consequently his verse does not interest me, it is non-existent, whereas Laforgue is always with us, a poet even when he errs.' [28] Rimbaud's efforts in this direction having consisted of two brief poems only, Laforgue is pre-eminently the poet of free verse in France during the nineteenth century, and it is of particular interest to the American reader that his earliest ventures were translations from Walt Whitman.

In this as in many other domains, Laforgue was *avant-gardiste*. No one of consequence had translated Whitman into French. The enthusiasm of André Gide and the Naturist poets for *Leaves of Grass* was all to come; even in Germany, where fervor for the American poet was one day to approach the proportions of a cult, he was known only to the few.

One experiences a certain mild surprise, coming upon Laforgue's translations in that highly artistic periodical which was the first *Vogue*.[29] Walt seems to be keeping queer company with the last of the Decadents, the first of the Symbolists, and the barbaric yawp of several 'Inscriptions' and 'A Woman Waits for Me' somehow jars with the usual tone of the retiring reader to the Empress of Germany.

It is I, you women, I make my way,
I am stern, acrid, large, undissuadable, but I love you,
I do not hurt you any more than is necessary for you,
I pour the stuff to start sons and daughters fit for these States,
    I press with slow rude muscle. . .

This Laforgue translates manfully:

C'est moi, femme, je vois mon chemin;
Je suis austère, âpre, immense, inébranlable, mais je t'aime;
Allons, je ne te blesse pas plus qu'il ne faut,
Je verse l'essence qui engendrera des garçons et des filles dignes
    de ces Etats-Unis; j'y vais d'un muscle rude et attentionné.

The differences between the two poets, however, are not as great as they appear at first. Whitman was a Byronic dandy, although an inverted one. Laforgue was a Baudelairian dandy. Whitman saw in nature a vague automatic impulse resembling the

Hartmannian Unconscious. And Whitman's verse is as strongly impregnated throughout by the ideas of nineteenth-century science as Laforgue's was at the beginning. Whitman also wrote about the nebular hypothesis and universal evolution, about planets and suns biologically conceived. Thus, in one of the poems that Laforgue translated:

Star crucified—by traitors sold,
Star panting o'er a land of death, heroic land . . .

Sure as the ship of all, the Earth itself,
Product of deathly fire and turbulent chaos,
Forth from its spasms of fury and its poisons . . .

Etoile crucifiée, vendue, par des traîtres,
Etoile palpitante sur un pays de mort, héroïque pays . . .

Aussi sûrement que le vaisseau de tout, la Terre elle-même,
Produit d'un incendie de mort et du tumultueux chaos,
Se dégageant de ses spasmes de rage et de ses déjections . . .

The lines of this free verse are rhythmic units tending to compose a stanza-sentence:

O star of France,
The brightness of thy hope and strength and fame,
Like some proud ship that led the fleet so long,
Beseems today a wreck driven by the gale, a mastless hulk,
And 'mid its teeming maddened half-drowned crowds,
Nor helm nor helmsman.

O Etoile de France,
Le rayonnement de ta foi, de ta puissance, de ta gloire,
Comme quelque orgueilleux vaisseau qui si longtemps mena toute
*   l'escadre,*
Tu es aujourd'hui, désastre poussé par la tourmente, une carcasse
*   démâtée;*
Et au milieu de ton équipage affolé, demi-submergé,
Ni timon, ni timonier.

At critical points these rhythms are strengthened both by alliteration and by assonance, though there is less need for either in
English than in French:

> O star! O ship of France, beat back and baffled long!
> Bear up O smitten orb! O ship continue on. . .

Words are reiterated at points of different stress in the rhythmic
units:

> Star crucified—by traitors sold,
> Star panting o'er a land of death, heroic land,
> Strange, passionate, mocking, frivolous land . . .

Here, in short, are all the main characteristics of free verse. It
would be unprofitable to argue that Laforgue learned to write
vers libre from Whitman. Suffice it to say that at a critical stage
in his development as a poet he was studying Whitman with the
translator's concentrated attention.

The *Derniers Vers* have a rough kind of plot. 'L'Hiver qui
vient,' the opening section, treats autumn for the most part in
pastoral terms but has one stanza full of urban images. The motif
of the horn call makes its appearance, preparing the next section,
'Le Mystère des trois cors,' a little allegory on the fortunes of
introverts and extroverts. Poems III and IV, both entitled 'Dimanches,' work out Laforguian themes in a kind of Sunday-
imagery now familiar. Singly or in groups the young ladies go off
to church, while the 'Polar Bear,' the 'Lord High Chancellor of
Analysis,' observes them from afar. 'Pétition,' poem v, is a meditation on young girls, how they are

> *Jamais franches,*
> *Ou le poing sur la hanche . . .*

and a firm statement of opinion on how they ought to be—com-
radely—somewhat in the fashion of Whitman's Woman who
Waits. In vi, 'Simple Agonie,' we seem to have weathered 'les
années mortes,' the dying and dead part of the year, '. . . et re-
voici les sympathies de mai.' A phrase of this sixth poem introduces the next section, 'Solo de lune,' in which the speaker is
shown taking a long, heart-rending journey away from the be-

loved. 'Légende,' VIII, is a dream-like respite. For after these 'clots of memories,' after strangely poignant evocation of loss,

> *Ah! ce n'est plus l'automne, alors,*
> *Ce n'est plus l'exil.*
> *C'est la douceur des légendes, de l'âge d'or,*
> *Des légendes des Antigones,*
> *Douceur qui fait qu'on se demande:*
> *'Quand donc cela se passait-il?'*

> Ah! it is no longer autumn then,
> Nor any longer exile.
> Rather a legendary mildness, an age of gold
> Befitting legends of Antigones,
> Such gentleness as makes one ask,
> 'When did all this come to pass?'

After two more dreamlike interludes (or only one, for sections IX and X were published by the author as one poem, 'Les Amours,' later divided by the editors) in a different vein—ironic visions of love satisfied—autumn closes down again in the final sections:

> *Noire bise, averse glapissante,*
> *Et fleuve noir, et maisons closes,*
> *Et quartiers sinistres comme des Morgues,*
> *Et l'Attardé qui à la remorque traîne*
> *Toute la misère du coeur et des choses,*
> *Et la souillure des innocentes qui traînent,*
> *Et crie à l'averse. 'Oh? arrose, arrose*
> *Mon coeur si brûlant, ma chair si intéressante!'*

> Bitter blast and howling rain,
> Somber river, and houses shut,
> And quarters sinister as morgues,
> And the belated Soul who drags behind him
> His heart's misery and all creation's,
> And the defilement of strayed innocents,
> Who cries to the torrent, 'Oh, assuage, refresh
> My burning heart, my so exceptional flesh!'

The concluding lines are a fair example of the poet's latest manner of turning upon himself, averting the peril of overstatement.

Structure has seldom been as flexibly bent to materials. Thus, among many instances, these lines from the opening section:

> Soleils plénipotentiaires des travaux en blonds Pactoles
> Des spectacles agricoles,
> Où êtes-vous ensevelis?

> Plenipotentiary suns of labors in gold-bearing torrents
> Of agricultural landscapes,
> Where have you vanished to?

The broad burst of sixteen syllables stands for the energy of the summer sun and the works carried on beneath it; this energy dwindles visibly to the seven ironic syllables of the second line and the query of the third. Immediately afterward the 'picturesque star' of the poet's early writings—a star that is still personified— is treated offhandedly in lines tapering off a syllable at a time from the thirteen of the first:

> Ce soir un soleil fichu gît au haut du coteau,
> Gît sur le flanc, dans les genêts, sur son manteau.
> Un soleil blanc comme un crachat d'estaminet
> Sur une litière de jaunes genêts . . .

Again the diminution is communicated by the shape of the verses. We are better able to see the sun fading, declining on the hilltop, because the poet presents the scene in verses of thirteen, twelve, twelve, and eleven syllables. Thirteen- and eleven-syllable lines are especially hard to bring off because they are so likely to give the effect of alexandrines that have missed fire. Poetic success has come with the surmounting of two obstacles; and indeed the variants of these later poems, which Dujardin and Fénéon included in their edition of 1890, show the poet overcoming many and diverse difficulties. He rejected, picked, chose, happened on a more vivid word by the way and finally fitted it into the rhythmic frame that had first occurred to him, almost as though he had not been a poet writing by direct dictation of the Unconscious. Here, for instance, are the stages of one of the concluding lines of 'Avertissement,' the poem conceived at Elsinore, in which the poet sees his Hamletic hesitations in the guise of a weathercock's waverings:

> *Bonne girouette aux quatre saisons*
>
> *Ivre girouette aux quatre saisons*
>
> *Bonne girouette aux quatre saisons*
>
> *Bonne girouette aux trent' six saisons*
>
> *Girouette peinte aux trent' six saisons*
>
> *Bonne girouette aux trent'-six saisons*

In the extraordinarily plastic verse of the *Derniers Vers* the major Laforguian themes reappear, assuming the forms most peculiarly their own. Poems on autumn open and close a cycle; and with the death of the year is associated the death of the individual. Most often the death implied is tubercular. In 'Le Mystère des trois cors,' on the other hand, it is by suicide. Then there are the less radical forms of denial of life: the sense of separation from society, the sense of incapacity for life in society, the theme of exile.

These are the great Romantic subjects with which Laforgue deals in verse that contrives never to be portentous, since the theme is nothing without its embodiment. The expansive description of a season is purposely made overexpansive, grandiose, and we are shortly told of some quotidian consequence for human beings. Death, by whatever cause, is suggested in the barest of terms. The appreciation of the difference between Shaun the Postman and Shem the Penman, Fortinbras and Hamlet, extrovert and introvert, is profound, but is expressed by *ironic* manipulation of an image dear to the Romantic mind, the call of the hunting horn. And the life from which the speaker of these poems—a prolongation of Pierrot and an anticipation of Hamlet—sees himself cut off is most often represented by the girls' boarding school, the detachment being felt with certain reserves. 'Forever astonished' and astonishing, tempestuous, continually bursting free of the immediate design to which their author would subordinate them, the *jeunes filles* of Laforgue are the most vivid in French literature until we come to those of Jean Giraudoux. Without neglecting the Balzacian Woman of Thirty—an 'aging sinner' appears in both 'Légende' and 'Solo de lune'—Laforgue succeeds in turning attention to a woman of half that age.

The life of the world from which the poet sees himself divided finds other symbols, and memorable ones, including the casinos of 'Légende.' But Laforgue, who had pointed so knowingly to the spoiled children in Baudelaire and Corbière, understands perfectly well that his exile is self-inflicted.

> *Je suis la Gondole enfant chérie*
> *Qui arrive à la fin de la fête,*
> *Par je ne sais quoi, par bouderie,*
> (*Un soir trop beau me monte à la tête!*)
>
> *Me voici déjà près de la digue;*
> *Mais la foule sotte et pavoisée,*
> *Ah! n'accourt pas à l'Enfant Prodigue!*
> *Et danse, sans perdre une fusée. . .*
>
> *Ah! c'est comme ça, femmes volages!*
> *C'est bien. Je m'exile en ma gondole*
> (*Si frêle!*) *aux mouettes, aux orages,*
> *Vers les malheurs qu'on voit au Pôle!*
>
> *—Et puis, j'attends sous une arche noire . . .*
> *Mais nul ne vient; les lampions s'éteignent;*
> *Et je maudis la nuit et la gloire!*
> *Et ce coeur qui veut qu'on me dédaigne!*

I am the favorite child canoe
That arrives toward the party's end,
I couldn't say why, but sullenly,
(Too fine an evening goes to my head!)

Here I am almost at the water-wall,
But the foolish crowd in its finery
Doesn't rush out to welcome the Prodigal
And dances on giddily.

So that's the way of it, flighty females!
All right, I'll just take my frail vessel
(My fragile canoe!) toward the gulls and the gales
And the perils that lurk at the Pole.

Then I pause beneath a somber archway . . .
But nobody comes. The lanterns are dead.
And I execrate nighttime and glory,
And this heart that desires to be scorned!

The last line was a second or third thought. It had been:

> *Et tout ce qui fait qu'on me dédaigne!*
>
> *Mon coeur qui veut qu'on me dédaigne!*
>
> *Ce coeur qui veut qu'on me dédaigne!*

As it stands it is probably the weightiest one-line demonstration of Laforgue's ability to see around his own position, that clairvoyance that made him the greatest of French Romantic ironists.

Among the unpublished papers of Laforgue is the following note, inspired no doubt by his own and his brother's art studies: 'In the great glassed-in hall of ancient art, especially about midday, when he was alone sketching among the white and calm statues. The room was deserted. It was the great silence of noon. There were echoes of footsteps on the tiles as the pupils of the school went to lunch—But he stayed on, forgetting his hunger—A near-by bell (St.-Sulpice or St.-Germain-des-Prés) tolled, adding a further note of solemnity to the vast noonday calm under the full daylight falling from above, on the tranquillity of those white and motionless statues. Solemn thoughts came to him. He was in an ideal life far from the narrow and muddy streets of the clamorous left bank, far from garrets, far from greasy pub-keepers, tailors, tradesmen, he was there transported to other ages, far from our feverish democracy, delighting in a calm and noble life.—The bourgeois who stare you down in the street, casting glances at your shoes—a Jack of poverty on his arrival in Paris— dinners at fifty centimes—shoes down at heel—his health threatened—theadbare cuffs from which one snips the threads . . .' At the end of the passage, in the handwriting of a later period, is the comment: 'Hello, dear Jack! Still your little cosmic cares?' [30]

There could be no more graphic demonstration of the difference between the Laforgue of 1880 and the writer of 1885-6, when the bulk of the *Moralités légendaires* were composed. And we do not approach the later man and his works without certain misgivings. Was there something to the opinion of that doughty defender of good prose, H. L. Mencken, that no one can possess a prose style before the age of thirty? So much mysterious tissue, incarnate experience, enters into authentic prose. Its absence is less palpable so long as objectives are limited, models evident, as in the passage just quoted; it is only too apparent in a work such as the earliest *Moralité*, 'Le Miracle des roses.' The tales, however, are progressively better. 'Lohengrin' and 'Salomé,' dating from 1885, are inferior to 'Hamlet,' finished in 1886. 'Persée et Andromède' and 'Pan et la Syrinx,' the last written of these works, prove that Mencken, who applied quantitative measurements to the wrong kind of subject matter, was mistaken.

Half-realistic, 'Le Miracle des roses' is remarkable for its broadsides against Baden-Baden, that resort of valetudinarians and vacationers, and for its record of a bullfight witnessed at San Sebastian in 1883. There is a gossamer veil of plot. Ruth, a victim of advanced tuberculosis, spreads an even more baneful Romantic affliction about her: her path is strewn with suicides, from the Paris art amateur and the *presidente* of the bullfight to a young man of the Corpus Christi procession who works the final wry miracle permitting her to see roses rather than blood. Laforgue conveys the impression that Ruth is averse to none of the gore, or to the disembowelment of the horses either. Sound observations reminiscent of Mérimée and Maupassant are couched in an exasperatingly parenthetical style: 'Patrick s'assied au chevet de sa soeur: il tient son mouchoir diaphane comme un parfum, sa bonbonnière de cachou à l'orange, son éventail (un éventail, ô ironie et triste caprice de la dernière heure!) son flacon de musc naturel (le dernier réconfort des mourants). . .' Such a sentence merely shows that the style of

Stéphane Vassiliew has disintegrated, and that nothing has arisen in its place.

'Lohengrin, fils de Parsifal' has good touches: Elsa's apparent indifference to everything but her own image in a mirror as she awaits the knight whose defection would bring about her blinding; the transformation of the lordly executioners into shuffling yokels when Lohengrin flies in on his swan ('How rich and refined his family must be! Oh! in what magic groves must they be taking ices, at this very hour!'). There are more dated details, such as Lohengrin's introduction of himself to the dazzled company: 'No, I am not Endymion. I come directly from the Holy Grail. I am Lohengrin, Knight Errant, the lily of future crusades for the emancipation of woman. In the meantime, however, I was simply too bored in my father's offices (I am a trifle hypochondriac by nature).' The suspense in the nuptial villa is well managed, as Elsa impatiently invites the objectification of the Unconscious and Lohengrin resists until his swan-pillow bears him away, as he says, 'toward the Holy Grail where my father Parsifal is preparing a blueprint for the redemption of our little sister, so human and so down to earth . . . toward those glacier mirrors that no young girl will ever tarnish with her breath in order to trace her name and the date.' The dialogue of this piece is properly pointed, and the Laforguian word-mine is by this time in full production, turning out such high-grade ore as Elsa's 'Massacrilege me!' and her inquiry, 'Child, child, are you familiar with the voluptial rites?' A prose prolongation of themes and images of *L'Imitation de Notre-Dame la Lune*, 'Lohengrin' is weakened by a certain fundamental lack of control.

The satire of 'Salomé' is too obvious. This is the only Moralité that would justify an uncharitable description of the collection as the 'Parodies artificielles.' Style, characters, major and minor episodes of Flaubert's 'Hérodias' are aped in a manner verging dangerously on that of the class yearbook. Here, for instance, in a style meant to suggest Flaubert's packed sentences, is Laforgue's notion of an old Palestinian pleasantry: 'The followers of the Northern Princes could be heard laughing hugely, in the court where the gutters converged, laughing without understanding one another, playing at quoits, swapping tobaccos. The

Tetrarch's followers were showing their foreign colleagues how white elephants prefer to be curried. 'But back home we don't have any white elephants,' the visitors gave to understand. And they saw these stablemen cross themselves, as though to conjure impious thoughts.'

A clever sophomore turns 'Hérodias' upside down, changing Herod Antipas to Emeraude-Archetypas of the Esoteric White Isles, a weary aesthete; Vitellius to an emissary of the Prussian militarized state; John the Baptist to a deported socialist agitator, his spectacles tied up with bits of string; Salomé into yet another etiolated dilettante who exacts John's head after having trifled with his affections. It is all quite witty and it is all, considering the model, a little disappointing. Yet the most adverse critics of Laforgue could hardly deny the interest of the elements held in suspension by this none too limpid prose. At the fatal feast are the clowns of the Idea, the Will, and the Unconscious, characterizing clearly if summarily the Absolute according to the Hegelian, Schopenhauerian, and Hartmannian philosophies: 'Idea chattered about everything, Will knocked his head against the scenery, and Unconscious made the large mysterious gestures of someone who knows more than he is yet permitted to reveal. This trinity had, moreover, a single refrain:

> O promised land
> Of utter void!
>
> O void, a pox
> On all your books . . .'
>
> *O Chanaan*
> *Du bon Néant!*
>
> *Néant, la Mecque*
> *Des bibliothèques* . . .

This comes from *L'Imitation de Notre-Dame la Lune*. After the chorus of the clowns, Salomé, dressed in jonquil yellow chiffon with black dots, chants to the music of her little black lyre an ample discourse on the Unconscious. Here, too, inserted willy-nilly in the tale is a revised version of the prose poem 'L'Aquarium,' Laforgue's most sustained sequence of imagery treating of the unconscious mind. Here is satire on authority in the shape of those Princes of the North who have ejected Iaokanaan from their territories, who gloat over him in his dungeon. One of them cannot refrain from observing: 'Ah ha! There you are, ideologist, scribbler, ex-conscript, bastard of Jean-Jacques Rousseau. So this is where you came to get yourself hanged, you broken-down pamphleteer, you! And how nice your unwashed top-piece is going to look in some guillotine basket. . .' It appears that the revolution Iaokanaan had engineered in the North has failed, and the organizer, who for a moment imagined that this was a conciliatory mission sent by the royal family, dies thoroughly disillusioned. Like other community leaders of the period, the Princes of the North are Darwinians, convinced positivists, meliorists:

> *Et tout honnête homme, d'ailleurs, professe*
> *Le perfectionnement de l'Espèce.*

> Every gentleman, of course, believes
> In the perfecting of the species.

If 'Salomé' is a heterogeneous effort, 'Persée et Andromède' is as skillfully unified as so original a work could be. From the beginning we are struck by the symbolic value of the sea. Young, red-haired, nubile, Andromeda is surrounded, along with her guardian dragon, by a sea as profoundly monotonous as her life, a sea that is, in fact, the objective equivalent for a life. When, unspeakably bored and restless, she rushes out into the unfurling waves, she is returning to the mother and matrix of her being. The amiable dragon, who before the end of the story manages to identify himself with most of the dragons of antiquity, cherishes Andromeda with unrequited affection, until the day when a daintily elegant Perseus wings in on his hippogriff. Andromeda all but goes off with him instanter. But the dragon shows a little fight, and is not turned to stone because the Gorgon, at the critical moment, closes her eyes: 'The good Gorgon recognized our Monster. She recalled that rich and spacious time when she and her two sisters lived next door to this Dragon, at that time keeper of the Garden of the Hesperides, the marvelous Garden of the Hesperides located in the neighborhood of the Columns of Hercules. No, no, a thousand times no, she would not petrify her old friend!' Enraged because of his ill success and Andromeda's first skeptical smile, Perseus runs the dragon through, mutilating him unnecessarily—so much so that Andromeda realizes that he had been a fairly good dragon after all, had gratified all her caprices (within the limits of his income, of course), collecting and polishing a whole heap of precious stones for her sake. In the pinch she refuses to go off with the interloper, who flies away indignant and abusive. Andromeda weeps over her slain guardian. 'She recalls that he had been a good friend to her, an accomplished gentleman, an industrious scholar, an eloquent poet. And her little heart bursts with sobbing. . .' She even asks, in words that sound very much like Philoctetes on Lemnos, 'With what lamentations can I now make these stony shores resound?' Then, after opening one eye and telling his story, the Monster is transformed into a personable young man. 'Leaning against the entrance of the cave, his human skin inundated with the enchantment of moonlight, he speaks of the future.'

Penetrating thus deeply toward the mythical foundations, appropriating as much as he needed of the story of Perseus and Andromeda to tell the story of Beauty and the Beast (the Monster had hinted to his uncomprehending ward that he could not be changed into himself until she loved him, that he was imprisoned within a vicious circle), Laforgue is at his best and his most rewardingly complex. 'Pan et la Syrinx' is an equally graceful story, dealing with love and the artist's self-discovery in loss; but it does not alter the main lines of the myth. There is no fusion of legends as in 'Persée,' nor is the prose quite so prophetic. As unmistakably as the rhythms of Rimbaud's *Illuminations*, of Lautréamont's *Chants de Maldoror*, cadences of 'Persée et Andromède' are echoed by later writers. 'And then there came those strange Argonauts, whose likes we shall not see again,' the dragon reminisces. 'Splendid epochs! Jason was their leader, Hercules followed, and his friend Theseus, and Orpheus who undertook to charm me with his lyre (and who was later to come to such a tragic end!) and also the twins: Castor, tamer of horses, and Pollux, clever at fisticuffs. Vanished epochs! Oh, their bivouacs, and the fires they kindled in the evenings!' [31] Some of the grandeur and none of the bourdon of Saint-John Perse are in these lines. Glimmering throughout is the fantasy, the irony of the greatest of Fargue, the best of Supervielle. And more important even than intonations so distinct that they could not but be caught and repeated is the step taken beyond realism, toward mythic structure.

The importance of the *Moralités légendaires* is due partly to their chronological place. Laforgue's inventive power, increasing steadily throughout his career, found its freest play in his last-written works. In his verse, too, he had been in search of the fundamental though changeful figure. His hero, 'un Philippe de Champaigne/Mais né Pierrot,' [32] belonged to 'L'école des cromlechs/Et des tuyaux d'usine,' and fished in troubled waters for her who is at once 'Eve, Joconde, et Dalila.' [33] The Romantic pair escaped together toward an isle that was simultaneously Eden, the Pole, and Eldorado. The evolution of a passage in *Derniers Vers* shows Laforgue accumulating fables. He begins by thinking of 'un cimetière plein d'Antigones,' adds a reference to a gravedigger suggesting *Hamlet*, then a mention of Philomela, and finally the words 'Alas, poor Yorick!' to clinch matters. He ends with:

> *C'est l'automne, l'automne, l'automne,*
> *Le grand vent et toute sa séquelle*
> *De représailles! Et de musiques! . . .*
> *Rideaux tirés, clôture annuelle,*
> *Chute des feuilles, des Antigones, des Philomèles:*
> *Mon fossoyeur, Alas poor Yorick!*
> *Les remue à la pelle! . . .*

> Now it is autumn, autumn, autumn,
> The wind in earnest and all its crew
> Of reprisals and concertos! . . .
> Drawn curtains, yearly closing-down,

Fall of leaves, Antigones, and Philomelas:
My gravedigger, *Alas poor Yorick!*
Turns them by shovelsful!

Figures from three tragedies combine with the falling leaves,
high wind, drawn curtains, to yield one universal, the falling away
of everything. It is primarily the last written of the prose tales,
however, which convince us that Laforgue would, time allowing,
have employed on a larger scale a dramatic technique based on
the fluid shift of personage into related dramatic personage: this
Monster who is at once nearly all the dragons of antiquity and
the Beast transformed by Beauty's liberating love; this Andromeda
who is also Beauty, who comforts and resurrects—the female
principle.

'Hamlet, ou les suites de la piété filiale' cannot be discussed
in quite the same way as the author's other works can. Laforgue
wrote 'Persée' in a short time during the spring of 1886. 'Pan' was
composed with dispatch, despite physical handicaps, in Paris the
following winter. Though 'Hamlet' was put down on paper in
1885-6 it had, in an important sense, been a work in progress
for at least seven years, ever since Laforgue's first mention of the
Shakespearian hero in an early poem. Jean-Aubry said with considerable justice that Hamlet was for Laforgue what Saint
Anthony was for Flaubert. The story whereby Laforgue sought
to lay one of his oldest ghosts is not his best; it was too close
to him, as another *Hamlet* may have been to its author; but
there is no doubt about its fascination.

This Hamlet is, if not a clown, at least the brother of a clown:
one of the gravediggers in the little cemetery reveals that the
prince and Yorick were sons of the late king by the same gypsy
mother. Since poor Yorick's remains are now being disinterred
to make room for Ophelia's, Hamlet strays over to the open
grave, picks up his brother's cranium, and soliloquizes in words
that are like an ironic echo to Laforgue's Pascalian apostrophe of
some years before. As far as content is concerned, the two speeches
to a skull are not very different: the underlying attitudes are
equally pessimistic; there is a similar lack of confidence in religion;
and in both the earth is dismissed as one of an overwhelming

number of planets. What is new is the tone, the defensive irony, the twist at the end: 'As for me, with my genius, I could have been what is commonly called a Messiah, but here I am, too, too spoiled, a veritable benjamin of Nature. I understand everything, I adore everything, I want to fecundate everything. That's why, as I have observed in a limping distich carved in my bed:

> My rare faculty of assimilation
> Cannot but thwart the course of my vocation.'

Ma rare faculté d'assimilation
Contrariera le cours de ma vocation.

Hamlet is also, if not a writer, at least one who aspires to be a writer, and even before he spies the band of strolling players across the stagnant bay we know that the play's the thing. What Hamlet would really like would be to unshoulder the few responsibilities he has not already disclaimed and be off to Paris, where a group of neo-Alexandrians is flourishing around Mount Sainte-Geneviève. Since that appears to be impossible, he has tackled the theme of his play in earnest; and the longer he has spent with this work designed, on one level, to ferret out the murderers' guilt, the more he has become convinced that he has got hold of a really first-rate subject. The arrival of William and Kate and their fellow players, his enthusiastic reading of his work, its performance and alarming repercussions, even his increasingly friendly feelings for the actress, are purely subordinate to his literary ambition, and toward the end we find him heading for Paris after all, with Kate. But on the way he stops off at the cemetery for just a moment, as an act of filial piety, is stabbed by a Laertes who does not seem too persuaded of the importance of what he is doing, and dies murmuring, '*Qualis . . . artifex . . . pereo!*'

If the rare faculty of assimilation displayed in 'Hamlet' works against its unity, if its somewhat haphazard ending makes it inferior to both 'Persée' and 'Pan,' it nonetheless encompasses more characteristically Laforguian themes and images, more ironic oppositions springing from inner contradictions, than any other

SKETCHES, C.1886

tale. Hamlet speaks of his 'dear Philoctetes,' and has had, he says, his 'moment of apostolic madness.' He is endowed with a 'sixth sense, a sense of the infinite,' and cherishes the 'immemorial sadness of a tiny chord struck on the piano.' His tower room, like his spirit, is invaded by 'an insoluble, an incurable autumn'— even in July, for 'today is the fourteenth of July 1601, a Saturday; tomorrow is Sunday and all over the world girls will go artlessly to church.' He had been fond of Ophelia, and yet— 'She would never have understood me. Whenever I stop to think of that!

No doubt she was adorable and mortally sensitive, but scratch
the surface and you would have found the Englishwoman tainted
from birth by the egotistical philosophy of Hobbes: "Nothing
is more agreeable about the possession of our own property than
the thought that it is superior to other people's." That was the
way Ophelia loved me, as a piece of property. . .' 'Method,
method,' he exclaims, 'what have you to do with me? You know
very well that I have eaten of the fruit of the Unconscious.' Yet
he remains in spite of that, as Gustave Kahn said, a reasoner, a
methodical doubter, a searcher. Over Hamlet, this final embodiment of Laforgue's irony exposed to all the winds of doubt, veers
the metaphorical weathercock of 'Avertissement,' the poem he
wrote the day he visited Elsinore:

> *Bonne girouette aux trent'-six saisons,*
> *Trop nombreux pour dire oui ou non . . .*

X

The Broken Citadel

LIFE in Germany became less and less bearable for Laforgue during the winter of 1885-6. The autumn had begun well enough, with a visit from Kahn in September. Two months later, however, the clatter and whistlings of the freight trains along the Rhine near Coblenz filled him with blank despair.[1] In December he came back to a Berlin without Théo Ysaÿe. The pianist was continuing his studies in Paris—the Paris of Charles Henry, the Paris where the star of Symbolism was rising over the café-table editorial office of Kahn's *Vogue*. Four winters and springs Laforgue had managed to contain his nostalgia for 'the galleries of the Odéon, the sickly skies one sees from the Pont de la Concorde, the fine puddles in the Place of that name, the funerals at the Madeleine and St. Augustine's, and the resigned and somnolent cab-nags.'[2] His homesickness, growing with his aversion for Germany, had filled letter after letter; but actual plans for throwing up his job had remained vague. Back in the Prinzessinnen-Palais in December the chore of reading and summarizing from the inevitable three newspapers, the eternal *Revue des deux mondes*, the novels that were changing as to title but constant in their mediocrity seemed intolerable as never before. He had complained about his ennui, had filled his copious correspondence with his dissatisfaction. Now he wrote few letters, and these were mostly perfunctory, laconic. In one he speaks of his 'nihilism,' the utter void of everything. Immediately after Christmas he fled to Denmark and meditated on Hamlet. In the second week of January he decided to take English lessons.

'Miss Lee, 57 Königgraezer Strasse' is one of the names and addresses written on the back flyleaf of the Agenda for 1883. It could easily have been jotted down there after the end of that year, and there is no reason to believe that Leah Lee had been in Berlin longer than Jules said in a letter of September 1886, 'for two years, living partly on what she receives from her father, partly on proceeds from English lessons.' [3]

Jules had always been an anglophile. He had liked the city of Hamburg because of the numerous English people there, had been equally devoted to the 'pensionnats de *young ladies*' at Coblenz and the diaphanous figures of Kate Greenaway albums. He had argued that there are 'three sexes, male, female, and the Englishwoman,' [4] and his writings leave us in no doubt about which of the two latter he preferred. Long before any mention of Leah Lee he had prophesied lightly to Théo Ysaÿe that he would marry an English schoolmistress.[5]

Leah was, Jules wrote to his sister, 'very thin, very, very English, with chestnut hair with reddish tints . . . a childish face, a mischievous smile and great, tar-colored, forever-astonished eyes . . . educated as all girls are, with, besides, what can be learned from travel and two foreign languages and whatever she may have been able to retain from our interminable conversations.' [6] The courtship proceeded slowly. Leah studied painting, so Jules took to bringing her engravings, books on art, and finally one of his articles about an exhibit in Berlin. One day in April he ventured to propose that they visit the museum together. 'She blushed, looked down, did not answer'—and Jules rushed home to write a letter of apology. Not long afterward Leah suggested that they visit the museum. Then Jules, who for some time had been giving her the opera tickets that fell to him as court reader, began to keep one of them, the adjacent seat, for himself.

By the end of April Laforgue was perfectly certain that he was spending his last months in Berlin. 'It is decided, definitely decided,' he wrote in an unpublished and finely Laforguian letter to Théodore Lindenlaub in Paris: 'I am going to start sending my books and trinkets along to Kahn's. I've had enough. The prospect of spending another winter here, between Oberwall-strasse, Renz [the café], Bauer and the Brandenburger Tor and the Schutzmann before my window and the same carts hitched to the same famished beasts, and the guard-house across the way, and all the valets' mugs with whiskers and coffee-colored gaiters, etc., etc., that prospect would certainly drive me to join the Mormons or to get myself castrated for the Sistine. This is my last winter!' True, he has no clear notion of how he will earn his living in Paris. But in spite of past extravagances, now regretted, he counts on arriving there with at least two thousand francs, enough to give him time to look around. In any case, 'Better squat as a typesetter in some cellar than spend another winter here! Five years of facing the same heads is too long for one who is not always perfectly sure of keeping his own.' [7]

He left Berlin as usual for Baden-Baden and did not see Leah again until the first of September. Having resigned as reader and made all preparations to leave, he kept putting off his departure until that day, the sixth of September, when they were out walking and he asked her 'with many circumlocutions' if she would like to pass her life with him. 'I remember my strangled voice and the tears in my eyes, and I did not give her time to answer but launched forthwith into protestations. She said yes, looking at me in an extraordinary way.' [8] Even now, and indeed until some time afterward, Jules did not call her by her first name, only 'petit personnage.'

One can understand why Paul Bourget, who refrained from writing about Laforgue because of the scant admiration he felt for his young friend's poems and stories, 'si peu traditionnels,' [9] should have felt moved to do so after reading Jules' letter to his sister announcing his engagement. Here the tormented ironic defenses are down, revealing all the childlike charm, not without its wiles. From this letter one gathers that Jules had not deeply changed since the night in the great apartment at Coblenz almost five years before, when he had had to write first to his sister about the broad staircases, the silver dishes, and the servants, but above all about his resolve to write many books and support two of his younger brothers.

Des ans vont passer là-dessus,
On s'endurcira chacun pour soi . . .

The years will have their way with this,
We will grow hard, each one for each . . .

But Jules did not harden, despite the German court, despite his
straining for the *suraigu,* despite the rigidity and poverty of the
reigning philosophies. And that constancy, whether Paul Bourget
could perceive it or not, is apparent in his poetry:

Je ne suis point 'ce gaillard-là!' ni Le Superbe!
Mais mon âme, qu'un cri un peu cru exacerbe,
Est au fond distinguée et fraîche comme une herbe.

I am not 'that fellow there!' nor The Superb.
But my soul, which the slightest shrillness can disturb,
Is at bottom distinguished and fresh as an herb.

The 'petit personnage' stayed on in Berlin till the end of September to teach some last English lessons. Jules went to Belgium
for the wedding of Eugène Ysaÿe. Afterward, waiting for Leah
at Verviers, he wrote Théo a letter quite different in tone and
content from the one to his sister: '. . . More than ever I feel
myself to be the slave of destiny. What we agree to call our
normal state is at the mercy of passing, overwhelming intoxication. It is frightening and divine at the same time. What does our
fate depend on, I was thinking. On pathetic (and terrifying)
chances, a stray smile in a village awakening the Shakespearean
in us, crystallizing our destiny. And I thought about our mad
mortal aspirations after the Unique. . . Ironically I breathed the
proud air of long journeys. Then twilight came and with it an
hour's wait in a little station. I strolled about, looking now and
then at the sky, so astonishingly full of stars. A lamp was burning in the window of a ponderous bourgeois house (a lamp with
a pink shade, I remember), and I fell to meditating again. The
Corinnes, the Ophelias, and so on, all that is a snare and a delusion.
After all is said and done we have nothing but the little Adriennes
with kind hearts and long eyelashes, with ephemeral and child-

ish smiles, the little Adriennes with beautiful complexions whom chance (and there is nothing but chance) sets upon our path. Yes, everything is chance, for if there hadn't been an Adrienne there would have been a Leah, and if there hadn't been a Leah there would have been a Nini, and so on. That's why we are enjoined to devote ourselves to the first one chance presents to us, and we will love her alone, because she was the first, forsaking all others. . . I will see her in half an hour. My heart is pounding, and forty years from now I will remember how slow the moment was in coming.' [10]

Laforgue's expectations were high, his mood positive, when he came down to Paris from Belgium. Kahn, his closest friend during the last years of his life, tells of his serene and creative gaiety, the period of plenitude into which he seemed to be entering. He tells of Laforgue's enthusiasm and that of his fellow poets: their forgetfulness of time, their oblivious working all night, the dawn of Symbolism coinciding with dawns breaking over the Bois de Boulogne. From Kahn we learn what Laforgue hoped from marriage, 'an ordering of life that would prevent waste of time, vague restless moods, and create a citadel about the writer.' [11]

Jules and Leah were married in the Church of St. Barnabas, Addison Road, London, on the last day of December 1886. R. R. Bolgar,[12] who consulted the parish register and learned what he could about Leah's family, has shown that she misrepresented more or less innocently when she gave Jules to understand that she had a brother who was a lawyer in Folkestone, another who was a clergyman in New Zealand, another an officer in Zululand. Leah Lee gave as her London address a poor neighborhood. She was probably the daughter of a blacksmith, had certainly suffered more hardships than her husband, and can hardly be blamed for wanting to forget about them.

Théo Ysaÿe, Kahn, and Emile Laforgue had found an apartment on the top floor of a building at 8 rue de Commaille, just off the rue de Babylone, and Jules had furnished it. There were some gaps in the furnishings, but there were also *objets d'art*, collected during prosperous years; and on the table stood a resplendent silver tea service, a gift from the Empress who had been so unwilling to let her reader go. The apartment building was handsome, with a fine carved doorway opening on the Square. It is still the property of the family who built it three years before Jules and Leah came there to live. This street and square are associated with the memory of another Celt, René de Chateaubriand, a glaring white bust of whom now stands opposite Laforgue's doorway. Five minutes away was Paul Bourget's apartment in the rue Monsieur. Laforgue had brought his bride to that richly interesting quarter of Paris that he must have admired the most as an uncertain apprentice writer when he had come to visit Bourget on Sunday afternoons seven years before.

Jules, who had such good reasons for feeling hopeful about his artistic future, was quite unarmed for the bourgeois present. Little in his studious and sheltered life had prepared him for the plunge into Grub Street. The struggle began immediately—for he had not, of course, arrived in Paris with anything like the two thousand francs he had counted on—and continued relentlessly. Of his thirty notes and letters written during 1887, all but half a dozen are entreaties for payment, or advances, or loans. The editors of the newly founded *Revue indépendante* 'endeavored to pay their contributors,' as one of them explained a little mealily later on, but on condition that they contribute their first article for nothing. Laforgue had to beg advance payment for his second 'Chronique parisienne' (a genre of article in which he parodied his own manner), promising to make it especially good.

Henri de Régnier recorded that one evening he was at the home of an amateur of letters when 'little Laforgue' appeared, wanting to know what the fee would be for translating some articles into English. Puffing on his pipe, the friend of literature replied that he, fortunately, was not obliged to earn his living and that such small sums did not interest him. Laforgue listened, head bent, obviously very weary, and from time to time he coughed.[13]

Severe though such difficulties were, they could have been weathered. Bourget and Ephrussi, angry at first because Jules had given up his job without warning them, began to help with sums of money. Téodor de Wyzewa arranged for the sale of articles to a nonexistent Polish periodical. What could not be met or apparently even gauged was the swift and terrible onslaught of disease; here, very close to the end, lies the true pathos, the real waste and shame of Laforgue's story. During all the years in Germany he had shown few signs of tuberculosis. But now the 'stubborn cold' caught in January on the English Channel on the way back from London refused to yield. Bourget arranged for treatments by his own doctor, one of the best known of the time; yet the illness seems to have been ignorantly diagnosed and treated principally with opium pills.

Jules continued to go about his business as best he could. All through the spring and torrid early summer he walked to the doctor's, to the publishers' where he was trying to place articles, stories, and especially his book about Germany, to the art dealers' where he sold one by one his well-loved albums and curios. An artist and connoisseur to the last, he lingered before the art dealers' windows along the boulevards. Nearly every afternoon he met fellow writers at the Café Julien. Some of them noticed that his old cheerfulness was gone, his pace slower. He was like someone who had been obliged to wait a long time. However, he would still speak, if asked, about *L'Ile,* the novel he had begun in Germany. Most of these men had known him during his carefree vacations of earlier years. Few of them knew how poor he was now, and none how ill. Jules had always been a good keeper of secrets, during his schooldays in Tarbes and Paris, and at the German court, where he had been sent because of his native reserve. No one had ever been able to guess his deeper feelings, or about his poetry, unless he chose to tell. Now he faithfully kept his last secret.

In July he wrote to Marie that he would not be able to spend the winter in Paris, that he and Leah would soon be leaving, probably for Algeria, where Bourget was trying to find him work as a translator. The second of August he asked if she remembered their father's coughing fits and suffocations—'well, mine are like that now, they keep on half the night. . .' On 20 August, four days after Jules' twenty-seventh birthday, Leah Laforgue awoke to find her husband dead. He had died quietly, perhaps from sheer drugged exhaustion.

Bourget arranged for the funeral, 'a plain funeral,' as Kahn recorded, 'without any kind of hanging at the door, a hurried funeral, the procession leaving without an instant's delay for any possible latecomer.' Leah Laforgue rode in a carriage with some distant relatives. Bourget, Félix Fénéon, Jean Moréas, Paul Adam, and Kahn walked behind, across the rue des Plantes, 'through the sordid quarters, the quarters of grinding poverty, negligence and indifference. . .' [14] It was a long walk, beyond the limits of Paris. Bagneux Cemetery was new at that time. The grave gaped ugly and lonely in the ground, under a brackish, low-hanging yellow fog. As the brief ceremony ended Leah burst into hysterical laughter, was shut in the carriage and taken away. A few days less than a year before, Jules Laforgue had asked her to become his wife.

We all but lose sight of Leah Laforgue after that. In December she was living in the Hôtel de Londres et de Milan, whence, on the seventh, she wrote to Téodor de Wyzewa asking him to call the next day, for she had a favor to ask regarding her husband's papers. She handed Wyzewa that bulging valise full of Jules' manuscripts which, sadly diminished after a long odyssey, was to find its way back into Wyzewa's hands some twenty years later.

'Le petit personnage' died at Menton the year after her husband's death, of the same disease. Thus ended Jules Laforgue's modest dream of living by his own work in the city that had drawn him back after five years of partial exile.

> Eh bien, ayant pleuré l'Histoire,
> J'ai voulu vivre un brin heureux;
> C'était trop demander, faut croire;
> J'avais l'air de parler hébreu.

XI

'Furtive Foster Father'

—Laforgue, furtif nourricier,
Vois-moi, je dépéris, daigne enfin me sevrer. . .
Délivre-moi de la tutelle
De tes rigueurs spirituelles;
Souffre que je sois Supervielle!
Enseigne-moi l'ingratitude,
Nécessaire béatitude;
Loin de ta chère Ombre importune
Ah! fais-moi une
Petite place dans la Lune! [1]

—Laforgue, furtive foster father,
Look down, I beg of you, deliver
Your wasting pupil from the spell
Of your rigors spiritual
And let me be Supervielle!
Instruct me in ingratitude,
Requisite beatitude;
Far from your dear importune
Spirit grant me as a boon
Just a little place in the moon!

IN France only Jules Supervielle has publicly confessed the importunity of Laforgue's shade and besought deliverance from it. But one suspects that several others must have done so silently, or privately, or at the very least ought to have done so.

In the white winter of that plain-speaking old age which finally rendered him one of the most fascinating of the Symbolists, Gustave Kahn used to complain that the friend of his youth had been 'pillaged.' The word is probably too strong. Nevertheless the presence of Laforgue has been one of the most vital since 1887. Kahn was only stating negatively what could have been expressed positively.

It was natural that a poet whose most important verse did not appear in volume form until three years after his death, whose unpublished manuscripts passed through many hands to be portioned out to editors and publishers for more than sixty years, should exert an influence somehow subterranean, germinal. The fragmentary thoughts printed in the magazines, giving literary form to some of the most fecund of modern ideas, set minds in motion, invited continuation. The impressions and sketches intended as notes for stories sometimes served that purpose after all. Meanwhile, if Laforgue was changed into himself by eternity, as Mallarmé said that the poet is transformed, he became something a little different from himself in time: one of the founders, the initiators, to whom the new writers look back, seeing what they must see and taking what they need. Laforgue's exaltation of the ephemeral was a preliminary to André Gide's enthusiasm for the momentary in *Les Nourritures terrestres*. His passages about the Unconscious had more than a little to do with Théodule Ribot's and Rémy de Gourmont's inquiries into the role of the subconscious in artistic creation. In the surrealist mind the distinction between the Laforguian Unconscious and the Freudian unconscious was pretty well lost; Laforgue was, in any case, one of the explorers of interior Africas. His writings became pretexts, turned up facets that the poet himself might not have suspected; and that, as always, was a guarantee of authenticity. From whatever angle one viewed his work it was obvious that Laforgue was one of the authentic moderns, one of the breakers of molds, those whom Nietzsche called 'the great destroyers.' His principal lever of destruction—and of the affirmation attendant thereon—was his irony.

The *Moralités légendaires* had already appeared in magazines. With some of his last energy Laforgue made them ready for publication in volume form. Inevitably the Symbolists praised them highly, even hyperbolically. Mallarmé called them the 'contes de Voltaire du Symbolisme,' apparently mindful of Voltaire's virtues and especially of his irony. Téodor de Wyzewa's approval of the *Complaintes* had been qualified, his praise of the later verse restrained; but he did not hesitate to proclaim the author of the *Moralités* a genius.[2] And it was chiefly the *Moralités* that prompted similar judgments from many contemporaries. Alain-Fournier, one of Laforgue's firmest admirers, took the trouble to count the mentions of his name in Jules Huret's gossipy *Enquête sur l'évolution littéraire,* a series of interviews with literary figures of the day. He reported that Laforgue's name appeared no less than thirteen times, and that when asked who in their opinion were the world's great men the Symbolists were likely to reply, 'Shakespeare—Pascal—Laforgue. . .'[3] The harm done by such rash comparisons was considerable; and yet Laforgue had discovered something new, or new for the time, in the *Moralités,* the best of which took a light and springy step beyond realism. A small host of writers armed with irony sprang up, perhaps from the blood of the dragon Perseus slew on the coast of Ethiopia.

Marcel Schwob advanced beyond realism, though with no special lightness. Undoubtedly he profited from Laforgue's example, as from that of Gautier, Robert Louis Stevenson, Mark Twain, and a number of others including the arch-realist Defoe; for it was Schwob, with his characteristic lucidity of mind, who gave the prescription for the fantastic tale—to describe with utmost meticulousness the most impossible events. Schwob's creative powers were not equal to his analytical ones, and it was only by palpable effort, by a laying-on of thick colors, by unremitting appeal to fundamental passions, that he lent vitality to the *Vies imaginaires.* Yet Schwob was genuinely concerned with the nature of tragedy (witness the thought-provoking essay, 'Terror and Pity'), and he was capable of a grotesque intensity reminiscent of that English dramatist to whom he devoted one of his imaginary lives, Cyril Tourneur.

'He sought to free himself from his youthful sentimentalism,' Rémy de Gourmont wrote of Laforgue. 'As a tool he used irony;

but the sentimentalism resisted and he was never able to conquer it.' [4] Gourmont had nothing to fear on the score of sentimentality. He had, as an artist, nothing to 'conquer' but his sensuality; it resisted so stubbornly, so pertinaciously that his tales have little but aphrodisiac value nowadays. Pathetic as were the circumstances that brought on this intense single-mindedness—Gourmont, like Schwob, was a grievously afflicted man—we cannot but wonder why so impatient a critic should have allowed himself to be so repetitive.

Se répéter, quel mal de tête,

as Laforgue observed. At the same time, Gourmont definitely made use of the same instrument Laforgue used, irony, and in fantastic tales, such as the *Histoires magiques;* and it seems to have occurred to Gourmont himself that he and Laforgue had somewhat similar techniques of ratiocination. His deep-rooted irony was refreshed by many living springs, among which may well have been the *Complaintes* and the *Moralités.*

Paul-Jean Toulet, who translated Arthur Machen and belonged to the group of poets who styled themselves Fantaisistes, told the story of Jason and Medea in the vein of the *Moralités,* calling it 'La Princesse de Colchide.' ('Then I passed over to Colchis, where the Golden Fleece would land . . .' the Monster had said in 'Persée.') Laforguian themes and images crop up in the quatrains inserted in that tale. The stanza is of a form that Toulet devised and called a *contrerime:* lines of eight, six, eight, and six syllables rhyming *abba* subtly confound the effects of the *abba* and *abab* quatrains. Here are some samples, Laforguian in substance and imagery, from the volume *Contrerimes:*

> *Dans le silencieux automne*
> *D'un jour mol et soyeux,*
> *Je t'écoute en fermant les yeux,*
> *Voisine monotone.*

> *Ces gammes de tes doigts hardis,*
> *C'était déjà des gammes*
> *Quand n'étaient pas encor des dames*
> *Mes cousines, jadis . . .*

Toulet turned these witty quatrains to a remarkable variety of purposes, the most characteristic being satire of an objectivity that Laforgue might eventually have attained.

Different facets of Laforgue's work shone again fitfully in that of other writers. Théo Varlet entitled an interplanetary novel *L'Agonie de la terre*, and the speaker of his poems is often an ironically self-deprecating hero of the kind Laforgue made familiar. Tristan Derème shared with Laforgue an ironic tone, systematic use of assonance, and differed from him in that Derème came to deploy these through longer, more discursive poems. Another Fantaisiste, he prized 'les choses minuscules,'—we almost translate this by the famous 'small, dry things' of T. E. Hulme, which had so much to do with the objectives of the Imagists—the poetry of the quotidian. At about the same time that Derème was discussing Laforgue sensitively in *Vers et Prose*, a periodical that was instrumental in molding the critical mind of Jacques Rivière, he published *Les Ironies sentimentales*. The promises of that early work were realized in *L'Enlèvement au clair de lune* and *Le Zodiaque ou les étoiles sur Paris*, verse as pleasant as it is unpretentious. Finally, we must mention among the lesser ironists the art critic who called himself Tristan Klingsor and demonstrated knowledge of the cadences of the *Derniers Vers* in the poems of *Shéhérazade*, set to music by Darius Milhaud.

In Léon-Paul Fargue we are confronted with a poet of a stature quite different from that of the poets just mentioned. This disciple of Mallarmé—academically as well as artistically, since he sat in the class of that reluctant schoolmaster—followed the well-charted course of a *symboliste moyen sensuel* until he emerged rather suddenly in the 'twenties as one of the major poets of his time. An early lyric tale, *Tancrède*, was beclouded by a vaporous Symbolist vocabulary. He combined an ingenuousness suggestive of Francis Jammes with a Verlainian music in the slender collection that comprised the total of his poems until he was more than forty years old. During this time his most Laforguian productions were probably the *Ludions*, swift ironic ripostes. Here, however, from *Poèmes*, is a reconciliation of the spirits of geometry and finesse reminiscent of Laforgue's 'la somme des angles d'un triangle, chère âme':

En vain la mer fait le voyage
Du fond de l'horizon pour baiser tes pieds sages.
    Tu les retires
        Toujours à temps.

Une méduse blonde et bleue
Qui veut s'instruire en s'attristant
Traverse les étages bondés de la mer,
Nette et claire comme un ascenseur,
Et décoiffe sa lampe à fleur d'eau
Pour te voir feindre sur le sable
Avec ton ombrelle, en pleurant,
Les trois cas d'égalité des triangles.

In vain the ocean journeys up
From the horizon's rim to kiss your cautious feet
    Which you withdraw
        Always in time.

A blond and blue medusa
Desiring wisdom with experience
Traverses the thronged storeys of the sea
Clear and light like an elevator,
And unshades its lamp at water level
To see you simulate upon the sand
With your parasol, in tears,
The three instances of equality of triangles.

The important poetry that Fargue finally found it in him to write is as memorable for its Dostoevskyan breadth and depth of perception as for its realization of long-standing Symbolist aims. The cult of the Word is there; Fargue is the only important modern coiner of vocables in a language that resists such innovation much more stoutly than Joyce's English. Incidentally, he appropriates more than his share of the technical and special vocabularies in which modern poets rejoice—the language of trainmen, for example, in his finest poem, 'La Gare.' With Mallarmé and the Symbolists generally, he refuses to distinguish between poetry in verse and poetry in prose, and his most peculiarly personal expression was in prose poems, stray cadences of which recall the *Moralités légendaires*. But Laforgue was chiefly for Fargue what he has been for several other poets in full possession of their powers, a sort of witty monitor challenging the authenticity of this or that lyric flight.

The twentieth-century French poet having most in common with Laforgue is undoubtedly his fellow Béarnais Jules Supervielle. Like Laforgue, Supervielle is an inveterate storyteller, finding it natural to spin a yarn whether in verse or in prose. Some of his best poems revive the narrative form too generally neglected by modern poets. And his fanciful prose tales, such as 'L'Arche de Noé,' have added nearly as much to his reputation as has his verse. The stories written after the beginning of the Second World War, versions of classic myths collected in *Le Petit Bois* and *Orphée*, are not his best. No doubt for that reason the models, the *Moralités* among them, are the more apparent.

In its own way Supervielle's verse illustrates something proved several times over by that of North Americans: the catalyzing power of Laforgue. Poetic worlds separate the early *Poèmes de l'humour triste* from the important *Gravitations;* the poet whose quality is so much to be felt in the first title had his part in Supervielle's discovery of himself. The autonomous verse lines of the *Derniers Vers* were at the back of Supervielle's mind when he wrote, still comparatively early, the lovely 'San Bernardino':

> *Que j'enferme en ma mémoire,*
> *Ma mémoire et mon amour,*
> *Le parfum féminin des courbes Colonies,*
> *Cet enfant nu-fleuri dans la mantille noire*
> *De sa mère passant sous la conque du jour,*
> *Ces plantes à l'envi, et ces feuilles qui plient,*
> *Ces verts mouvants, ces rouges frais,*
> *Ces oiseaux inespérés,*
> *Et ces houles d'harmonies,*
> *J'en aurai besoin un jour.*
>
> *J'aurais besoin de vous, souvenirs que je veux*
> *Modelés dans l'honneur lisse des ciels heureux,*

Vous me visiterez secourables audaces,
Azur vivace d'un espace . . .

May I in memory enfold,
In memory and love enfold,
The feminine fragrance of the swelling Colonies,
This child nude-blooming in the black mantilla
Of his mother passing beneath the shell of day,
These emulous plants, these bending leaves,
These moving greens, these cool reds,
These birds beyond all dreams
And these surging harmonies,
I will have need of them one day.

I will have need of you, memories
Shaped in flowing praise of happy skies,
You will come back to me, good braveries,
Undying azure, azure of a place . . .

Gravitations contains much *vers libre*. But the distinctive virtue of Laforgue's verse has been to engender something quite different from itself: 'tighter, more concentrated form,'[5] as Supervielle has testified, the alexandrine and the octosyllable. The compactly wrought eight-syllable lines of *Oublieuse Mémoire* are in particularly sharp contrast to all the varieties of free verse, just as the brooding gentleness of Supervielle's later poetry leaves adolescent ironies and despairs far behind.

The passage quoted at the beginning of this chapter is probably an overhandsome acknowledgement of indebtedness. One of the most honest of poets, anxious to escape a dominion he was the readiest to admit, Supervielle was never possessed by Laforgue to the same degree as T. S. Eliot was. Nor, for that matter, were any other French poets. For something comparable to Eliot's fellow feeling with Laforgue, we must turn to a prose writer who, incidentally, acted as Eliot's French tutor during his stay in France after leaving Harvard—Alain-Fournier, author of *Le Grand Meaulnes*. There is no more attractive story of a young man's devotion to a favorite writer than that of Alain-Fournier for Laforgue as revealed by his letters. Jacques Rivière, Fournier's correspondent, did not share his friend's enthusiasm. The letters exchanged by one of the most authentic creators and one of the most acute critics of the century weigh Laforgue's merits better than any of the literary histories or formal criticisms have done.

Born in the Sologne, that profoundly rural region east of Tours and south of Paris, the son of a country schoolmaster, Fournier had spent two years in naval school (to no one's satisfaction) before becoming a student at the Lycée Lakanal in the southern outskirts of Paris. When in the summer of 1905 he went to England to learn the language, he wrote long letters to Rivière, his schoolfellow at Lakanal, letters full of talk about literature and especially about Laforgue. His opinions are fervent but not immature. The half-peasant childhood of which he was to tell in *Le Grand Meaulnes,* experience more varied than that of most schoolboys, the creator's jealous concern for everything touching his craft—all combined to toughen his literary mind, to arm his judgment.

He had, to begin with, little use for Rimbaud (compare with Eliot's similar opinion). Rimbaud is an "incomplete genius . . . a foil for unrestricted admiration for Laforgue,' [6] who is remarkable for his completeness, for the abundance of resources on which he draws, for his 'strange diversity of means of evocation.'

His enthusiasm begins with Laforgue's letters, especially the one of September 1881 in which the poet tells his sister of his shifts for keeping body and soul together. (Rivière replied that a satiric writer does not have the right to pity himself.) Fournier falters with *Le Sanglot de la terre:* 'Why should the fellow wear himself out with a lot of nonsense about the revolutions of the earth, the life of the planets, the rottenness of life, the vileness of bodies, etc., etc. . . . why didn't idealism cure him of all that?' Enthusiasm is revived more vigorously than ever with the *Complaintes* and *Des Fleurs de bonne volonté,* especially the 'Complainte d'une convalescence en mai' and the 'Dimanche' that begins, 'Le fleuve a son repos dominical.' But then on almost every page of Laforgue's poems, Fournier finds verses, phrases expressing something poignantly, perfectly, evoking a 'vision.' These verses, these fragments gave the effect for which Fournier was looking in his own work: something to make him forget the words. And he copied out for his friend some of the bits that gave him this intense impression of things seen:

> *O cloîtres blancs perdus*
>
> *Soleils soufrés croulant dans les bois dépouillés*
>
> *S'entrer un crucifix maigre et nu dans le coeur*
>
> *Puis les squelettes de glycines aux ficelles*
>
> *O lendemains de noce! ô brides de dentelle!*
>
> *Soeur faisait du crochet,*
> *Mère montait la lampe . . .*

> O lost white cloisters
>
> Sulphur suns crumbling in the leafless woods
>
> To plunge a naked crucifix in the heart
>
> Then the wisteria skeletons on strings
>
> O wedding morrows! Bridle reins of lace!
>
> Sister was crocheting,
> Mother brought up the lamp . . .

With a humdrum word Laforgue was able 'to give a profound and even gentle impression.'

> *Premiers soirs, sans pardessus, chaste flânerie . . .*
>
> First evenings, coatless, innocent excursion . . .

The element of the commonplace is exaggerated because Laforgue 'lives in dread of poetry which is merely beautiful, while right at hand is life itself, including probably a large share of ugliness.' But when Laforgue goes further and definitely assumes the ironic tone, Fournier confesses he can no longer follow, 'because he saw the painful everywhere and tried to exasperate his pain by pretending to make fun of it, because by dint of his efforts to see the painful and the stupid, he saw falsely.'

This attempt to see around a literary hero was occasioned by Rivière's accusation that he had 'created his own Laforgue out of whole cloth.' From beginning to end of these epistolary conversations covering a full year, Rivière's position underwent no real change; and his position remains that of the average cultivated French reader right down to the present day. He confesses himself offended 'in his need (a very French need) for literary decorum.' He knows that it is a 'slightly bourgeois need,' but there is nothing he can do about it. Laforgue rubs him the wrong way. 'I am shocked by the incoherence, calculated though it be. . . I find it all somewhat facile and bewildering. The ideas make such enormous, giddy leaps. . .' He concedes certain happy touches in the 'Convalescence en mai.' He realizes what Laforgue was trying to get at, the blurred and haggard dreams of a sick man getting well. The trouble seems to be that for Rivière this poet is a perpetual convalescent or even a chronic invalid. His complaints reek with self-pity. Rivière has no patience with a personality that Fournier defends on the grounds of extreme sensitiveness.

Such divergent views could be reconciled only by the calmest of deliberation, and this Rivière undertook with all the clairvoyance of his critical mind. Leaving to his friend 'the superior intuitions of enthusiasm,' aspiring to no more liking for the poet than might be acquired by methodical industry, he set about examining Laforgue. He found in him 'an admirable spirit, one that refused to be crushed by the pressure of environing mediocrity; an extraordinary capacity for expression, incomparable verbal skill; an uncommon knack for subjecting the whole of history, literature, and fantasy to his own personal vision.' And he found three corollary objections: 'a spirit not quite admirable enough to adjust itself to the mediocrity of existence and transfigure it; an excess of verbal skill, glibness almost, intoxication with words—he has so many words at his disposal that he is forever expressing the same thought in different dress; the very fact that he reduces the whole of history, literature, and fantasy to his own personal vision. . . That *idée fixe* of his is really exasperating. After all, the misunderstanding between the sexes is all right, but . . . there are so many other things.'

The hostile historians—of whom René Lalou is the chief—have added little but violence of tone to this estimate, and the foreign reader of French verse must dissent with proper circumspection. There is no doubt that Laforgue is primarily the poet of the quarrel between the sexes as seen by a twenty-year-old, too steadily and hence not whole. Laforgue's verse is, to use one of his own words, a trifle 'monocorde.' Poets are not celebrated, however, for their neglect of the most powerful of metaphors, the sexual one. If the poet happens to be a Romantic, even though a late-blooming and ironical one, the misunderstanding between the sexes may stand for other misapprehensions, the one between the poet and society, for example. The attentive reader must seek to discover the meanings of that personal vision of the world to which Laforgue, like any true writer, reduced history and experience. Rivière failed to allow for all the values of La-forgue's *idée fixe*. He had no intimation of the depth and breadth of Laforgue's intellectual world. It is true that Laforgue was not, spiritually speaking, quite admirable enough. The boredom of which he complained (until the last year of his life) was, unfortunately, more than a worldly posture; it betrayed a certain lack of spiritual energy, a refusal of life and experience, deficiency in that grain of heroism that would have enabled him to accept and transform the commonplace.

Two of Rivière's remarks bear on Laforgue the man, and upon the ostensible content of his verse. As for the single judgment passed on the vital question of Laforgue's artistic form, one cannot deny that the abundance verges on glibness. Yet the critic must resist the temptation to condemn the writer who does his work easily, to revenge the difficulty of his own lucubrations. Having conceded that an author's verbal skill is extraordinary, incom-parable, it would seem that an indispensable next step is to examine the curiously rich language that has somehow got down on paper, the language that is so obviously the poetic heart of the matter. Rivière gets only a little beyond Laforgue's person and his own personal prejudices. Fournier's enthusiasm, his creative impulse in search of a master, is more fruitful, nor does it merely manu-facture a private Laforgue. The nascent novelist perceives the 'vision,' the lack of 'written' quality, the poetry of the quotidian, the assimilation of the ugly, the grotesque. He remarks correctly that where Laforgue saw only the ugly, the grotesque, he falsified his vision. Having his special reasons for being interested in the narrative technique of the *Moralités*, he observes that there is no 'petite histoire,' that the points of view are multiple. 'With Laforgue there is no character at all, that is, he says to the devil with characters. He is at once author, character, and reader.' Rivière acknowledged with some reluctance the technical 'franchise' of these pieces.

In this dialogue between the finely poised critical mind of Rivière and the creative mind of Fournier, destined to grope its way for several years yet, it is the latter who sees the more clearly, the more deeply—and who was insufficiently aware that he did so. Apparently overawed by the critic's authentic-sounding remarks, Fournier was writing before the year was out about 'the glorified mediocrity, the worried mediocrity prone to burst out in a few irremediable words, the self-exalting mediocrity' of the man whom he had so lately been defending and justifying. We find him abusing Laforgue as 'Homais devant la science.' This in the same letter in which he speaks of 'the pure and passionate soul' of Laforgue. No one having such a soul was, in Fournier's scheme of things, mediocre.

Rivière's taste, which seems to have prevailed, is correct but limited, as he himself obscurely felt it to be. Bewildered by the qualities that failed to fit into a closed national tradition, by the ellipses, by the disregard of canons and decorum, Rivière missed the Laforgue that proved most stimulating to the creative mind in general and the Anglo-Saxon mind in particular. He saluted his friend's 'superior intuitions' a little ironically. As it happens, such intuitions, the enthusiasm that prompted them, the current that passed between creative minds not once but many times, far outweighs in importance such cautious classicist judgments as Rivière's.

In spite of his announced change of mind, Fournier continued to look for that which was new, which was capable of renewing, for what he had already found. 'For the moment,' he had said, 'I would like to start from Laforgue, but write a *novel*. This sounds contradictory. But it would not be contradictory if one made up, out of the lives and stories of one's characters, only dreams that cross (*des rêves qui se rencontrent*). I use this word "dream" because it is right at hand, even though a trifle irritating and threadbare. What I understand by "dream" is this: a vision of the past, of past hopes, a past day, that returns to meet a vision disappearing, the memory of a meeting of an afternoon, the remembered whiteness of a parasol and the freshness of another thought.' The work that lay at the end of this route taken from Laforgue was *Le Grand Meaulnes*, one of the minor masterpieces of twentieth-century literature because it fuses the visionary with the waking world, because it takes in its own way the step beyond realism. So many important works have begun with a departure from Laforgue that we may well ask ourselves whether his peculiarly animating poetry was not even more important for its consequences than for its intrinsic merits. In any case it becomes clear that Fournier was right and that the adverse critics have consistently missed the point.

XII

Irony and Legend

WHAT has Laforgue meant to the American literary mind? What, more specifically, did he mean to our most active poets over a period of some twenty years, from about 1908 until the late 'twenties? Mallarmé is a much greater poet than Laforgue. Corbière seems, on a first or second reading, to be a more vigorous one; and after several readings and miscellaneous inquiries it seems clear that Laforgue had from Corbière some of what seemed newest in the *Complaintes*. Rimbaud was a more intense creator, with some glimmer of the Romantic vision. Yet the poetry of Mallarmé was met with comments having many of the marks of vague incomprehension. Corbière has remained a curiosity. Rimbaud, read with enthusiasm, has provoked enthusiasm, but not for Rimbaud. Rather than any of these less equivocal creators it was the evasive, understating, ironic Laforgue, a prophet insufficiently honored in his own country even today, who exerted the unmistakable influence in ours. The best explanation is still the succinct one given by Ezra Pound: Laforgue was an angel with whom the American poetic Jacob had to wrestle. The evidence shows that those who wrestled were those who found the strength to affirm themselves, sometimes in a Laforguian, sometimes in a quite different way.

'I myself owe Mr. Symons a great debt,' Eliot was to say. 'But for having read his book . . . I should not, in the year 1908, have heard of Laforgue or Rimbaud.' [1] *The Symbolist Movement in Literature* (1899) represented a change of heart. Six years earlier Arthur Symons had published an article not calculated to

introduce anyone to any very significant aspect of French literature. In a carping essay entitled 'The Decadent Movement in
Literature,' he had touched on none of the more wholesome
connotations of the term 'decadent,' had lumped Decadence,
Symbolism and Impressionism all together as badges of 'little
separate cliques, noisy, brain-sick young people who haunt the
brasseries of the Boulevard Saint-Michel, and exhaust their in-
genuities theorizing over the works they cannot write.' [2] He had
made tentative gestures in the direction of Huysmans, the Goncourts (on whom he is the least unsatisfying), Verlaine, Maeter-
linck and Mallarmé. But he was quite unable to make up his mind
about *vers libre*, 'this apparently structureless rhythm . . . in the
hands of most of the experimenters it becomes mere rhymeless
irregular prose . . . in the hands of Gustave Kahn and Edouard
Dujardin it has, it must be admitted, attained a certain beauty of
its own.' [3]

From such nay-saying and exquisite error to Symons' valuable
introductory volume is no small distance. Well chosen quotations
in the chapter on Laforgue must have become imbedded in Eliot's
memory; they became, at any rate, the models of lines in 'Portrait
of a Lady' and *The Waste Land*. There is no mistaking the
provenience of

> Well! and what if she should die some afternoon,

in

> *Mais voici qu'un beau soir, infortunée à point,*
> *Elle meurt!*
> —'Pierrots—(On a des principes)'

or at least from these lines in combination with

> *Enfin, si, par un soir, elle meurt dans mes livres . . .*
> —'Autre Complainte de Lord Pierrot'

Another passage quoted by Symons, the solemn monition ending
a section of the *Derniers Vers*:

> *O vous qui m'écoutez, rentrez chacun chez vous,*

leads directly to 'O you who turn the wheel and look to wind-
ward' in *The Waste Land*.

But there are other good things in Symons' article—remarks
on what some would call Laforgue's death wish, his macabre
imagery, and on his paradox, especially paradox in the prose.
'We learn from books of medieval magic that the embraces of
the devil are of a coldness so intense that it may be called, by
an allowable figure of speech, fiery. Everything may be as
strongly its opposite as itself, and that is why this balanced, chill,
colloquial style of Laforgue has, in the paradox of its intensity,
the essential heat of the most obviously emotional prose.' [4] Symons
translates gracefully from Hamlet's monologue (he seems to
have more feeling for the prose than for the poetry). His position
regarding free verse remains mystifying. We are told that Laforgue writes '*vers libre*, but at the same time correct verse,
before *vers libre* had been invented.' [5] Toward the end he remarks that Laforgue, 'coming as he does after Rimbaud, turning
the divination of the other into achieved results, is the eternally
grown up, mature to the point of self-negation, as the other is
the eternal *enfant terrible*.' [6] The statement has been properly
disputed. Laforgue was never more than prematurely mature, except perhaps during the last two years of his life, when the
artificial airs Symons wrongly takes to be adult begin to disappear.
But this mistaken pronouncement is by way of digression from
Symons' main argument: that Laforgue, an artist 'of the nerves'
in the Goncourtian sense of that term, found release in utterance
fundamentally paradoxical. And this chapter has more illuminating
criticism of Laforgue than any that Eliot, inhibited by his
polemical classicism and his instinct to yoke Laforgue with the
English Metaphysicals, has been able to produce.

In the same year as Symons' essay on Decadence there had
appeared in *Scribner's* a remarkable study by Aline Gorren, an
all but forgotten translator of Rimbaud. 'The French Symbolists,' [7] as her article is called, has extremely interesting things to
say about Laforgue's tales, about Symbolist aesthetic doctrine,
even about Mallarmé. We find, for example, the valuable distinction, made by too few critics early or late, that 'the anachronism of the *Moralités légendaires* never degenerates into parody.'

Laforgue's anachronism is something altogether more far-reaching.

The pre-eminence of Pound and Eliot among Americans who have learned from Laforgue should not make us overlook lesser, independently formed poets who profited from the French ironist. Walter Conrad Arensberg, a contributor to Alfred Kreymborg's *Others*, translated 'Autre Complainte de Lord Pierrot' and 'Jeux' adroitly, and some of his own poems, like 'The Inner Significance of the Statues Outside the Boston Public Library,' live up to their Laforguian promise. Maxwell Bodenheim lit upon Laforguian themes in poems such as 'Sunday in a Certain City Suburb.' But the best of the *minores* is certainly Donald Evans. Particularly in his second book, bizarrely entitled *Sonnets from the Patagonian* (1914), when he was no longer unduly influenced by his French models and had not yet begun to repeat himself, Evans gave proof of unmistakable visionary intensity. He imitates neither Laforgue nor any other poet. We are reminded, if of anyone at all, of Rimbaud or Hart Crane. In his poetry as in the conduct of his life Evans sought 'systematic derangement of the senses.' That may have been partly the reason for such verse as this:

> And she was sad since she could not be glad,
> And every star fled amorous from the sky,
> Her pampered knees fell under her keen eye
> And it came to her she would not go mad.
> The gaucheries were turning the last screw,
> But there was still the island in the sea,
> The harridan chorus of eternity,
> That let her smile because he saw she knew . . .

What we have is a bodying-forth of emotional depths that might never have been accomplished without exposure to French (or Patagonian) examples.

Malcolm Cowley was one of those who, sensitive to Pound and Eliot, Amy Lowell and the Imagists, began to write in the years immediately following the First World War. 'After the war we drifted to New York,' he has recorded, 'to the district south of Fourteenth Street, where we could occupy a hall bed-

room for two or three dollars weekly . . . Our college textbooks
and the complete works of Jules Laforgue gathered dust on the
mantelpiece. . .' [8] Dusty but symbolic, the works of Laforgue
helped provoke 'a sort of crooked sentiment, a self-protective
smirk' characteristic, as Cowley says, of the postwar writers. And
though Cowley ceased to believe in his own verse he was capable,
when he dusted off the volumes on his mantelpiece, of turning
out two of the best English renderings of Laforgue. We do not
soon forget his adaptation of 'Dimanches' in which life is compared to a potato peeling; Laforgue did not think of that simile,
but he undoubtedly would have if he had ever occupied a hall
bedroom south of Fourteenth Street. And the following varia-
tion on the theme of the 'Complainte des pianos' is deft:

NOCTURNE

Mother has washed the dishes, limped upstairs;
Mother has disappeared into the light;
porches are filled where wicker rocking chairs
creak . . . through the emptiness of night
. . . creak . . . scrape, as if they would repeat
the chorus of the daughters of the street:

> *Hamburg steak for dinner, runs in our hose,*
> *nobody speaks of them, everybody knows:*
> *meeting me at twilight he handed me a rose:*
> *will he come?*

'Will he come with gallant eyebrows, chestnut hair;
will he come and rock beside me in the chair;
will he press my fingers neatly, say discreetly,
life is real,
life is true, will he tell its every secret,
but discreetly,
having realized how sacredly I feel?' [9]

The subject is the same as that of Laforgue's *Complainte*, the
cribbed, cabined, and confined life of the girls, and so is the
treatment, the voices of the girls and a meditative young man

alternating. Here even are equivalents for the dashing Rolands of Laforgue's poem and an echo of his memorable line, 'La vie est vraie et criminelle.'

Hart Crane was the principal poet among those who kept Laforgue's works on the mantelpiece; Allen Tate, who wrote a Laforguian 'Elegy for Eugenesis,' [10] was another. But we are primarily concerned with two older poets responsible for the conspicuous position of Laforgue.

'Have found a new good poet named Eliot,' Pound wrote to his father 2 October 1914. And the next day, to H. L. Mencken: 'I enclose a poem by the last intelligent man I've found—a young American, T. S. Eliot (you can write him direct, Merton College, Oxford). I think him worth watching—mind not "primitive." His "lady" is very nicely drawn.' [11]

'Portrait of a Lady' was the second-composed of the four poems Eliot himself has ranged 'sous le signe de Laforgue.' 'Conversation galante' had been the first, 'Prufrock' and 'La Figlia che Piange' were the third and fourth.[12] These pieces were preceded by three less familiar and equally Laforguian ventures written while Eliot was at Harvard, published in the *Harvard Advocate*. Here is one of them:

SPLEEN

Sunday: this satisfied procession
Of definite Sunday faces;
Bonnets, silk hats, and conscious graces
In repetition that displaces
Your mental self-possession
By this unwarranted digression.

Evening, lights, and tea!
Children and cats in the alley;
Dejection unable to rally
Against this dull conspiracy.

And life, a little bald and gray,
Languid, fastidious, and bland,
Waits, hat and gloves in hand,

Punctilious to tie and suit
(Somewhat impatient of delay)
On the doorstep of the Absolute.[13]

The theme is, at the outset, peculiarly Laforguian. But what
begins as the lyric expansion of a mood becomes, before the
end, a poem about a personified abstraction capable of passing
such splenetic Sundays, 'unable to rally/Against this dull conspiracy.' 'Life' has some of the distinctive traits of J. Alfred
Prufrock. A second poem, 'Nocturne,' has in it the germ of 'Conversation Galante.'

The third of these experimental poems is avowedly Laforguian;
it is also the most complex, the most interesting of the three.

HUMOURESQUE (after J. Laforgue)

One of my marionettes is dead,
Though not yet tired of the game,—
But weak in body as in head,
(A jumping-jack has such a frame).

But this deceaséd marionette
I rather liked: a common face,
(The kind of face that we forget)
Pinched in a comic, dull grimace;

Half bullying, half imploring air,
Mouth twisted to the latest tune;
His who-the-devil-are-you stare;
Translated, maybe, to the moon.

With Limbo's other useless things
Haranguing spectres, set him there;
'The snappiest fashion since last spring's,
'The newest style on Earth, I swear.

'Why don't you people get some class?
(Feebly contemptuous of nose),
'Your damned thin moonlight, worse than gas—
'Now in New York'—and so it goes.

Logic a marionette's, all wrong
Of premises; yet in some star
A hero!—Where would he belong?
But, even at that, what mask *bizarre!* [14]

This poem seems to have grown out of a single stanza of 'Encore un Livre' (quoted by Symons in his *Symbolist Movement*):

> *Encore un de mes pierrots mort;*
> *Mort d'un chronique orphelinisme;*
> *C'était un coeur plein de dandysme*
> *Lunaire, en un drôle de corps.*

All the pierrotic traits noted in Laforgue's quatrain are preserved. The 'chronic orphelinism' leads to the 'half bullying, half imploring air.' The 'heart full of dandyism' passes over into 'the snappiest fashions since last spring's . . .'—a 'dandysme lunaire,' translated, maybe, to the moon. Meanwhile a Pierrot is happily metamorphosed into a marionette—translated successfully to Anglo-Saxondom. And Eliot's try at colloquial speech is more successful here than in some other places, the second part of *The Waste Land*, for example. Altogether an extremely interesting poem, though too much Laforgue's to be quite Eliot's.

At twenty-two Eliot was proceeding with characteristic deliberation, and he was to 'work out the implications of Laforgue,' [15] as he has said, for several years, with the most significant consequences. What would have happened or failed to happen *pour tel coche manqué*, if he had not subjected himself to the discipline of fresh artistic forms? Conrad Aiken was writing fluently, with undeniable melodic gift, in the *Advocate* during the same years, and at least one of his college poems is a little better than anything Eliot did while at Harvard.

Eliot has called the relation between Laforgue and himself 'a sort of possession by a stronger personality.' [16] He took from the French poet images, rhythmic patterns, the designs of whole poems, finding in Laforgue a plastic imagination and an instinct for dramatic situation akin to his own. In so far as we are ever indebted to more than one poet at a time, Laforgue had a part

in the 'sawdust restaurants with oyster-shells,' the yellow smoke
that 'licked its tongue into the corners of the evening,' the 'head
[grown slightly bald] brought in upon a platter' and other images
inextirpably imbedded in our consciousness.

The debt to specific lines is manifest. 'Rhapsody on a Windy
Night' is not one of the poems recognized by Eliot as particularly
Laforguian. There, however,

> Midnight shakes the memory
> As a madman shakes a dead geranium.
>
> The reminiscence comes
> Of sunless dry geraniums.

The geranium image, and probably the meaning attached to it,
comes from *Des Fleurs de bonne volonté:*

> *Dans un album,*
> *Mourait fossile*
> *Un géranium*
> *Cueilli aux Iles*
>
> *Un fin Jongleur*
> *En vieil ivoire*
> *Raillait la fleur*
> *Et ses histoires. . .*
>
> *—'Un requiem!'*
> *Demandait-elle*
> *—'Vous n'aurez rien,*
> *'Mademoiselle!'*

> In an album
> A-dying lay
> A geranium
> Picked far away
>
> A fine old singer
> In ivory

Scoffed at the flower
And at her story. . .

'A threnody!'
The flower implored
'No, young lady,
'Never a word!'

Add to this the title of the next poem but one in this collection, 'Maniaque,' and we have the elements of another Eliotic syncretism. 'Maniaque de bonheur,' [17] writes Laforgue in *Derniers Vers*, and elsewhere, 'Pauvre maniaque de bonheur.'

Between those two mentions of the geranium in Eliot's poem comes

'Regard the moon,
La lune ne garde aucune rancune,'

a revision of Laforgue's

—*Là, voyons, mam'zelle la Lune,*
Ne gardons pas ainsi rancune . . .
                    —'Complainte de cette
                    bonne lune'

And this is followed by just the kind of acidulous description of the planet to be found in *L'Imitation de Notre-Dame la Lune*.

Was Eliot inspired by Laforgue to use underwater imagery? Did he find the foetus image in the *Complaintes?* Mr. Apollinax laughs like

an irresponsible foetus.
His laughter was submarine and profound. . .

Quite as interesting as the borrowings, in any case, are the coincidences. It is unlikely that Eliot ever delved into *La Vogue*, and he could not otherwise have known of the following lines, part of the prose poem prompted by visits to the Berlin Aquarium:

et moi, serais-je donc si déplacé, sur le dos,
parmi ces limules? [18]

and I, would I have been so out of place, upon my back,
among those king crabs?

This bit was cut out when the 'Aquarium' was revised and fitted
into 'Salomé.' But the lines that sum up Prufrock's hesitations,

> I should have been a pair of ragged claws
> Scuttling across the floors of silent seas,

have a good deal more in common with Laforgue's lines than, as
has been suggested, [19] with Shakespeare's 'Yourself, sir, should
grow old as I am, if like a crab you could go backward.' [20] Prufrock and the speaker of Laforgue's prose poem express the same
desire to be hidden from the light of upper day.

The four poems Eliot placed 'under the sign of Laforgue' even
retrace in miniature the curve of development seen in Laforgue's
versification. 'Conversation Galante' is a compactly wrought col-
loquy in iambic pentameters varied by lines of three and four feet
at the stanza ends; the poems of which 'Autre Complainte de
Lord Pierrot' is the model are dialogues in alexandrines with brief
lines ending the strophes. 'Portrait of a Lady,' 'Prufrock' and 'La
Figlia che Piange' are all in free verse of the kind toward which
Laforgue's poetry evolved: irregular lines representing emotive
ideas compose a stanza-sentence, with irregular rhyme and assonance lending firmness to fluid structure. Two poets anxious to
capture the 'ephemeral,' to 'borrow every changing shape/To find
expression,' felt the need for stretched and broken rhythms, for
verses contracted or distended. Through most of his first book
Eliot exploits the instrument developed by Laforgue in his last.
The free verse forms discursive soliloquies of a thoroughly modern sort, images simulating the flow of ideas within the consciousness. The *vers libre* of Eliot and Laforgue realizes many of the
possibilities of associational form, stream-of-consciousness technique.

Formal resemblances between Laforgue and the early Eliot
are far more important than thematic similarities. The moon
would not have figured as conspicuously in 'Conversation Galante'
and 'Rhapsody on a Windy Night,' however, without Our Lady

the Moon. Nor would womankind have been dismissed quite as roundly as 'eternal enemy of the Absolute,' without a number of pessimistic poems whose female personage is clearly an ancestor of the lady in Eliot's 'Portrait.'

Eliot's criticism has been as fertile in new associations, 'new objects caught in new intuitions' as Santayana might have said, as has his poetry. It obliges us to compare Laforgue's free verse and the blank verse of the later Elizabethan and Jacobean play-rights; they are, Eliot tells us, 'free verse in much the same way.' [21] Not quite the same: the lines of *Derniers Vers* are more self-sufficient, more cohesive, not constructed out of two or three 'emotive ideas' as Webster's frequently are. Nevertheless, there is a rough kind of parallel between the evolution of the alexandrine during the nineteenth century and that of the blank verse line during the Elizabethan period, between two kinds of verse made increasingly free by growing awareness of the techniques of perception. Is there as much resemblance between Laforgue's psychological notation and the conceit, the fancifully elaborated image of the English Metaphysicals? Eliot tells us that the two are 'curiously similar' [22] and quotes the first ten lines of the *Derniers Vers*, Section x, as evidence that Laforgue is close to 'the school of Donne.' G. M. Turnell, on the contrary, argues that the resemblance is slight. [23] Offhand there would seem to be little in common between the associationist, enthusiastic poet that was Laforgue and the imposer of rational design that was Donne. To associate the authors of the *Derniers Vers* and the *Songs and Sonnets* this closely is to leave out of account the modern revolution of sensibility begun by Diderot. However, if the new combinations, the new 'objects' of Eliot's criticism carry less conviction than his poetry, if his criticism here illumines Eliot more than his subject matter, it has the great merit of making us think about the two kinds of verse in question and shows what diverse faces Laforgue's work has turned up to a great modern poet. Nothing is more important, in conclusion, than to recall where Eliot began. 'The form in which I began to write, in 1908 or '09,' he said in an introduction to the *Selected Poems* of Ezra Pound, 'was directly drawn from the study of Laforgue together with the later Elizabethan drama; and I do not know anyone who started from exactly that point.' [24]

Another important poet had come upon Laforgue somewhat later in his career. 'I was a man in a hurry,' Pound remarked in 1948. 'When I got to London in 1908 I was an extremely unsophisticated individual. Eliot was born with all that, Laforgue and so on. I had to acquire it.' Pound thereby demonstrates once more a capacity for self-examination that has enabled him to move restlessly from stage to stage of artistic development. He gives evidence of a certain absence of vanity

> But to have done instead of not doing
> this is not vanity . . .

that must always have gone along with his superb role as the principal animator of Anglo-American poetry in the twentieth century. And he pays proper heed to a poet, Eliot, whose history is inseparable from his own.

The framework of Pound's relationship with Laforgue is fairly familiar. Pound began to read the *Complaintes* and *L'Imitation de Notre-Dame la Lune* about 1914, probably having been introduced to them by F. S. Flint,[25] and certainly being reminded of them by Eliot's early poems. In the preceding half a dozen years spent in London, in Italy, in the United States, he had published his first verse, in which the manner of the early William Butler Yeats is evident. *A Lume Spento*, the *Personae* of 1909, and *Exultations* are full of 'still forest pools' and the very 'Crepuscular Spirit in Modern Poetry' which Pound deplores in one of these very poems. The following passage,

> By the still pool of Mar-nan-otha
> Have I found me a bride
> That was a dog-wood tree some syne.
> She hath called me from mine old ways,
> She hath hushed my rancour of council,
> Bidding me praise
>
> Naught but the wind that flutters in the leaves,

is hardly Pound as we think of him. Despite a poem in praise of Robert Browning, this passage is a fair sample of *Personae* as a whole.

These lines are not representative of Pound as he wished to be thought of, even as early as 1912, when *Ripostes* appeared. First and last, Pound valued the final letter on 'Imagiste' and 'Imagisme' mentioned in this volume; it served to fix a great gulf between the movement as he conceived it and the avatar animated by Amy Lowell. In his pronouncements concerning the nature of the Image, Pound did not limit valid poetic imagery to the visual. But T. E. Hulme, on whose aesthetic speculations Pound and his friends leaned more or less heavily, virtually makes this limitation; and so does the 1915 manifesto of the Imagist group, a document based in great part on Pound's oral criticisms and the principles deducible from his famous blue-pencilings of his fellow craftsmen's efforts. In practice the Imagists were poets of objects clearly seen. Having learned the poetic value of small, dry things, they ordinarily avoided the graceful picturesque. On the other hand, they were rarely able to suggest realities beneath appearances. Structurally speaking, the Imagist poem tends to be the elaboration of a single visual image, or else it places end to end a series of such images, in a compound but not a complex relationship. The ambitious poets among the Imagists—Pound in so far as he was an Imagist—sensed limitations of method, straitness of viewpoint, within their program, and began to cast about for techniques that would permit them to respond to complex realities in a complex way. It was at about this point of creative dissatisfaction that Pound began to read Laforgue.

He saw in the work of the French poet, primarily, an intellectual element which he called 'logopoeia' and defined as 'the dance of the intellect among words.' Using the term first in 1918, he came to reserve it almost exclusively for Laforgue. 'Unless I am right in discovering it in Propertius,' he remarks in *How to Read*, 'we must almost say that Laforgue invented *logopoeia*, observing that there had been a limited range of logopoeia in all satire, and that Heine occasionally uses something like it. . . At any rate Laforgue found or refound logopoeia.'

Thus Pound instituted a critical term of some value, in addition to making a bolder and more accurate estimate of Laforgue's dynamic significance than anyone had made up to that time, in France or elsewhere. Laforgue, said Pound, was a finer artist than either Corbière or Rimbaud: not as vigorous a draftsman as the former or as firm a colorist as the latter, he was the most discriminating of the three and accordingly had the most to teach.

It has been generally agreed that Pound, most active of poet-pedagogues, contrived to instruct others concerning Laforgue, to transmit lessons of craftsmanship inherent in the French poet's verse and particularly applicable to the American poetic mind. Beginning to write about Laforgue in 1917, in the London *Egoist* and in Harriet Monroe's *Poetry*, he loaded 1918 numbers of the *Little Review* with translation from Laforgue's verse, with a prose pastiche based on one of the tales, with seven poems reprinted in French along with critical comment. As a result of this determined presentation Hart Crane, Allen Tate, and an undetermined number of young American writers made their first acquaintance with Laforgue.

A more contested point has been how much direct influence Laforgue exerted on Pound's own poetic practice. René Taupin in his *Influence du symbolisme français sur la poésie américaine* found little or none. The contrary could, I believe, be shown; and one could begin by contrasting an earlier quatrain with two later ones.

The first is taken from Pound's Imagist volume *Ripostes*, the poem with the good Imagist title 'Apparuit,' and is characteristic of that volume:

> Half the carven shoulder, the throat aflash with
> strands of light inwoven about it, loveli-
> est of all things, frail alabaster, ah me!
> swift in departing.

The second and third are chosen almost at random from *Hugh Selwyn Mauberley*:

'Siena mi fe'; disfecemi
Maremma'

Among the pickled foetuses and bottled bones,
Engaged in perfecting the catalogue,
I found the last scion of the
Senatorial families of Strasbourg, Monsieur Verog,

and from the first poem of the group, with its title borrowed from
Ronsard, 'Ode pour l'élection de son sépulcre,'

Unaffected by the 'march of events,'
He passed from man's memory in *l'an trentiesme*
De son eage; the case presents
No adjunct to the Muses' diadem.

These and other quatrains of *Mauberley* lead back to the French
poet whom Pound had been studying in the years since the publication of *Ripostes.* They represent a kind of intellectual discussion that can be pertinently described as 'logopoeia.' One of Laforgue's favorite images, that of the foetus, turns up. The cliché,
'march of events,' is pressed into ironic service, according to characteristic Laforguian procedure. The verse depends on the literary reference as Laforgue's does, with 'l'an trentiesme de son
eage' woven in. Here too are the long 'international' words out
of Latin, the sort of polysyllables to which Laforgue resorted on
slight pretext. At the end of the third quatrain, 'No adjunct to
the Muses' diadem' furnishes a familiar ironic sparkle of grandeur.
Taken singly, no one of these traits would justify the term 'Laforguian.' Occurring all together, sustained by the ironically
learned tone which was Laforgue's contribution to nineteenth-
century verse, they send us back to the Pierrot poems.

No one, I think, would be more likely than Pound to maintain
that the structure of the literary work of art begins with and
comes round again to the quality of the disengaged word. It is
not irrelevant to recall that Mauberley's 'true Penelope was
Flaubert'—Mauberley's, Pound's and several other North and
South American poets' who would recognize no difference in
kind between the 'musical phrases' of their own verse and the

fragments from 'Un Coeur simple' which Pound fits into Canto VII. One could profitably dwell on the distance separating the falsely archaic, unduly simplified diction of the early *Personae* from the properly complex, ironic wording of *Mauberley*, bearing witness to activity on the intellectual level, eliciting more than one kind of response from the reader.

But wording does not make the poem, even though Pound would say that the men of his group were primarily concerned with that rather than with 'imagery.' Symbolists in several places have reiterated the lesson of the eighth chapter of Aristotle's *Poetics;* the structural order of the incidents also counts, especially in the poem of epic or dramatic pretensions. Stefan George, whose poems are mostly brief, wrote that the worth of a body of poetry is not to be determined on the basis of isolated beauties, however unmistakable, in lines, strophes or longer passages. . . 'die zusammenstellung, the relation of separate parts to one another, the inevitable development one out of another—these are the distinguishing marks of high poetry.' [26] Paul Valéry, some of whose poems are lengthy, remarked on the many beautiful lines written by bad poets. We must think of how a poem is or is not held together. Pound's reputation will in the long run depend not on any alleged accord between his poetic practice and farfetched poetic theories of his own, but on whether he has ever achieved that interrelation of diverse parts in which the best work of the Symbolists resembles that of their best European predecessors.

The larger problems of composition arise with particular force when a poet has written verse suffused with Celtic twilight, then Imagistic *croquis,* equally brief epigrammatic poems, and finally undertakes 'a poem of some length,' the *Cantos.* In the long work he is faced with the necessity of rising from image and remark to some kind of general design. The unsuccessful Cantos will be those in which the poet fails to rise from the particular to the general—those, I would say, in which he follows most faithfully his so-called 'ideographic' or Chinese-picture-writing method of heaping disconnected particulars together. Granting that the cluttered Cantos are too numerous, it is nonetheless uncritical to speak, as is quite commonly done, of all the Cantos as equally scrappy, evenly graced with exquisite but gratuitous passages. There is a good deal of difference in quality between Canto and Canto. In some of them Pound achieves compositional order, general design.

Ordinarily he does it by finding the common denominators in Greek and Provençal legends. In Canto IV, for example, he compels us to recall that the boy Itys was given to his father Tereus to eat, by way of revenge for the rape of Philomela; and that an outraged husband served the baked heart of the troubadour Cabestan to Soremonda. The common theme of both legends is that of the loved object offered to the lover to eat. Very adroitly Pound shows figures melting into corresponding figures and then with a bilingual pun

> Tis. Tis. 'Ytis!
> Actaeon . . .

introduces the figure of the mortal hunted by hounds. This figure is at once Actaeon and Peire Vidal, a slightly extravagant troubadour who out of pure devotion to his lady, whose name suggested 'she-wolf,' donned a thick wolfskin and invited pursuit by dogs and mastiffs and greyhounds. If Achaia is Provence, it is not unreasonable to find 'Troy in Auvergnat,' where the fifth and twenty-third Cantos put it. Pound recalls that still another troubadour, Peire de Maensac, stole away the wife of a certain Bernart de Tierci. The latter, identified with Menelaus, pursued the seducer northward, where he had taken refuge with the powerful Dauphin of Auvergne. The parallel breaks down at one point: the Dauphin protected the lovers successfully for the rest of their days, and this second Ilion did not fall. When Pound writes near the end of Canto XXIII

> . . . that was when Troy was down, all right,
> superbo Ilion . . .

before packing Aeneas off with Anchises, he can only mean the original Troy.

Several times in the early Cantos the poet hints at the identification of Eleanor of Aquitaine with Helen of Troy. The convergence is clearest in II and VII. But it is nearly as definite in VI, and the reiterated epithets *helenaus, helandros, heleptolis*—'ship-, man- and city-destroying'—apply to the composite figure.

Canto VI begins:

> What you have done, Odysseus,
>   We know what you have done . . .
> And that Guillaume sold out his ground rents . . .

Guillaume, duke of Aquitaine, 'sold out his ground rents' in order to take part in the First Crusade: to participate, that is, in war financed by mortgage or sale of real estate, in war the breeder of Usura and much else of what Pound detests. Another Crusader mentioned in the same Canto, Louis VII of France, Eleanor's first husband, dealt similarly with his possessions. Obviously Pound is looking to the Middle Ages for originals of the modern mort-gaged warrior. Is he looking to antiquity as well? He was un-doubtedly familiar with those accounts that would make of the Trojan War merely another commercial incursion, an attack on the rich citadel of the Hellespont by seafaring Greeks, some of them homeless. Yet there is no escaping the catalogue of the ships in the second book of the *Iliad:* many of the leaders and their men were associated with specific localities. Odysseus, along with other heroes, is returning to a fixed abode. Pound may have imagined him setting forth from home under circumstances not much different from those governing Guillaume of Aquitaine, Louis VII, and all the feudal lords who sold or pledged their property, giving modern capitalism one of its main impulses. If this were the case, we should have a plausible explanation for the placing of a long translation from the *Odyssey* as the first Canto. Canto I would relate to Usura, the main theme of all the *Cantos.*

In many other places Pound thus brings one out of many. His thoughts turn to the retributive murderer (Canto V) and Loren-zino de' Medici's assassination. Duke Alessandro reminds him of Clytemnestra's slaying of Agamemnon. Lorenzino appears again in the seventh and twenty-fifth Cantos, and there is a certain appropriateness in Pound's preoccupation with this character. For Lorenzino 'pondered Brutus,' as Pound tells us; or rather, he pondered two Brutuses, the earlier one who brought about the exile of the proud Tarquins and the later one who put an end to Caesar. Lorenzino imagined that he was both Brutuses and one heroic tyrannicide, achieving in his mind, if not in the mediocre verse he composed, something like that bold fusion of figures in a telescoped time which characterizes Pound at his best.

There was more in common between Pound and Laforgue in early stages of development than has been appreciated. Both had plastic imaginations of great vividness, were deft at rendering visual particulars. Lift certain passages out of Laforgue's early poems and those of his middle period and they would do quite well as Imagist poems. In the course of their development, both poets were more and more moved to comment in rather bare, conceptual terms, to assimilate refractory materials into verse that tore loose from traditional prosodic moorings, a *vers libre* founded on the autonomy of the rhythmic unit. The degree of freedom attained by the *Derniers Vers* in the 'eighties was no less remarkable than that of the *Cantos* in our time. If there is little similarity of tone between the early *Cantos* and the *Derniers Vers*, tone, for craftsmen like Pound and Laforgue, is a secondary consideration. In any case more tonal resemblance can be detected between the *Derniers Vers* and the *Pisan Cantos*, where the *vae soli*, the cry of loneliness running through Laforgue's last poems, is echoed in the lines presenting the gorilla cage, the deal table, and other emblems of Pound's captivity:

> a man on whom the sun has gone down
> and the wind came as hamadryas under the sun-beat
> Vae soli
> are never alone
> amid the slaves learning slavery
> LXXIV

Finally, Pound and Laforgue derive unity from diversity by similar means. For we have seen Laforgue arriving at fusion of legendary figures in just such a 'continuous present' as Pound's: Lohengrin and Endymion dissolved in a single moonstruck image of masculine beauty; a feminine figure who is at once Eve, la Gioconda, and Delilah; a monster who is most of the dragons of antiquity besides being the Beast liberated by an Andromeda metamorphosed into Beauty.

Two bodies of imaginative work, Pound's and Laforgue's, show a development from more or less haphazard allusiveness toward increasing correlation of allusions. In two bodies of verse, for the most part loosely woven, faithful to the inconclusiveness of the interior conversation, the same kind of knot is occasionally tied very tightly. Both of these modern poets find in the metamorphosis of mythical figures the bases of dramatic unity. Beyond them lies the tauter unity imposed by the synthesizing personage, by Tiresias in *The Waste Land*, of whom Eliot could say: 'Tiresias, although a mere spectator and not indeed a "character," is yet the most important personage in the poem, uniting all the rest. Just as the one-eyed merchant, seller of currants, melts into the Phoenician Sailor, and the latter is not wholly distinct from Ferdinand Prince of Naples, so all the women are one woman and the two sexes meet in Tiresias.' Neither Pound in the *Cantos* nor Laforgue in any of his works presents a central figure of whom it could be said, as Eliot says of Tiresias, that what he *sees* is, in fact, the poem. Pound lacked the sure instinct that led Eliot to devise such a personage, and Laforgue did not have time to develop an instinct he certainly possessed (witness his multiple points of view in the *Moralités légendaires* as noted by Alain-Fournier). Yet the *Cantos* and the *Moralités* furnish precedents for the one-eyed merchant, the Phoenician Sailor, the Prince of Naples; and Éleanor of Aquitaine, Tierci's wife, Soremonda, and a multitude of other female figures do tend—like Eve, la Gioconda, and Delilah—to compose one Helen.

XIII

Crane and Laforgue

In April 1920 Hart Crane wrote a poem called 'Episode of Hands.' A warmhearted autobiographical narrative reminiscent of Walt Whitman and Sherwood Anderson, it tells of the bandaging of a factory worker's damaged hand by the factory owner's son that was Hart Crane. The sentiment and the pictorial detail come out equally clearly; but 'Episode of Hands' is the kind of free and easy verse that unnumbered young Americans were to be writing in the 'twenties and 'thirties. Like most of what Crane wrote before 1920, it is distinctly minor in quality.

Just a year after 'Episode of Hands,' in April 1921, Crane wrote another poem, 'The Bridge of Estador, an Impromptu Aesthetic Tirade.' Taken as a whole, it is as ill-assured as its subtitle. But 'The Bridge of Estador' contains such intimations,

> Awaiting
> far consummations of the tides to throw
> clean on the shore some wreck of dreams . . .
>
> But some are twisted with the love
> of things irreconcilable,—
>
> The everlasting eyes of Pierrot,
> Or, of Gargantua, the laughter,

in which we recognize respectively 'At Melville's Tomb,' 'For the Marriage of Faustus and Helen,' and 'Praise for an Urn,' that this early poem about a bridge has undeniable significance. It is characterized by a rude but healthy irony,

> High on the bridge of Estador
> Where no one has ever been before,
> I do not know what you'll see,—your vision
> May slumber yet in the moon,

a manifest desire to include rather than exclude the elements of experience, to increase rather than diminish the lyric total. There is a fine new precision of observation:

> . . . a lake, perhaps with the sun
> Lapped under it . . .

Much, to quote another compact phrase from this poem, has here been 'tied bundle-wise.' *Poeta nascitur.* And without any wish to violate the mystery of what has occurred, it is important to note that between 'Episode of Hands' and 'The Bridge of Estador,' in the fall of 1920, Crane had ordered and received from Paris the works of Rimbaud, Vildrac, and Laforgue.

Crane's reading was presumably not limited to books he purchased. His poem of 1918, 'Modern Craft,' with its opening line, 'Though I have touched her flesh of moons,' and its preoccupation further on with a Gallicized Ophelia, would tend to show that he had come by a copy of Laforgue earlier. A good deal of the Laforguian quality must have reached Crane by way of *Prufrock and Other Observations* in 1917. The time at which he took verifiable contact with French verse is of interest, however, the more so because it seems to have coincided with a fallow period of great importance to his development. From October 1920 till the end of the following January he wrote little or no verse. 'It was,' Brom Weber, his most recent biographer, has written, 'as if he were resting quietly, summing himself up, endeavoring to ascertain just who and what he was.'[1] And in February of 1921 he produced the first poem in his mature manner, 'Black Tambourine.'

No doubt it would be difficult to find two poets presenting greater temperamental, environmental, intellectual differences: Laforgue like his own Hamlet; Crane bearing some resemblance

to what the 'indigent et positif Prince Fortimbras' might have
been if we had seen more of him in the same tale. Laforgue,
ardent, but on another plane, nourished at his most intense by
the regime of a Buddhist ascetic and by the Bibliothèque Nationale; Crane, far simpler, ignorant as the visionary is ignorant,
not sealed by 'la marque complexe de l'intellectuel.'

And there is another, equally fundamental dissimilarity. The
poetry of Crane imposes a vision on the imagination, is 'phano-
poetic,' to use the word Pound applied to Rimbaud's verse; while
the poetry of Laforgue is 'logopoetic,' something like 'a dance
of the intellect among words.' Thus it happens that Crane's
verbalism, a trait for which he may have found a sort of authori-
zation in Laforgue, comes off much less well than Laforgue's. In
the *Complaintes* and the *Derniers Vers* the apparently prolix passages, the seemingly idle exhibitions of verbal virtuosity, are almost always for a good reason, and are usually balanced by some
calculated leanness not far away. In 'Atlantis' the swollen diction
blurs the edges of a poetic vision.

Differences recognized, it becomes all the more significant that
Crane, in a word, *liked* Laforgue, and that he imitated and translated him during the decisive years when his own dissimilar style
was being formed. 'Certain educated friends of mine,' he wrote
to Allen Tate in 1922, 'have lamented my scant education, not
in the academic sense, but as regards my acceptance of and
enthusiasm about some Modern French work without having
placed it in relation to most of the older "classics," which I
haven't read. I have offered apologies, but continue to accept
fate, which seems to limit me continually in some direction.
Nevertheless, my affection for Laforgue is none the less genuine
for being led to him through Pound and T. S. Eliot than it would
have been through Baudelaire. There are always people to class
one's admirations and enthusiasms illegitimate, and though I still
have to have the dictionary close by when I take up a French
book, a certain sympathy with Laforgue's attitude made me an
easier translator of the three poems in the D. D. than perhaps
an accomplished linguist might have been. However, no one
ought to be particularly happy about a successful translation. I
did them for fun. . .' [2]

'D. D.' stands for the *Double Dealer*, one of the most imaginative of the little magazines of the time, published in New Orleans between 1921 and 1926. The poems are three 'Locutions des Pierrots' (the first three in the series), translated during 1921 and published in May 1922. In them Crane confronts typical Laforguian attitudes and themes: Pierrot half deprecating, half exalting himself, Pierrot suffering defeat in and detachment from romantic love. Crane's translations were long neglected. Left out of the *Collected Poems*, they were published at last by Brom Weber in an appendix to his study of Crane.

LOCUTIONS DES PIERROTS

I

Your eyes, those pools with soft rushes,
O prodigal and wholly dilatory lady,
Come now, when will they restore me
The orient moon of my dapper affections.

For imminent is that moment when,
Because of your perverse austerities,
My crisp soul will be flooded by a languor
Bland as the wide gaze of a Newfoundland.

Ah, madame! truly it's not right
When one isn't the real Gioconda,
To adaptate her methods and deportment
For snaring the poor world in a blue funk.

II

Ah! the divine infatuation
That I nurse for Cydalise
Now that she has fled the capture
Of my lunar sensibility!

True, I nibble at despondencies
Among the flowers of her domain
To the sole end of discovering
What is her unique propensity!

—Which is to be mine, you say?
Alas, you know how much I oppose
A stiff denial to postures
That seem too much impromptu.

III

Ah! without the moon, what white nights,
What nightmares rich with ingenuity!
Don't I see your white swans there?
Doesn't someone come to turn the knob?

And it's your fault that I'm this way,
That my conscience sees double,
And my heart fishes in troubled waters
For Eve, Gioconda and Dalila.

Oh, by the infinite circumflex
Of the archbeam of my cross-legged labors
Come now—appease me just a little
With the why-and-wherefore of Your Sex!

Crane's dictionary was sometimes at fault. The second quatrain should have been something like, 'It will soon be an hour now that my crisp soul languorously slakes, with the bland gaze of a Newfoundland, its thirst for your perverse austerities.' In the last line of that poem 'poor chaps' might be read for 'poor world,' since Laforgue wrote 'pauv' monde.' III, 4, could be changed to 'Didn't someone just now turn the latch?' for 'Vient-on pas de tourner la clenche?'

Such flaws would not be sufficient to destroy the effect of an otherwise successful rendering. And it is perfectly true, as Crane said in a note, that 'a strictly literal translation of Laforgue is meaningless. The native implications of his idiosyncratic style have to be recast in English garments.' But when we set the English beside the French we see that the poems have not quite been recast. Several rereadings do not discover a firm rhythmical armature in such lines as 'When one isn't the real Gioconda.' More successful translations than these demonstrate that the evasive rhythms of French verse have to be rendered by more decided stress rhythms in English. Moreover, while Laforgue's tendency was to break the basic verse line of his language into a multitude of curiously shaped fragments, Crane's natural technical progression was away from free verse toward a steady and assured meter. In the drafts of 'Chaplinesque,' of 'Garden Abstract,' again and again in the worksheets of his poems, the development is away from free verse and in the direction of blank verse, Marlovian by preference. Confronted by the relaxed rhythms of Laforgue's lines, Crane is technically ill at ease. Formally, as intellectually and morally, he struggles counter to Laforgue. The most successful line in the translations, a line worthy and characteristic of Crane at his best, is certainly

> What nightmares rich with ingenuity!

And if we set this line, with its rich tones and overtones, its near-absence of irony, beside the original

> *Quels cauchemars pleins de talent!*

we have already taken a long step toward comparing Crane and Laforgue.

These differences and difficulties considered, Crane did reasonably well at conveying pierrotic moods and outbursts. He was to do still better: he was to reinforce a tradition of Romantic clownishness with the figure of an authentic popular artist. Under the double impact of Laforgue and Chaplin's *The Kid*, in the fall of 1921, he wrote 'Chaplinesque,' capturing what D. H. Lawrence once called 'the flash of pure beauty' in the gentle-hearted misfit. In his own way and on his own terms Crane approached the most advanced stage of Laforgue's irony, the attitude of pathetic buffoonery for which Laforgue found a precedent in Shakespeare's clowns.

Laforgue would certainly have approved 'Chaplinesque.' The devoted amateur of the Reinz Circus in Berlin, the young poet who once wrote to a friend that he had gone to the circus five nights in a row and who further declared that he had missed his manifest destiny as a clown, would have underlined the 'we' in the opening line of each of the first three stanzas,

We make our meek adjustments . . .

For we can still love the world . . .

We will sidestep, and to the final smirk . . .

The 'we' bobs up again in strophes four and five,

We can evade you, and all else but the heart . . .

> but we have seen
> The moon in lonely alleys . . .

This 'we' pleasantly and conclusively equates poet and comedian
and sets him off against the machine-tooled general obtuseness
represented by the 'you.' Here is, of course, the romantic rebel-
lion against environment which is at the bottom of both Crane
and Laforgue in spite of all their differences. The earlier Pierrot
who had not seen Charlot would have liked everything about this
poem—the 'random consolations' with which 'we' take up and
comfort the famished kitten in 'warm torn elbow coverts'; the
fine identification of the 'you' with the gendarmery, which, as
in *The Kid*, 'slowly chafes its puckered index toward us' ('index'
being, we imagine, both the index finger, as in *The Kid*, and an
index of forbidden things). He would have appreciated 'our' vic-
tories, since 'we' somehow do get away after all, tyrannized ultimately only by the heart itself. Laforgue would have been
enthusiastic about the fine generalization of 'our' smirks into a
'grail of laughter' in the last strophe, where the grail is redeemed,
so to speak, made up-to-date and American by its identification
with an empty ash can:

> The game enforces smirks; but we have seen
> The moon in lonely alleys make
> A grail of laughter of an empty ash can
> And through all sounds of gaiety and quest
> Have heard a kitten in the wilderness.

If 'Chaplinesque' is Crane's best poem in what may honestly
be called a Laforguian vein, 'For the Marriage of Faustus and

Helen' was his first lengthy and very ambitious poem, and one whose style Allen Tate found to be 'heavily influenced' by Laforgue.[3] There may or may not be Laforguian irony in the choice and kind of epigraph. The expansive and solemn bit of rhetoric from Ben Jonson's *Alchemist* which Crane puts at the head of his poem is the kind of passage with which Laforgue liked to prepare an ironic catastrophe. The passage, in itself serious-seeming enough,

> And so we may arrive by Talmud skill
> And profane Greek to raise the building up
> Of Helen's house against the Ismaelite. . .

occurs at a curious point in Jonson's play, spoken by a parodied Helen to a satirized Faust. Crane may have had an ironical intention; personally, I doubt that he did. 'Hypogeum,' meaning cellar and air-raid cellar in the explosive third part, is taken either from Laforgue or from Noah Webster. In the lovely passage beginning 'The earth may glide diaphanous to death,' Crane may have been responding to Laforgue's use of the word 'diaphane' at the most intense point of all his love poetry, the beginning of the tenth poem in *Derniers Vers*. And in the remarkably syncopated second part of 'Faustus and Helen,' among the 'snarling hails of melody' on a penthouse dance floor, there is the hypnotically poised passage which might be a thoroughly naturalized bit of Laforguian unexpectedness:

> And you may fall downstairs with me
> With perfect grace and equanimity.
> Or, plaintively scud past shores
> Where, by strange harmonic laws
> All relatives, serene and cool,
> Sit rocked in patent armchairs.

But even these lines make us think, quite as much as of Laforgue, of hypnosis as one of the means mentioned by P. D. Ouspensky (to whose *Tertium Organum* Crane was so devoted) for entry into the noumenal world. There can be no question that throughout this poem full of such splendid dynamic imagery Crane is looking hopefully for something that Laforgue, once

his period of mortification in Paris was over, resigned quite hopelessly: a point of view that can only be described as religious.
Crane's heroic desire to throw a bridge from one world to the
other is already evident. The intention of his poetry turning
out to be radically different from Laforgue's, structure and style
will be different too. Resemblances will be incidental, in the
choice of a word, the placing of a passage; this is already the
case in 'Faustus and Helen.' And what concerns us most about
'Faustus and Helen' is a four-line passage which did not, as a
whole, enter into the poem, but contributed elements thereto.
It is the beginning of a projected poem on adolescence written
in 1921 and soon discarded as too derivative. Brom Weber rightly
attaches considerable importance to the quatrain as the first sample
of Crane's mature style. Two of the lines are particularly important:

> The mind shall burst its aquarium vagueness,
> Its melon opacity of graduate dawn.

Part of the second line passed into 'Faustus and Helen I,'

> Until the graduate opacities of evening,

part of it also, I believe, into the second section of the poem,

> Let us take her on the incandescent wax
> Striated with nuances, nervosities,

for Crane seems to have been much possessed by images of
gradation, of regular succession.

The first of these two verses was not assimilated into Crane's
published poems. But it is very significant even where it is, among
the rejected fragments. For the noun-turned-adjective in this line
is highly Laforguian. Laforgue developed the aquarium symbol
at length in two places, as a prose poem published separately in
Gustave Kahn's *Vogue*, then, radically revised, in 'Salomé.' With
Laforgue as with Crane the aquarium stands for the uncertainty,
the vagueness—very precisely noted by Laforgue—of the poet's
youthful mind. It is more than likely that Crane came upon the
aquarium passages in the three thin volumes of Laforgue's work

that he got from Paris. Whether he did or not, the aquarium of Laforgue, with its scrupulous notation of strangely wavering, vacillating, submerged life, is an appropriate symbol of that imaginative world which Crane explored and from which he turned with a clearer understanding of his own.

XIV

Lunar Prose

Good prose is founded on doubts.

FRANCES NEWMAN

AT the same time that Laforgue was exerting a direct or galvaniz-
ing influence on American poets, his *Moralités légendaires* was
being appreciated in different quarters. Ever since the 'nineties
there had existed in the United States a succession of writers and
critics who, without much patience for poetry as they saw it
practiced about them, were seriously devoted to an ideal of good
prose. Such was the prophet crying in the turn-of-the-century
wilderness, James Gibbons Huneker. He proclaimed the importance of Baudelaire before anyone else in America and wrote
about the lives and works of post-Baudelairian poets too, but with
none of the passion that he focused on Flaubert. Huneker seems
to have felt about the verse of his time what Stendhal felt about
the poetry of his epoch, that it did not express 'les nuances du
coeur,' that it 'always said too little or too much and regularly
beat a retreat before the appropriate word.' Such were the opinions of the critic on whom Huneker's mantle descended, H. L.
Mencken, whose ineptitude when confronted by a book of verse
was notorious, who declined to publish Eliot's 'Portrait of a Lady'
and heaped superb scorn on Hart Crane, yet did stout service for
the cause of American prose, to which he added some notable
pages himself.

Huneker was not exactly responsible for the fact that the true
Penelope of the foremost American writers became Flaubert.

That could not have come about without an invincible attraction on the part of Pound and Eliot, Cowley, and the postwar group for French prose represented ultimately by Flaubert. But Huneker, archetype of those Americans who went abroad to study their craft and see what they could see, was in prose as in other domains a great lever of discovery. He first got to Paris in 1878 and was afterward able to describe the artistic climate of the time and place with unequaled gusto. Driven back to the United States by cruel exigencies, obliged to write without letup at a time when criticism (not just criticism 'aux Etats-Unis, ou plutôt dans ce coin des Etats-Unis où l'on pense,' as someone remarked apropos of Huneker in the *Mercure de France*) had thrown itself into the arms of the Impressionists in order to avoid those of Brunetière, Huneker was guilty of many an ill-organized article. Yet by his persistence in calling attention to what he felt to be good and his stubbornness in dismissing what he knew to be bad, by his trained taste in several arts, his imagination often 'lunary,' * Huneker lifted untold dead weight from creative minds in America. During the last forty or fifty years there must have been few Americans, interested in all that Eliot meant by 'the

---

* To use a word of T. S. Eliot's, in a review of *Egoists:* 'Now that Arthur Symons is no longer active in English letters, Mr. James Huneker alone represents modernity in criticism. Few critics are possessed of so much erudition, yet there are few so determined to consider subjects only of the most modern interest. In fact, he is far too alert to be an American; in his style and in his temper he is French. Then, too, he is a musician; plays himself, and has written an interesting life of Chopin; has written also a volume on contemporary European drama, and can speak intelligently of art. All of this, in an American (or English) critic of literature, is quite unusual.

'Huneker's style may impress us as unpardonably hasty, crammed, staccato; a notebook and journalistic style. But (among American writers, still further distinction) a style it decidedly is, and shares with that of Mr. Henry James (from which, we need not add, it differs in almost every other respect) what I should call a conversational quality; not conversational in admitting the slipshod and maladroit, or a meagre vocabulary, but by a certain informality, abandoning all the ordinary rhetorical hoaxes for securing attention. In the matter of English style, by the way, his criticism, in *Overtones*, of the later Henry James is illuminating.

'. . . the Egoists are all men—French and German—of highly individual, some of perverse and lunary, genius. Particularly good is the critique of Huysmans, the genius of faith, also the note on Francis Poictevin, a forgotten literary specialist.' *Harvard Advocate*, 5 October 1909, p. 16.

Gallic mind,' who have not devoured at least a dozen of the neat
volumes of unsystematized articles and incurred a great debt to
the only important American critic of the twenty years or so
leading up to the World War. Only Huneker among productive
American critics had an unfailing sense of the contemporary;
only Huneker steadily kept European works of art before American eyes, looking forward to a day when American artists should
cease to be provincial.

He wrote twice at some length on Laforgue, and on both
occasions had much more to say about the prose than about the
poetry. The first was best: 'A Masterpiece of Irony, the Hamlet
of Jules Laforgue,' in the *New York Sun* for 11 January 1903.
Having gone over different versions of the Hamlet legend,
Huneker makes the none too startling suggestion that Frédéric
Moreau of Flaubert's *Education sentimentale* is also a kind of
Hamlet suffering in a bourgeois milieu from impairment of the
will. But the Hamlet of Jules Laforgue, he says, is the one that
will be 'nearest and dearest to the children of this age,' the
Hamlet who instinctively knows Nietzsche and his joyless joy-
ousness, though he has not read Nietzsche. This Hamlet is a
moral anarch, pure and complex, despising all methods. He 'be-
haves as a man trepanned, the moral nature removed.' And therein
lies his significance. The essay that Huneker wrote a dozen years
later on Laforgue is less vivid; the veteran of hundreds of thou-
sands of enforced critical words is a little weary, and perhaps
chilled by the thought that his effort is destined to appear in
that quite un-Nietzschean if sufficiently Hamletic aegis of respect-
ability, *The North American Review*. 'The Buffoon of the New
Eternities: Jules Laforgue' jumbles too many impressions and
musical analogies together. However, Huneker's honesty of reaction before a difficult subject is undiminished. He had said that
George Moore had done a poor job of introducing the poet of
the *Complaintes* to the English public because Laforgue was above
all The Man of Fine Shades—whereas George Moore was not.
Now he observes truly that 'one never gets Laforgue with his
back to the wall; he vanishes in the shining cloud of a witty
abstraction.' Huneker insists on Laforgue's importance as an idealist ('the spirit in him, the "shadow," devoured his soul, pulverized

his will, made of him a Hamlet without a propelling cause, a doubter in a world of cheap certitudes and insolent fatuities, but barred his proffering his pearls to pigs') and as an ante-Nietzschean transvaluer of values. Of the relative merits of Laforgue's poetry and prose he has this to say: 'Perhaps Laforgue's verse is doomed; it was born with the hectic flush of early dissolution; but it is safe to predict that as long as lovers of rare literature exist the volume of prose will survive.' In both these essays Huneker is preponderantly concerned with the contents and qualities of Laforgue's prose. And if we follow him back to *M'lle New York,* the gaudy, arty little periodical which he and his friend Vance Thompson held together for a time, we find that Huneker's penchant for prose was revealed early. Thompson, a poet of sorts, prints snatches of Laforgue's poems in the margins and translates others in the text. Huneker contributes a prose episode, 'Venus Victrix,' suggestive of Rémy de Gourmont in the subject matter and Laforgue in the manner.

A poet advanced the reputation in America of Laforgue's prose when Ezra Pound, in the famous 1918 volume of the *Little Review,* published 'Our Tetrarchal Précieuse (A Divagation from Jules Laforgue),' a translation of 'Salomé' with much omitted. In fact, too much is omitted, for example practically all the pages describing the attachment of Salomé, bluestocking of the Esoteric White Isles, for Jao Kanaan, the incarcerated labor agitator. Pound apparently wished to preserve Laforgue's name from any stain of sentimentality. And that is a pity, because if we do not know about Salomé's tender sentiments we cannot understand why Jao kept his head as long as he did or why he finally lost it. Moreover, we cannot understand Salomé, for whom such emotions were momentous. Notwithstanding all the whimsical appearances, the theme of 'Salomé' is the rather serious one central to Laforgue's work: purity and how it shall be retained. The erudite tomboy Salomé, who recites canticles to Buddhistic renunciation and the Unconscious (which Pound also deletes as non-essential), defends her virginity just as Lohengrin, Pierrot *fumiste* and many a Pierrot of the poems defend theirs. Despite the sparkling beginning of Pound's piece we have a feeling that even a divagation ought to divagate in some direction, and that

Pound has made a mere rhetorical exercise out of a tale with a main point and several subordinate ones. He understands perfectly that Laforgue is taking off Flaubert's marmoreal manner and successfully takes over the take-off: 'There arose, as from a great ossified sponge, the comic-opera Florence-Nightingale light-house, with junks beneath it clicking in vesperial meretricious monotony; behind them the great cliff obtruding solitary into the oily, poluphloisbious ocean, lifting its confection of pylons; the poplar rows, sunk yards, Luna Parks, etc., of the Tetrarchal Palace, polished jasper and basalt, funereal, undertakerial, lugubrious, blistering in the high-lights under a pale esoteric sun-beat; encrusted, bespattered and damascened with cynocephali, sphinxes, winged bulls, bulbuls, and other sculptural by-laws. The screech-owls from their jungle could only look out upon the shadowed parts of the sea, which they did without optic inconvenience, so deep was the obscured contagion of their afforested blackness.' This is approximately as effective as the corresponding passage from 'Salomé' and only half the length. But here, as in so many other places, Pound is too easily satisfied with exclusively verbal and stylistic aspects of a work. Frances Newman, even if she had only paraphrased 'Salomé'—she translated it instead—would not have failed to get across the point of the work. Nor would she have missed certain significant details. She would never, for example, have rendered 'double file de peupliers violet-gros-deuil en caisses' flatly and meagerly by 'poplar rows,' as Pound does in the passage cited above.

A native of Atlanta, Georgia, who labored as a librarian during most of her life, Frances (not Cardinal) Newman, as she delighted in signing herself, wrote her first reviews for Carnegie Library quarterlies. Thereafter she published many reviews, remarkably good ones, in a variety of periodicals. She was first and last a critic, perhaps even, in a flattering sense of the term, a reviewer. Next to being installed in a garden seat with the *Moralités légendaires*, a thin crescent moon beginning to show over the poplars, Frances Newman was never so happy as when narrowly scanning a reviewer's copy of some contemporary claim to immortality. She could not forbear to judge a great many bad books by the standards of a great many good books she had read as an ugly-duckling child in a large family. There can be no doubt that her Alcestian frankness obstructed recognition of her own books both during her lifetime and afterward. Few of her victims were as charitable as James Branch Cabell, who sought her out after a violent attack on one of his books and became her firm friend.

Her first appearance in print was with *The Short Story's Mutations* (1924), an anthology of tales mainly fantastic, with critical introductions. Some of the choices are irreproachable: Petronius's 'Matron of Ephesus,' the fabliau 'Le Vilain qui conquit paradis par plait,' Hans Christian Andersen's 'The Shepherdess and the Chimney Sweep.' On the other hand, why the anthologist should have chosen Chekhov's 'The Darling' and Laforgue's 'Miracle of Roses' out of many more likely possibilities is almost as difficult to say as why Paul Morand should be there at all (represented by his 'Nuit Nordique'). As her choice from Maupassant ('Les Bijoux') and several of the other authors indicates, Frances Newman was partial to stories illustrating recognition and reversal—narratives that finish smartly and a little trickily. At bottom it was probably the influence of O. Henry and his endings.

She seems to be critical of preciosity of style, when it is derivative, remarking accurately that 'Osbert Sitwell is still decorating limping Henry James stories with the interjections and the curves and almost the very phrases of Laforgue. . . "Every morning at twelve o'clock, to the droning snort of a brass band, Mr. Dearborn, in white flannel trousers (oh! how long ago was that day in the garden of Walter Pater. . . !) would descend the steps of the sugar-pink terrace" . . .' The trouble is that there are too many curves, conceits, and conscious graces in Frances Newman's own style. The critical comment is both learned and alive; yet the book is marked and marred by a 'self-protective smirk.'

After the *Mutations*, Frances Newman published two novels. *The Hard-Boiled Virgin* (1925) was resolutely experimental with never a word of conversation, purporting to tell the thoughts and feeling of *ces jeunes filles—jeunes filles* such as the type with which Laforgue endowed French literature. It was followed in the spring of 1928 by *Dead Lovers Are Faithful*

Lovers, which Cabell described as the dying sparks of the earlier novel's brilliance. Meanwhile Frances Newman was planning the translation of one of the books she had read the oftenest and admired the most. 'I am bent on translating Laforgue,' she had written to Cabell in 1924, 'and on doing an introduction and getting it published beautifully with a picture for each one [of the *Moralités*] perhaps. . .' And to Horace Liveright four years later: 'I have been wondering if you would let me do the Jules Laforgue *Moralités légendaires.* I talked to you a little about them the very first time I ever saw you. . .' In the spring of 1928 she went to France to consult with Paul Morand about the translation of puzzling passages, to acquire a remarkably complete knowledge of Laforgue's biography in a short time, and to look for some 'ethereal and indigent young artist who will be able to illustrate Laforgue without imitating Aubrey Beardsley.' It was during this trip that her eyes began to trouble her severely. In July she returned to the United States, where American doctors were as helpless as the French had been to relieve the 'rumblings and roarings' in her head. Unable to use her eyes at all, working with a secretary, suffering from excruciating headaches, she had just time to finish her translations and introduction before she died in September, one of the most honest of American writers, in her way, and one of those whose death has been least lamented.

Six Moral Tales is neither wholly correct as translation nor as lucid and gracious prose as Miss Newman was capable of writing when she stopped trying to be clever. But the English is very good just the same, full of a dash and relish astonishing when one considers the circumstances in which the work was done. The versions do not constitute implicit criticism of style, as does Pound's pastiche. In fact, Frances Newman liked least among the moral tales the one that is most obviously a stylistic exercise, and at the beginning of 'Salomé,' without regard for Laforgue's satiric intent, she pruned and tidied the long, choked sentences. On the other hand, there is full translation of the abstract passages that Pound ignored, and the problem of the Unconscious is tackled in the introduction.

'Laforgue knew the Unconscious about which we have just begun to learn,' she tells us, 'and his Hamlet's play contains a quatrain which might have been written by a Freudian of the second generation.' She quotes:

> *Dans le jardin*
> *de nos instincts,*
> *allons cueillir*
> *de quoi nous guérir.*

This quatrain might have served as a program for several writers who emerged during or soon after the First World War, valetudinarians who wandered in the garden of the instinctive. We think of the lyrical self-revelations of D. H. Lawrence, Sherwood Anderson, and others. And Laforgue probably did 'know the unconscious,' as any good writer does, better than any psychoanalyst. However, Frances Newman is here guilty of the confusion of the surrealists—of whom she luckily is not one: the confusion between the Unconscious as metaphysical Absolute and the unconscious as a region of the human mind.

This quatrain represents only one of many conflicting impulses that find expression in Laforgue's 'Hamlet.' There were more currents of Buddhistic renunciation and pessimistic indifference to cure in Laforgue than were dreamed of in any second-generation Freudian's philosophy. So were there in Frances Newman, though her discourse is larded with Freudian terms, though she rails against 'the ladies who are finding that an Electra complex, and a talent for lawn tennis, and a taste for poulticing the souls of the poor, will excuse celibacy in the eyes of their contemporaries.' She says that Lohengrin ('as complex as any hero conceived in the complex brain of a Freudian of the second generation') may be viewed as 'one of those young gentlemen who used to be given two years in Reading Gaol, but who are now given literary prizes.' But she admits that 'it is also possible . . . to believe that he was only suffering from the stigmata of a soul and body pierced by the chaste emerald rays of the Holy Grail.'

It is impossible to read Frances Newman's *Hard-Boiled Virgin*, or her introduction to *Six Moral Tales*, without concluding, by a process of analysis Freudians have made familiar, that she was haunted by the ideal of purity that she made a point of condemning. In her own twisted and embittered way she felt, like Alain-

Fournier, that Laforgue cherished a certain intactness; and in that feeling she herself was involved. Of 'Hamlet' she has little to say beyond making grotesque claims for her author's wit as superior to Shakespeare's, and for nontheatrical writing as *ipso facto* superior to drama. But about 'Lohengrin' (which she puts first in her collection instead of 'Hamlet,' altering Laforgue's order), about 'The Miracle of Roses,' 'Pan and the Syrinx,' she has much to say. The theme of all these stories is purity.

The prose of Laforgue and Rimbaud, in Frances Newman's opinion, 'created the English prose of the eighteen-nineties which is creating the English prose of the nineteen-twenties. . . . Laforgue has literary descendants who have probably never read one of his beautiful sentences and who are not likely to have heard his name.' The relationship between these French poets, the English 'nineties, and the American 'twenties, while close, was hardly that of the degrees of a genealogical tree. This exaggeration reminds us of all that was overdrawn about Frances Newman, the high price she placed on the fanciful, the wearisome play of conceits in her early prose, her novels in which we are never allowed to forget an experimental form determined in advance—form that does not grow out of her subject but is imposed upon it. In short we are reminded that Frances Newman was not one of the prose artists of her time, only one of those craftsmen in whom the excesses of a period are betrayed. Her work is one of those stony surfaces against which the living flood of genuinely imaginative writing rises and breaks, without which it might never rise at all. This rock is curiously carved—'curieusement taillée,' as Laforgue might have said.

Writers of the 'twenties were in search of techniques, of *expertise*, even of a certain skepticism indispensable, as Gourmont said, to the work of the artist. They found, among other writers and attitudes, Laforgue and 'irony.' Laforgue's poetry provided major poets with models that had the fascination of the unfamiliar, were imitated, and had soon served their purpose. The *Moralités légendaires* made a more lasting impression on at least one prose writer, Frances Newman, who should probably not be rebuked, as she was by John Macy, for 'ruining a fine intelligence by a false and flashy brilliance.' Such critics of Cabell,

Joseph Hergesheimer, Frances Newman, and a score of writers who cultivated the hypertrophic image, the striking phrase that militates against a total effect, forget that at a certain period in the development of a literature preciosity has its place. There was a salutary preciosity in the American writing of the 'twenties. Much unformed talent was stimulated, provoked to action and reaction, educated, by such writing as we find in Frances Newman's essays and reviews.

With the kind of writing that Frances Newman did, Laforgue had more than a little to do. And her fragmentary vision of Laforgue as a sort of preternaturally clever artist-psychologist of the 'twenties serves to complete the views of Laforgue as the Nietzschean transvaluer of values, as the moonlit astronomer of the ivory tower, as the type of incisive creator-critic, which Huneker, Symons, and Pound respectively provide.

XV

Music of Ideas

THIS book began with the assumption that a life is symbolic; and Laforgue's life fits several representative patterns of personal history. He was, first of all, the 'American' as that term is understood in a region of France—the Béarnais born abroad like Lautréamont and Supervielle, who came back to make contact with 'la ville de ses pères.' In a more general way he resembled a number of French poets of the past century who have had good reason to be preoccupied with exotic imagery—poets such as Leconte de Lisle and Saint-John Perse, born on their remote colonial islands, or Heredia who came from Cuba, Moréas from Greece, Apollinaire from Rome and Poland, Stuart Merrill and Francis Vielé-Griffin from the United States—for Symbolism in particular has called its own from a distance.

Laforgue further belongs to that even more inclusive and influential group that D. H. Lawrence described simply as those who 'must be willing to go away'; he was one of the modern exiles. If he was not obliged, like Lawrence's apprentice writer, 'to live on three pounds a week,' that sum is symbolic too, standing for a sloughing-off of the accustomed. This, for Laforgue, was brought about by the reversal of his former fortunes. He was less at home with his 1,800,000 francs a year (as it would be in terms of today) than he would have been with something like his old wage as Ephrussi's assistant. In any case, the Laforgue that we remember, the admirable poet, the prose writer whose inventions anticipate those of Proust and Joyce, the first-rate critic, would

233

almost certainly not have existed without the bitterly lamented absence from France. Laforgue went to Germany a bewildered boy, an avid private scholar whose psychological development was not nearly so advanced as his reading. At twenty he was well along the way to continuing Ephrussi's work as an art historian, but his poetry and imaginative prose lagged far behind his learning. He returned from Berlin five years later, a worldly-wise young man with two important published books to his credit and notes for several more. In and around the German court he had rubbed shoulders with people he did not like, but who had much to teach a bookish young poet all the same, whose very difference from himself had stimulated him to self-discovery. Laforgue takes his place in the company of those who have gone away to discover, if not the uncreated consciousness of a race, at least a distinct personal consciousness.

We can see the German sojourn now in the light of what it brought forth. Otherwise it might strike us as a futile period indeed. The top-hatted figure that Skarbina painted *unter den Linden* in 1885, the pallid young man in black intellectual livery, lackey to the literary pretensions of a seventy-year-old monarch, seems at first glance to be stuff of which revolutions are made. It is stuff of which revolutions *have been* made. Nothing could be much more remote from our own time and place than those scenes of German imperial grandeur in which Laforgue spent the better part of five years—the palaces bursting with cumbrous furniture, intrigue and stagnation, the comic-opera watering-places, the parade-ground soldiery, all flourishing at the expense of an intimidated and stupefied citizenry. Yet we must not forget that such leisure, however unenlightened on the whole, did foster the excrescence that is art. Our 'feverish democracy,' as Laforgue called it, is well calculated to make the poetic mind heroic, conscious of its obligation to live in the midst of suffering; but it rarely allows the time, the detachment, the Romantic irony that makes first-rate work possible. The fraudulent social system sheltered a poet.

It is to Laforgue's lasting credit as a man that he hated more and more fervidly the position of patronized eighteenth-century intellectual into which he had been thrust, that he broke away from it as soon as he was able, or sooner. The leap cost him his life and his generation its most gifted writer. But it gave to this frail post-Baudelairian poet his universal significance and his particular claim to our attention. By his marriage and return to Paris, Laforgue sought to take his proper place in society. He revealed himself as Faustian man, the modern man par excellence, who wants something of the world: not a great deal, to be sure, nothing like the total possession, the grand desires, of the earlier Fausts; only a tiny corner of the world, a hearth, a chance to earn his bread by doing the kind of work that comes naturally to him; or if it cannot be exactly his own work, something not too unlike it—*Chroniques parisiennes*, let us say, or articles about French literature for exportation, such as he was trying to have translated the day not long before his death when Henri de Régnier encountered him. If modern man cannot work as a land surveyor he is willing to labor as a janitor, like K. in Kafka's story which Max Brod (also a critic and translator of Laforgue) has interpreted. He will make almost any compromise with the mysterious Castle, will efface himself to almost any extent to protect his shrinking fraction of the world. But if he is like K. or Laforgue, a man symbolic of man's modern condition, he is likely to be crowded off even the bare floor of the classroom it is his duty to sweep out.

If a telling of Laforgue's personal story is essential to any appreciation of his significance, so certainly is some inquiry into his thought. For this young man with the meditative forward tilt of the head was a significant artist only for the last five years of his life, a hero only toward the end, but a penetrating student of ideas for a full decade. He was the only creative writer of his time to follow the evolutionary doctrine, circulating everywhere in 1880, through works of history, criticism, and philosophy, back to its source in Spencer and Darwin. This was only one evidence of his desire to come to grips with ideas. He admired Taine sincerely and sympathized with the Tainean impulse to write history showing parallels between activities of the human mind. Yet he felt profoundly that Taine's determinism, his accounting for the work of art by its milieu, was mistaken. Through Hartmann and the Unconscious, Laforgue found his way back to Schelling, the liv-

ing source of nineteenth-century philosophizing about the imagination; and there are passages in his notebooks that tend to show
that he might one day have written something comparable to
the *Biographia Literaria*, the work of another poet-aesthetician
equally imbued with the ideas of Schelling. Certainly Laforgue
would have written more incisively about artistic intuition than
his fellow-student at the Lycée Condorcet, Henri Bergson; he
would have spoken out of more direct artistic experience, and
would have been as effective a transmitter of Romantic philosophy. We cannot know what Laforgue might have done as a
thinker on aesthetic subjects, since he did not reach the age when
such ideas become clear. His thoughts on art are occasionally as
entangled as those of Paul-Joseph Chenavard, the painter-aesthe-
tician after whom he traced a Wheel of Life. However, we can
test the quality of his literary judgments by his notes on Hugo,
Rimbaud, Corbière, and particularly on Baudelaire. In possession
of a sound critical judgment from the age of eighteen, he leaped
full-armed into lists dotted mainly with feeble Impressionists.
Rounded out, his 'Notes on Baudelaire' would have made a
formidable essay. As they stand, in telegraphic style, they are un-
excelled among criticisms of Baudelaire, for no others so combine perceptiveness with historical immediacy.

According to the system of ideas which Laforgue made his
own, the supreme activity of the human mind is the poetic. In
the last analysis, this has been the story of a poet who, like the
best of the earlier Romantics, sought to unify much knowledge
into an artistic vision. We have seen how his early verse characterized by direct expression of emotion is succeeded by a different kind of utterance—less satisfying, the first of it, than the
candid expressions of feeling had been. *Le Sanglot de la terre* may
have been somewhat underestimated by Bourget and by Laforgue
himself. More lyrical than the verse of Sully-Prudhomme and
representing a more serious attempt to broaden the subject matter of poetry, it impresses us nowadays as the best poetry of ideas
that had been written in France since Vigny's *Destinées*. Published
earlier than 1903, when it appeared as part of the first *Oeuvres
complètes* (so far from complete), it could not have been popular
any more than were Vigny's poems. To one of the best and most

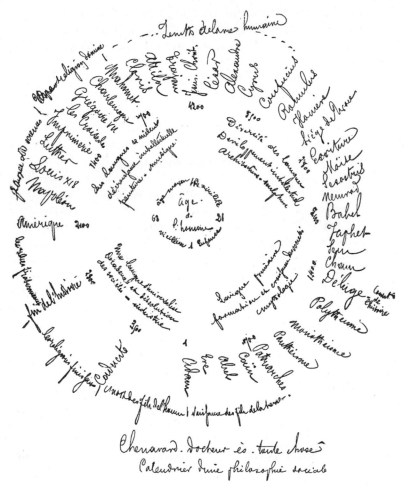

A WHEEL OF LIFE
As conceived by Paul-Joseph Chenavard and Jules Laforgue

recent historians of Symbolism, Guy Michaud, on the other hand, some of the lyric and meditative verse of Laforgue's first collection seems superior to later pieces in which he finds the humor forced.

Too many of the *Complaintes* are merely complicated, full of obviously jarring voices. *L'Imitation de Notre-Dame la Lune* is better, but the tensions of that work are inordinate, the tone shrill, the conceits strained. Before the end of his brief career, however, Laforgue had written some poems, in *Des Fleurs de bonne volonté* and especially in *Derniers Vers*, which finely reconcile the familiar and the remote, the offhand and the tender, the dissenting voices of instinct and judgment, and reflect the author's experience fairly.

Since he was in the habit of using the same images over and over again with variations, embellishments, changed angles of view, it is possible to observe the shift from direct to oblique presentation. The central concern of this book has been to show how this change took place, offering later writers the example of a new technique, a fresh attitude. The realistic description of a sunset in *Stéphane Vassiliew* leads to the burlesque magniloquence of the sea sunset in 'Persée et Andromède.' In *Le Sanglot de la terre* the center of the solar system is treated with distinct, even positivistic, respect. But in the collection of verse that followed, the sun has become a *soleil malade,* and the innocent moon has acquired a cracked complexion that she does not lose until the *Derniers Vers.* Specific situations are reversed: the poet was much possessed by the thought of a man apostrophizing a skull, and the ironic passage in which Hamlet caresses Yorick's cranium has a solemn avatar, an early prose fragment.

As the poet's imagery and ideas become more diverse, so do his rhythms. The staunch traditional alexandrines of *Le Sanglot* give way. Less and less attempt is made to satisfy the arbitrary rules 'for the eye,' and we find false rhymes, slurred mute 'e's,' alexandrines with caesuras in unheard-of places, lines with uneven numbers of syllables in novel groupings. The alexandrine had been subject to much stretching and straining since the first flush of Romanticism, and Verlaine's name had become associated with 'liberated' verse. But Laforgue with his Impressionistic ideal of fidelity to the instantaneousness of perception, carried the fragmentation much further. He was the author, indeed, of most of the authentic free verse written in France during the nineteenth century. For Rimbaud composed only two poems in *vers libre,* both of them brief; Gustave Kahn and Edouard Dujardin can no longer be regarded as poets, if they ever were; and it is hard for the dispassionate observer to work up enthusiasm for the verse of Henri de Régnier or Francis Vielé-Griffin. An American can hardly fail to be interested in Laforgue's free verse, on the other hand. Walt Whitman had at least a little finger in the concoction, and any reader of T. S. Eliot's *Prufrock and Other Observations* will feel at home with Laforgue's irregular lines, sudden rhymes, and assonances.

Little distinction need be made between a poet's imaginative prose and his verse. But Laforgue found himself first in the more relaxed rhythms of prose, early examples of which might have compelled more attention—if Bourget had not discouraged publication—than his apprentice verse. It has a competence, a limpidity of flow within its Flaubertian frame, which are evidence of an impressive word sense. And perhaps because *Moralités légendaires* was his last work, it gives evidence of a bolder technique than does his verse—a fusion and reduction of characters in a continuous present, a simplification in the direction of mythology, of which his verse contains only hints. Stream-of-consciousness composition is anticipated in Hamlet's rambling meditations even more than in the fluid stanzas of the *Derniers Vers*. Loosely woven and inconclusive as *monologue intérieur* must be, for the most part, the emotive ideas are sometimes unified by the means that has proved most fruitful in twentieth-century writing: dissolving of several figures into a single figure that assumes mythical proportions. Experimenting with stream-of-consciousness construction, as Edouard Dujardin was to do in *Les Lauriers sont coupés* a few years later, Laforgue was taking a step beyond the realism of Stendhal, Flaubert, and their followers. The fluid transitions of his later writings suggest developments in the work of recent English and American writers who have won through realism in much the same way. But the way back to the prime poetic foundations has to be rediscovered after each epoch of realism. Laforgue found early and surely the route taken by important writers since his time.

Hasty impressions of his life and works have seldom been either favorable or revealing, as several histories of literature testify. Laforgue's superficial traits are against him. He looks much like a weary *fin de siècle* dandy, plunged in an 'à-quoi-bonisme' exactly contemporary with the German Empire. He seems to have written poems that are hopelessly sentimental or uneasily flippant, crammed with undigested ideas. And Laforgue undoubtedly did write some ill-poised verse. But when this much has been said, only the surface has been scratched. Beneath the adolescent mannerisms is the Laforgue who possessed Eliot 'like a stronger personality,' daemonically, for a decade; who had an almost equal fascination for Alain-Fournier and half a dozen significant French poets; who exerted, thanks to Ezra Pound, a curious attraction for Americans of quite dissimilar temperament. As we look more closely at this undeniably influential, superficially bewildering writer, we see that each negative trait co-existed with a positive one. The fashionable pessimism was only exterior, the Romantic preliminary to genuine intellectual inquiry. This poetry is charged with intellectual life. Laforgue's ironical attitude is, at best, the irony with which Fichte believed that a true poet was bound to regard his own work, because to the extent that a work of art is complete, its author must be detached from it. Even as quotidian a matter as the poet's life is a riddle that must be read, since the ironist's deeds, like his words, might readily lead us to miss an inner meaning. And so much sentiment could hardly have existed without lapses into sentimentality.

Laforgue having raised so many more questions than he had time to answer, the problem of the 'Laforguian' writers assumes peculiar importance. It is not precisely a matter of assessing influence; it is almost a question of seeing how certain poetic discoveries were put to account. T. S. Eliot, who, as Malcolm Cowley has said, had a faculty for looking at each new poem as a problem to be solved, was much the largest inheritor. It is hardly necessary to say that he was far from being a Classicist, either aesthetically or poetically at the time of *Prufrock and Other Observations*, where long-standing Romantic attitudes are worked out in poems with many Romantic trappings. Not even in *L'Imitation de Notre-Dame la Lune* are there more essentially Laforguian poems than those four in *Prufrock* which Eliot placed 'under the sign of Laforgue,' whose implications, more than any other poet, he grasped and worked out. Yet we cannot leave out of any study of the Laforguian inheritance those for whom 'Laforgue' was something a little vague but perfectly real, a sort of synonym for 'irony.' American writers who came of age about 1920 learned, sometimes in a rather dramatic way, the advantages of the indirect approach. Laforgue, more than any other single writer with the exception of the Laforguian early Eliot, was the lever of this discovery.

F. O. Matthiessen describes Eliot's poetry—without reference to Laforgue's—as 'music of ideas.' Better than any other, the term seems to apply to the verse of Eliot's first master, verse that does not answer to any of the meaningful descriptions of Symbolism, that develops concepts as well as images in a freely associative medium. Laforgue was not a musician of the Word in the Symbolist sense; had he been, he would have effaced concepts from his poetry as Mallarmé did, leaving only the pure multivalent shell of imagery. But Laforgue was a singer at least to the extent that the Romantics were, and Matthiessen's term has the great merit of recognizing in a certain kind of verse ideas not to be found in pure Symbolist poetry. To put the matter simply, it seems to me that the poetry of Eliot and Laforgue develops lines of thought, an argument, as Mallarmé's sonnets (and Hart Crane's 'Voyages') do not. With a little attention we can follow these lines of thought. His poems have exact meaning; they are not vases of election for any of several meanings. This is not to raise the question as to whether poetry presenting concepts is better or worse than essentially Symbolist poetry (it is less intense, because less pure), but simply to say that such verse is different from the Mallarméan variety, and fully as alive today.

Indeed, Laforgue's poetry, which preceded by a little that of the historical Symbolists, has far more in common with the poetry of the post-Symbolists than has Mallarmé's. In France there has appeared what the critic Gabriel Bounoure calls 'poetry of the pure event'—conversational, phenomenological rather than archetypal. In America, Auden, Shapiro and others have written verse quite different from the Symbolist variety, distinguished from prose by its ellipses, by the quality of its wit, by its meter and movement, but not by its symbols. Much of the French and American poetry of recent years has in common with the poems of Laforgue the distinctive music, the peculiar dynamism lent by the development of ideas upon the page.

Such, seen in the light of our day, is the lunar poetry of Jules Laforgue. It is evidence of the inexhaustible abundance of works of art that this poetry is very much with us, turning a quite different face to us than it did even to such a devoted reader of the 'twenties as Frances Newman, not to mention readers of earlier decades. And it is Jules Laforgue's destiny as an artist to be forever contemporaneous, fixed neither in the attitudes of his own period nor in those of any other, to escape forever from all solemnizations of the words he wrote with a light heart. For that, all said and done, was the way he wrote—with more gentle humor than any other poet since Heine, and with the gaiety of the artist that transcends all circumstances.

NOTES

Chapter I

1. *The Symbolist Movement in Literature*, 1899, p. 105.
2. *Mélanges posthumes*, p. 119.
3. Notes on Baudelaire. *Entretiens politiques et littéraires*, II, April 1891.
4. 'Et dans Verlaine des roublardises de métier d'une innocence suprême.' *Lettres à un ami*, p. 178.
5. 'Rimbaud, fleur hâtive et absolue sans avant ni après.' *Mélanges posthumes*, p. 129.
6. 'L'oeuvre pure implique la disparition élocutoire du poète, qui cède l'initiative aux mots, par le heurt de leur inégalité mobilisés. . .' 'Variations sur un sujet,' *Oeuvres complètes*, Edition de la Pléiade, p. 366.
7. *Histoire de la littérature française de 1789 à nos jours*, 1936, p. 480.
8. *Approximations*, 1930, 4e série, p. 188.
9. *Histoire de la littérature française*, pp. 480-81.
10. 'Climat, faune et flore de la lune,' *L'Imitation de Notre-Dame la Lune*.
11. 'ce qui fut baptisé le symbolisme se résume très simplement dans l'intention commune à plusieurs familles de poètes (d'ailleurs ennemies entre elles) de reprendre à la Musique leur bien. . .' *Variétés*, I.
12. 'Ouïr l'indiscutable rayon—comme des traits dorent et déchirent un méandre de mélodies: ou la Musique rejoint le Vers pour former, depuis Wagner, la Poésie.' 'Variations sur un sujet,' *Oeuvres complètes*, p. 365.

Chapter II

1. 'Préludes autobiographiques,' *Les Complaintes, Oeuvres*, I, p. 62.
2. 'Il était né—ceci n'est pas une blague—d'une bretonne qui était

vraiment un brin gasconne et d'un gascon misanthrope, vagabond et pur comme un breton. Arrangez cela comme vous pourrez.' Prose fragment, *Revue blanche*, XII, 1 May 1897, p. 523.

3. Prose fragment, *Entretiens politiques et littéraires*, III, September 1891.

4. Loc. cit.

5. Marie Labat (née Laforgue) in an interview with Jean-Aubry at Tarbes.

6. To Charles Henry, December 1881, *Oeuvres*, IV, p. 65.

7. Unpublished manuscript.

8. 'D'une nature fantaisiste, peu travailleur, mais remarquablement intelligent, le jeune Laforgue n'était pas ce qu'on appelle au lycée un bon élève.' Letter to Jean-Aubry.

9. *Derniers Vers*, I.

10. Loc. cit.

11. Jean Pérès, 'Sur Jules Laforgue: Idées et souvenirs,' *Revue de l'Amérique latine*, June 1922, p. 132.

12. Edition Connaissance, I, pp. 31-6.

13. 'Agenda de l'année 1883,' *Oeuvres*, VI, p. 254.

14. Where two more poems were conceived than was generally known before 1931, when the volume of the *Complaintes* that Jules presented to Marie was put up for sale by a Paris bookseller. The dedication reads:

> *A ma chère et unique Marie (en attendant de te dédier par-ticulièrement quelque chose). J'ai daté la plupart des pièces. Tu reconnaîtras bien dans les Préludes, la Vigie, etc. . . le coeur de ton pauvre Jules du 5 rue Bertholet. Il n'a pas changé, ce coeur, il est toujours aussi gros. Il est devenu un peu plus littéraire, voilà tout.* Jules
>
> *Coblentz, Mardi 26 juillet 1885.*

The 'Préludes autobiographiques' are dated '1880, 5 rue Berthelot (misspelling of Berthollet in all editions; Laforgue corrected to '1881, 5 rue Berthollet'). In his sister's copy he dated by hand 'La Complainte de la vigie aux minuits polaires,' '(1881) 5 rue Berthollet'; 'Complainte des condoléances au soleil,' '5 rue Berthollet, 1881.'

15. 'Je te dirai à toi que ça m'est venu, la première idée, à la fête de l'inauguration du Lion de Belfort, carrefour de l'Observatoire.' Letter to Charles Henry, August 1885.

16. 'Une femme de la noce vomissait des flaques de vin, où un chien lappait. Une autre lui tapait maternellement dans le dos pour exciter, faciliter, bougonnant—il n'y avait pas de bon sens, après avoir bu et mangé toute la journée, à aller tourner sur des chevaux de bois— Des ménages d'ivrognes. . . Un souteneur faisant sortir une bande de filles dont l'une adorable et triste avait un bleu sous l'oeil—elles buvaient du vin. . . Odeurs de quinquets, glapissement des montreurs, mélancolie des orgues jouant des airs de carrefours d'automne, en haut les étoiles vierges et éternelles. Drôle de planète!' *Revue blanche*, x, 15 April 1896, p. 367.

17. 'Le paysage d'en face, un crépuscule splendide—mais trop tableau— un beau ciel tacheté de flocons cinabre tendre—les deux collines régulières hérissées de sapins noirs,—places vertes des jeunes sapins—au sommet la ruine rose—et plus loin sur le dévalement onduleux des collines vertes avec le serpentement d'un chemin poudreux, des arbres, et posées pittoresquement, les maisonettes blanches à tuiles vermillon—des fenêtres étincelant aux derniers rayons désespérés de l'astre pittoresque— Puis la cloche dans la vallée— C'est Calame, chanoine Schmidt, etc.—il fait beau et c'est beau; il n'y a rien à dire—le paysage de Fénelon "composé à souhait pour l'oeil"—cette nature pose par trop—oh! la Bièvre malingre, les sarments maigres des vignes, et les terrains vagues.' *Revue blanche*, x, 15 April 1896, p. 367.

Chapter III

1. This and following passages quoted from *Symbolistes et Déca-dents*, 1902, pp. 181-99.

2. 'avec, le samedi soir, le tumulte des cloches de Notre-Dame dans les deux tours sonores; le tapage du Boul' Mich' couvre la voix des cloches, c'est très philo. Ça symbolise la fin du christianisme. Ceci a tué cela. Ceci = les trompes des tramways; cela = la voix des cloches tristes.' *Lettres à un ami*, p. 18.

3. 'Noël! Noël! à Paris! Triste et froid, le vent souffle, chantent les cloches vers le ciel pluvieux et noir; mais l'incessant va-et-vient des piétons dans la boue des trottoirs, l'éternel roulement des pesants omnibus et des fiacres éreintés, le tapage des cafés et des restaurants, les cris des marchands de *Bel' Valence!* tout l'enfer du bouvelard couvre la voix des cloches solitaires.' Edition Connaissance, I, p. 13.

4. 'J'étais croyant. Depuis deux ans, je ne crois plus. Je suis un pessi-miste mystique. Les vitraux de Notre-Dame m'ont rendu malade

souvent. Pendant cinq mois, j'ai joué à l'ascète, au petit Bouddha avec deux oeufs et un verre d'eau par jour et cinq heures de bibliothèque. J'ai voulu aller pleurer sur le Saint-Sépulcre. Maintenant, dilettante, revenu de tout, j'irais fumer une cigarette sur le Golgotha en contemplant quelque couchant aux tons inédits.' *Oeuvres*, IV, p. 127.

5. 'Deux éventails de Pissarro bâtis solidement par petites touches patientes.—De Sisley, la Seine avec poteaux télégraphiques et ciel de printemps. Ou une berge des environs de Paris avec un voyou bucolisant par les sentiers.—Et les pommiers en fleurs escaladant une colline, de Monet.—Et la sauvageonne ébouriffée de Renoir, et de Berthe Morisot un sous-bois profond et frais, une femme assise, son enfant, un chien noir, un filet à papillons. . . Et de Renoir encore, la Parisienne aux lèvres rouges en jersey bleu. Et cette très capricieuse femme au manchon, une rose laque à la boutonnière, dans un fond spirituellement fouetté de neige. Et la danseuse de Mary Cassatt en jaune vert blond roux, fauteuils rouges, nu des épaules. Et les danseuses nerveuses de Degas, et le Duranty de Degas—et le Polichinelle de Manet avec les vers de Banville!' *Oeuvres*, IV, p. 42.

6. 'les douces heures passées là, à m'oublier sur les tables d'*Albert Dürer*, à rêver . . . dans votre chambre claire où éclatait la note d'un fauteuil jaune, jaune, très jaune!' Loc. cit.

7. *Oeuvres*, IV, pp. 6-8.

8. *Lettres à un ami*, p. 37.

9. 'Un charmant disciple de Schopenhauer, qui se tue de se sentir devenir fou de ne pouvoir arriver à réaliser cette oeuvre: l'épopée macabre de l'humanité (l'histoire et le XIXe siècle) en trois gds cartons correspondant aux trois stades de l'Illusion de Hartmann, plus un prologue (l'humanité des premiers jours), plus un épilogue (l'humanité des derniers jours quand l'Illusion sera morte, que les cités seront désertées, que l'homme, la tête rasée, couverte de cendres, attendra le néant), etc., etc., Que de plans! Mais la vie est courte.' Ibid. p. 22.

10. 'Je vous quitte pour relire mon ami H. Heine.' Ibid. p. 23.

11. 'J'ai 1.800 vers de mon volume. Mais il commence à me dégoûter parfois.' Ibid. p. 37.

Chapter IV

1. 'Deux ans de solitude dans les bibliothèques, sans amour, sans amis, la peur de la mort.' *Mélanges posthumes*, p. 7.

'Je demeurai presque pendant tout le siège de Troye seul, sans secours, sans espérance, sans soulagement.' *Les Aventures de Télémaque*, xv.

2. 'A quoi bon ta vie, tu ne sus rien de l'univers, du but de tout, des astres lointains, de l'histoire, de la Loi, de l'évolution universelle, rien des splendeurs solennelles, des angoisses, rien des renoncements, des prodiges, des vertiges, des contemplations, des épouvantes, des stupeurs, des frissons, des éblouissements de l'Etre unique, de la misère de tout, de l'éternité, de l'infini, du néant, de la Vie, des grandes tristesses, du temps, de l'espace, de la mort des soleils, tu partis sans avoir connu rien des sanglots de la terre, sa tragique odyssée, son histoire, ses Dieux, tu ne soupçonnas rien . . . rien de ton corps mécanisme prodigieux.' *Revue blanche*, x, 15 April 1896, p. 373.

3. *Mélanges posthumes*, p. 18.

4. 'Un Bouddhiste contemporain en Allemagne: Arthur Schopenhauer,' *Revue des deux mondes*, LXXXVI, 1870, pp. 296-332.

5. 'Par la contemplation sereine, esthétique, scientifique ou philosophique (ces deux dernières sont les plus sûres de quiétude) on échappe à soi, on est affranchi pour un instant du Temps, de l'Espace et des Nombres, on monte à la grande Liberté:—sortir de l'Illusoire.' *Mélanges posthumes*, p. 11.

6. *The World as Will and Idea*, translated by Haldane and Kemp, I, 1891, p. 485.

7. 'Il faut souffrir au moins deux ans: jeûner, souffrir de la continence, saigner de pitié et d'amour universel, visiter les hôpitaux, toutes les maladies hideuses ou tristes, toutes les saletés, se pénétrer de l'histoire générale et minutieuse, en se disant que cela est réel, que ces milliards d'individus avaient des coeurs, des sens, des aspirations au bonheur; la lire avec *sympathie* . . . comme Carlyle ou Michelet.' *Mélanges posthumes*, p. 12.

8. Letter to Sandah Mahali (Mme Mullezer), March 1882, *Oeuvres*, IV, p. 128.

9. J. M. Carrière, however, has drawn an interesting parallel between a Laforgue poem, 'Soir de Carnaval,' and Leopardi's 'La Sera del dì di festa.' 'Jules Laforgue and Leopardi,' *Romanic Review*, XXXIV, February 1943, pp. 50-53.

10. '. . . the dark impression of that nothingness which we discern behind all virtues and holiness as their final goal, and which we fear as children fear the dark.' *The World as Will and Idea*, I, p. 532.

11. *De Rerum Natura*, II, vv. 1051-75.

12. Flammarion improves his case slightly. Huygens writes: 'Fieri vix potest, Frater optime, si quis cum Copernico sentiat, Terramque, quam incolimus, è Planetarum numero unum esse existimet, qui circa solem circumferantur, ab eoque lucem omnem accipiant; quin interdum cogitet haud a ratione alienum esse ut, quimadmodum noster hic Globus, ita caeteri estu; cultu ornatuque, ac fortasse habitoribus non vacent.' *Oeuvres complètes*, XXI, 1944, p. 683.

13. *Allgemeine Naturgeschichte und Theorie des Himmels*, III, Kant's *Kleinere Schriften zur Naturphilosophie*, 1909, p. 178.

14. Laforgue reviewed Ephrussi's book two years later in his sixth published piece. *Gazette des Beaux-Arts*, XXV, 1 June 1882, pp. 608-16.

Chapter V

1. 'Je me souviens du temps où je portais à Bourget des pièces de théâtre, des chapitres de roman, et des masses de vers, en songeant: de ce coup-ci, il va être épaté! Et il me répondait le dimanche suivant: "Vous ne savez pas encore le français, ni le métier du vers, et vous n'en êtes pas encore à penser par vous-même." Quand je relis ce qui me reste des vieilles choses, je sens combien il avait raison et je me félicite de mon séjour ici en ce que cet éloignement de Paris m'a empêché de publier des sottises qui m'auraient ensuite fait faire du mauvais sang toute ma vie.' Letter of April 1886 (month changed from July to April by Jean-Aubry in his personal copy), *Oeuvres*, V, p. 146.

2. In an interview by Claudine Chonez, in *Une Semaine dans le monde*, 1 May 1948; summarized in the *Mercure de France*, July 1948, p. 551.

3. Sonnet enclosed in a letter to Mme Mullezer, 2 July 1882.

4. 'Je me suis aperçu que mon volume de vers était un ramassis de petites saletés banales et je le refais avec rage.' 2 February 1882, *Oeuvres*, IV, p. 112.

5. The first was Auguste Gérard, who became French ambassador to Japan. The second, Amédée Pigeon, was a critic and novelist.

6. 'Je pensais tout de suite à Laforgue; il avait de bonnes manières, un air correct et doux, un peu fragile et secret. Je jugeais qu'il pourrait travailler là à sa guise, à l'abri du besoin.' Quoted by Gerald Bauër, reviewing *Berlin, la cour et la ville*, *Echo de Paris*, 18 January 1923.

7. 'C'est un excellent père, va, bien qu'il ait trop lu Jean-Jacques Rousseau.' September 1881, *Oeuvres*, IV, p. 12.

8. 'Vois-tu, je serai triste pour toute la vie, si papa n'a pas dit un mot bon pour moi avant de mourir.' Ibid. p. 15.

9. Letter of 22 November 1881, ibid. p. 21.

10. Letter of 28 November 1881, ibid. p. 24.

11. Ibid. p. 33.

12. Ibid. p. 38.

13. Letter of 7 December 1881, ibid. p. 52.

14. *Berlin, la cour et la ville*, Appendix, p. 152.

15. Ibid. pp. 154-5.

16. To Ephrussi, 12 February 1882, *Oeuvres*, IV, p. 114.

17. To Ephrussi, 5 December 1881, *ibid.* p. 43.

18. 'Serré dans une redingote noire, rasé, le visage presque enfantin, mais si sérieux, et (par instants fugitifs) avec des plis si âgés, les yeux bretons, couleur de mer, et un regard au delà ou intérieur; je ne savais qui j'avais devant moi.

'Mon impression de la première seconde,—la plus nette de toutes, de beaucoup,—fut celle-ci: "La vieille impératrice, avec son goût pour les catholiques, aurait-elle fini par prendre pour lecteur un *petit prêtre rhénan?* Mais non, c'est impossible avec ces yeux-là!

'. . . Je n'ai jamais rencontré un être qui fût plus absolument dépaysé que Laforgue en ces premiers jours de là-bas, ni dominé par une plus intense phobie des êtres et des choses. . .

'Ce masque impénétrable, cette voix uniforme et calme recouvraient un état de timidité, d'incertitude presque morbide. Je suis encore à me demander par quel effort extraordinaire de volonté il put, du jour au lendemain, assurer le fonctionnement régulier et les dehors indispensables de sa "vie de cour": simplement s'habiller, ne pas oublier les heures, entrer, saluer, parler, c'est-à-dire répondre, sans qu'on remarquât rien de cette détresse d'oiseau effarouché.

'Dès les premières paroles, nous nous étions trouvé des connaissances ou amis communs: Paul Bourget . . . Charles Henry . . . d'autres encore. A chaque nom Laforgue ponctuait d'un: "C'est curieux! c'est singulier!" comme s'il y avait une harmonie préétablie ou je ne sais quel dessein commandant que je fusse venu justement à ce moment-là.

'Nous causâmes bien longtemps, et dès ce premier jour, il me dit presque tout de sa famille, de ses ascendances; jamais il ne se confia davantage; un besoin irrésistible de s'accrocher à quelqu'un de Paris et de son ancien milieu.' Letter from Théodore Lindenlaub to Jean-Aubry, 26 June 1921, quoted in the Introduction to *Berlin, la cour et la ville*, p. 35.

Chapter VI

1. 'Hier Taine (dont je suis régulièrement le cours malgré la fresque d'Ingres qu'on a devant les yeux), Taine a été étonnant sur Angelico.' Letter to Kahn, 27 January 1881, *Lettres à un ami*, p. 30.

2. 'Le cours de Taine—pantalons ridicules, trop courts avec la forte marque des genoux—Nourri de faits. Pendant une heure on est dans l'Italie parsemée du XVI siècle. Je regarde ces crânes penchées des auditeurs attentifs, sur qui tombe la lumière d'en haut sans nuance, février-blafarde. Ces gens mâchent des pâtes de guimauve, ont des foulards, des caoutchoucs aux pieds, de la flanelle, des parapluies. Ils écoutent les mémoires de Cellini, la vie des Borgias (v. Taine, *Philo. d'A. en Italie*).' Unpublished manuscript.

3. 'lequel aboutit au beau classique, à ce nu grec où la noblesse morale achève la perfection physique, et demeure insuffisant, par conséquent, devant ce qui n'est pas inspiration hellénique ou Renaissance.' Unpublished draft of 'L'Art moderne en Allemagne.'

4. 'que devient votre idéal devant les merveilles des arts chinois et japonais? devant des tapis persans?' *Mélanges posthumes*, p. 151.

5. 'M. Taine pose "un principe qui assigne à chaque oeuvre un rang dans l'échelle." Encore une fois un tapis est une oeuvre, une partie de notes est une oeuvre, un griffonnage de Rembrandt ou de Degas sont des oeuvres. Vous voyez qu'il n'y a plus qu'à tirer l'échelle.' Ibid. p. 161.

6. 'ce dehors m'importe à moi, peintre, autant que votre dedans, psychologue. Puis, ce dehors, ce décor (même en notre temps submergé, paralysé par la confection, c'est la physionomie, le geste, le beau, l'intéressant de mes personnages. . . On peut l'ôter en un tour de main? . . . Je vois des gens habillés avec d'infinies nuances selon le rang, la pose, le caractère individuel, l'heure, l'occupation. La toilette qu'on ôte en un tour de main est aussi précieuse que celle qu'on se greffe, la coupe de la barbe, des cheveux; le soin des ongles et des pieds, la toilette de la peau, la toilette du geste, les manières, l'allure sont une toilette aussi.' *Mélanges posthumes*, p. 150.

7. 'Le nu est-il toute la sculpture? Et cela étant, le nu d'une grisette

déformée par le métier ou le nu grêle d'un Donatello, n'est-il pas aussi intéressant que celui de la Diane chasseresse? Et les bustes des Césars de la décadence (voir Taine), si congénères des nôtres ne sont-ils pas aussi intéressants que les têtes des Niobides?' Ibid. p. 146.

8. 'La plume est grosse, point élégante et envolée, on dirait que c'est timide et tâtonnant; regardez comme c'est souple et savant. . . Ces génies à la plume inélégante et subtile sans le paraître . . . La plume est grosse, elle crache, elle est inexperte aux jolies hachures calligraphiques, aux profils enlevés d'un trait . . . oui, elle est grosse et crache, mais comme elle s'écrase bien à l'endroit *juste juste,* et avec un rien qui paraît sale et attrapé de hasard établit des physionomies d'une variété d'expressions étonnante.' Ibid. p. 174.

9. 'une cire de Cros qui me sourit maladivement, adossée à la lampe.' To Ephrussi, 5 November 1883 (not 6 November 1882), *Oeuvres,* IV, p. 203.

10. To Henry, 6 November 1883, *Oeuvres,* V, p. 55; *Lettres à un ami,* p. 44.

11. 'Agenda of 1883,' *Oeuvres,* VI, p. 257.

12. 'Mais de même qu'au-dessus d'une scène reproduite en gravure je mets cette même scène reproduite avec toute sa vie de tons et de valeurs dans l'atmosphère, autant je mets au-dessus d'un buste en marbre on en bronze, ce buste, en cire par exemple, avec les yeux bleus ou noirs . . . les cheveux et la parure, etc. . .' *Mélanges posthumes,* p. 147.

13. 'Eh bien, en art, non. Néron, être *anti-social,* vibrion, microbe monstrueux, avait raison de dire *qualis artifex pereo!'* Ibid. p. 152.

14. Loc. cit.

15. 'telle grisette de Paris, telle jeune fille de salon, telle tête de Burne-Jones, telle parisienne de Nittis, la jeune fille d'Orphée de Gustave Moreau,—nous fera seule sangloter, nous remuera jusqu'au tréfond de nos entrailles, parce qu'elles sont les soeurs immédiates de notre éphémère, et cela avec son allure d'aujourd'hui, sa coiffure, sa toilette, son regard moderne.' *Mélanges posthumes,* p. 161.

16. Letter from Théodore Lindenlaub to Jean-Aubry discussing Laforgue's reading while in Berlin, dated 16 July 1921.

17. 'Quant aux symbolistes, ne m'en parlez pas; ils ne soufflent plus mot de celui d'entre eux qui avait le plus de talent et qui est mort, c'est Jules Laforgue. . .' Joris-Karl Huysmans, *Enquêtes sur l'évolution littéraire,* Jules Huret, 1891, p. 184.

18. 'Un des personnages de son roman nous expose des théories d'art, aussi justes, à notre avis, que remarquables, à propos de ce qu'on appelle aujourd'hui la *modernité*. Son dernier ouvrage nous offre dans ce chapitre une abondance de documents précieux sur la vie de certains quartiers parisiens.' *Magazin für die Literatur des In- und Auslandes,* 28 May 1881; reprinted in Olive Jacobs' 'Une Page oubliée de Jules Laforgue,' *Mercure de France,* cccIV, 1 November 1948, p. 463.

19. These and quotations following are from *En Ménage,* 1881, pp. 109-14.

20. 'poètes trop chats, trop débiles pour être criminels . . . anarchistes, nihilistes—nourris dans l'école critique mais qui en sont sortis et se sont rejetés dans la vie—les seuls êtres qui ne reconnaissent plus aucune discipline ni de conscience ni de santé, ni de société.' *Mélanges posthumes,* p. 157.

21. 'Chaque homme est selon son moment dans le temps, son milieu de race et de condition sociale, son moment d'évolution individuelle, un certain clavier sur lequel le monde extérieur joue d'une certaine façon. Mon clavier est perpétuellement changeant et il n'y en a pas un autre identique au mien. Tous les claviers sont légitimes.' Ibid. p. 141.

22. This essay is included in Volume VII of the *Oeuvres complètes.*

23. December 1880, *Lettres à un ami,* pp. 22-3.

24. 'Un raté de génie. Et vierge, qui rêve quatre grandes fresques: l'épopée de l'humanité, la danse macabre des derniers temps de la planète, *les trois stades de l'Illusion.*' Fragments of 'Un Raté,' *Mélanges posthumes,* p. 9.

25. Author of *Arthur Schopenhauer, Philosopher of Pessimism,* 1946.

26. *Mélanges posthumes,* p. 201.

27. 'La rage de vouloir se connaître, de plonger sous sa culture consciente vers "l'Afrique intérieure" de notre inconscient domaine. Et c'étaient des épiements pas à pas, en écartant les branches, les broussailles des taillis, sans bruit, pour ne pas effaroucher ces lapins qui jouent au clair de lune, se croyant seuls. Je me sens si pauvre, si connu tel que je me connais moi, Laforgue, en relation avec le monde extérieur. Et j'ai des mines riches, des gisements, des mondes sous-marins qui fermentent inconnus. Ah! c'est là que je voudrais vivre, c'est là que je voudrais mourir! Des fleurs étranges qui tournent comme des têtes de cire de coiffeurs lentement sur leur tige, des pierreries féeriques comme celles où dort Galatée de Moreau surveillée par Polyphème, des coraux

heureux sans rêve, des lianes de rubis, des floraisons subtiles où l'oeil de la conscience n'a pas porté la hache et le feu. Il passait des journées à s'épier en dedans, avec l'immobilité des moines du Mont-Athos. . . *Épier des instincts avec autant que possible absence de calcul, de volonté, de peur de les faire dévier de leur naturel, de les influencer.' Entretiens politiques et littéraires,* IV, February 1892, p. 49.

28. 'Il est un domaine qui, on le sait, vient d'ouvrir à la science les forêts vierges de la vie. . .' *Mélanges posthumes,* p. 201.

29. 'le dernier divin, le principe mystique universel révélé dans la *Philosophie de l'Inconscient* de Hartmann, le seul divin minutieusement présent et veillant partout, le seul infaillible—de par son inconscience—, le seul vraiment et sereinement infini, le seul que l'homme n'ait pas créé à son image.' Ibid. pp. 201.

30. Ibid. p. 202.

31. Ibid. p. 179.

32. 'Le génie est la venue mystique, signe d'élu immédiat de l'Inconscient, pouvant parler immédiatement en son nom,'

33. *Mélanges posthumes,* p. 108.

34. 'La force transcendante qui pousse Beethoven à chanter, Delacroix à chercher des tons, Baudelaire à fouiller sa langue, Hugo à être énorme. . .' Ibid. p. 147.

35. 'Les arts n'ont qu'une importance secondaire, mais merveilleusement nécessaire, pour les fins divines: leur mission est de développer indéfiniment les organismes respectifs qu'ils exploitent et de concourir ainsi, dans un affinement sans frein de tout l'organisme, à l'état d'ivresse divinatoire du cerveau . . . en un mot, à l'épuration du miroir où se cherche l'Inconscient. . . Donc, en ce qui nous occupe, les arts optiques, la condition *sine qua non* du beau pour les oeuvres, sera avant tout le développement à outrance de l'organe exploité, l'Oeil. Est-il besoin de rappeler ici cette vérité d'hier, que, comme toute force de vie, chaque organe est en évolution? Que, par exemple, l'oeil, sens chromatique, primitivement en pleine achromatopsie, n'a appris que graduellement à connaître les ondes, de plus en plus rapides et de moins en moins longues, du rouge au violet, et continue son évolution vers l'ultra-violet. . . Que l'oeil . . . n'a appris que peu à peu à fouiller le compliqué des lignes et des perspectives mêlées et se combattant en riches vibrations. . .' *Mélanges posthumes,* pp. 205-6.

36. 'En somme l'oeil impressioniste est dans l'évolution humaine l'oeil le plus avancé, celui qui jusqu'ici a saisi et a rendu les combinaisons de nuances les plus compliquées connues.' *Mélanges posthumes,* p. 137. Bruce Morrissette points out this flaw in Laforgue's theory in his *Aspects fondamentaux de l'esthétique symboliste,* 1933, Chapter 3.

37. *Mélanges posthumes,* pp. 196-9.

38. 'La philosophie comme l'expression dernière des idées dominantes à telle période de civilisation comme la fleur consciente en laquelle s'épanouit d'elle-même la Vertu Inconsciente de l'Histoire peut seule donner dans quelques formules concises et accessibles l'âme de cette période.'

39. '. . . un point commun à tous les êtres, c'est le mécontentement de la stagnation de leur être présent, la possession de monter, etc. . . Ce plasma rêve vaguement de ce monde inouï: deux valves d'huitre à charnière qui jouent . . . L'homme est tourmenté de progrès, etc. . . Ce point commun est d'être possédé du démon de l'infini. Ce point est leur âme—Toutes ces âmes sont non seulement de la même famille, mais une même âme unique. Et la fleur universelle est le tourment indéfini de l'Idéal.'

40. 'L'objet et le sujet sont donc irrémédiablement mouvants. . . Les éclairs d'identité entre le sujet et l'objet, c'est le propre du génie.' *Mélanges posthumes,* p. 141.

41. 'La vraie philosophie—en dépit de l'émancipation autonome des sciences (un Dieu est au-dessus des castors) doit toujours rester la science première et universelle et dernière. . . Rien de la cathédrale Herbert Spencer—Il faut des poètes. Les sciences doivent rester les *ancillae diligentes* de la philosophie, de la métaphysique, dans leur anarchie bornée. Toutes ces pauvres sciences sont basées sur le sens commun, sur l'arbitraire. Elles ne doivent pas se peiner de premiers principes.—D'ailleurs ce n'est qu'une fugue de gamins qui jettent leur gourme. Le progrès des sciences spécialisées ne peut à la longue que les ramener à la science première et dernière, à la métaphysique.—Le vice radical des sciences c'est qu'elles sont impersonnelles—Tandis qu'une métaphysique vient d'une âme.'

Chapter VII

1. *Revue universitaire,* 1903, II, p. 424.
2. Ibid. 1904, I, p. 322.

3. 'L'ennui de ces périodiques pavés roulés du Sinaï coutumier, trois cent cinquante pages de gros papier, en gros caractères . . . Il n'y a pas de raison pour que ça finisse. . . [Mais] la strophe, et le vers, et la rime et les césures . . . disciplinés et aisés . . . Et à presque tous les tournants de page, faisant oublier un peu le parasitisme des adjectifs, les tortils de fantaisies techniques des *Chansons des rues et des bois.' Mélanges posthumes*, p. 130.

4. 'C'est la Bastille, la liberté et les divagations humanitaires. (Quelle corvée!)' Ibid. p. 131.

5. 'Ça va parce que c'est de la prose et que la sienne est encore seule en ce genre. Mais songez à ces livres mis en vers par un poète équivalent au prosateur Flaubert. Ce serait décidément honorablement pauvre.' Ibid. p. 131.

6. *Lettres à un ami*, p. 105.

7. 'L'Inconscient; le principe, après l'effort, l'apothéose de la conscience artistique parnassienne se consolant dans des protestations bouddhiques, le principe en poésie du bégaiement, de l'en allé.' *Mélanges posthumes*, p. 128.

8. 'ce n'est pas le bégaiement de l'enfant qui a mal, mais le *Sage qui divague;* ce n'est jamais une divagation d'images comme dans le rêve et l'extase inconsciente, c'est-à-dire de sentiments exprimés avec l'immédiat de l'enfant qui n'a à sa disposition que le répertoire de ses besoins, mais de la divagation *raisonneuse.* Sa technique est également *raisonnée,* consciente et l'on voit souvent qu'elle n'est pas de premier jet.' Ibid. p. 128.

9. 'Mes idées en poésie changent. Après avoir aimé les développements éloquents, puis Coppée, puis la *Justice* de Sully, puis baudelairien: je deviens (comme forme) kahnesque et mallarméen.' Letter of December 1881, *Oeuvres,* IV, p. 66.

10. 'Frisson d'hiver,' 'Plainte d'automne,' 'Le Phénomène futur.'

11. 'Rimbaud, fleur hâtive et absolue sans avant ni après . . . le *seul isomère* de Baudelaire.' *Mélanges posthumes*, p. 129.

12. 'Une poésie n'est pas un sentiment que l'on communique tel que conçu avant la plume. Avouons le petit bonheur de la rime, et les déviations occasionnées par les trouvailles, la symphonie imprévue vient escorter le *motif;* tout comme un peintre est amené là—à ce gris perle à propos de bottes, à ce géranium . . . tel le musicien avec ses harmonies qui ont l'air parasites.' Loc. cit.

13. 'Corbière a du chic et j'ai de l'humour; Corbière papillotte et je ronronne; je vis d'une philosophie absolue et non de tics; je suis bon à tous et non insaisissable de fringance; je n'ai pas l'amour

jaune; mais blanc et violet gros deuil. Enfin, Corbière ne s'occupe ni de la strophe ni des rimes (sauf comme un tremplin à concetti) et jamais de rythmes, et je m'en suis préoccupé au point d'en apporter de nouvelles et de nouveaux; j'ai voulu faire de la symphonie et de la mélodie, et Corbière joue de l'éternel crincrin que vous savez.' *Oeuvres*, v, p. 137.

14. 'Tout ça, c'est fait de chic, je pose. Je vais même vous expliquer comment ça se fabrique.' *Mélanges posthumes*, p. 120.

15. Loc. cit.

16. 'Un Hugo au fond avec son énorme cerveau ne vivait que pour cette seule volupté des rimes drôles.' Notes on Baudelaire, *Entretiens politiques et littéraires*, ii, April 1891.

17. *Mélanges posthumes*, pp. 123, 124.

18. Ibid. p. 125.

19. Loc. cit.

20. These and following passages on Baudelaire are translated from 'Notes,' *Entretiens politiques et littéraires*, ii, April 1891, pp. 97-120.

Chapter VIII

1. 'Je déchiquette la fougère amère du spleen.' *Oeuvres*, iv, p. 119.

2. *Oeuvres*, vi, p. 228.

3. 'La placidité berlinoise m'exaspère et j'en ai peur, aussi je n'écris pas une phrase, un vers sans vouloir du suraigu, pour me prouver que je ne m'en vais pas. Mais sans doute l'alcool à Berlin est tisane à Paris.' Letter to Henry, January 1882, *Oeuvres*, iv, p. 91.

4. Ibid. p. 208.

5. 'J'ai voulu te recopier quelques vers . . . Ils te paraîtront peut-être bizarres. Mais j'ai abandonné mon idéal de la rue Berthollet, mes poèmes philosophiques. Je trouve stupide de faire la grosse voix et de jouer de l'éloquence. Aujourd'hui que je suis plus sceptique et que je m'emballe moins aisément et que, d'autre part, je possède ma langue d'une façon plus minutieuse, plus clown-esque, j'écris de petits poèmes de fantaisie, n'ayant qu'un but: faire de l'original à tout prix.' To Marie, *Oeuvres*, v, p. 20.

6. 'Je crois me rappeler, vaguement, une *seule et unique allusion* à une jeune fille de l'entourage de l'impératrice-reine que L. m'avait dit, sans la nommer, distinguée, intellectuelle, analyste, ultra-sensible, presque orageuse . . . Elle aurait été fille d'un bourg-mestre de Cologne (ou Coblentz??). . . . L. ne m'en avait dit que ce seul mot. "Nous sommes deux malheureux . . ." lui avait-elle

dit un jour. . .' Letter from Théodore Lindenlaub to Jean-Aubry, 28 July 1921.

7. '—Lecture—puis chez R.—scène interminable.—Banquise et tison . . .' '—Promenade folle avec R. lamentations d'ambitieux esclave—' 'Scène avec R.! projets de fortune, Halle aux tableaux et dessins. Impressionisme et cire!' 'Grande scène avec R. . . Elle était née pour être mère—' '—Ereinté—Tendresses chez R. Explosion.' 'R. devant ma mine—' '—Scène de l'indigne.' *Oeuvres*, VI, pp. 223-38.

8. 'Le rendez-vous où elle ne vient pas—Il erre encore une heure après l'heure fixée, les yeux suintants, les dents serrées. Il revient du coin de la rue voir l'horloge—enseigne de l'horloger. Il est bel et bien 10^h—Il erre encore, quelque chagrin il y a, il veut en amasser avant de rentrer chez lui, jusqu'à déborder, jusqu'aux larmes. Il erre imaginant mot à mot la scène qu'il lui fera demain, et sa physionomie prend la mimique de ses paroles mentales. Que répondra-t-elle? C'est le second rendez-vous dans cette semaine qu'elle manque. Il jouera l'irréparable—Lui, quand le ciel eût croulé, n'aurait pas manqué un rendez-vous, eût fait signe etc. . . En rentrant par les rues, il s'aperçut qu'il l'adorait comme un fou—il se promettait d'en finir, dès le lendemain il lui proposerait de l'épouser, ou de l'enlever. Elle l'aimait. Cela irait seul. Il n'avait que trop hésité. Elle s'en était sans doute attiédie. Il imaginait la scène de larmes et d'amour éternel que cela ferait demain. Je t'en avais comblée, je t'en veux accabler.' Unpublished prose fragment.

9. 'Je commence à croire que c'est toute ma personne qui a déplu à l'illustre R. . ." October 1885, *Oeuvres*, V, p. 140.

10. Letter to Charles Henry, 27 July 1883, *Oeuvres*, V, p. 42.

11. Unpublished letter of 14 March 1884 to Vanier.

12. 'Quelles étranges machines vous avez publiées dans votre numéro d'aujourd'hui! Je parle des vers [de Laforgue]. Cet . . . de Verlaine, en publiant ses poètes maudits, aura fait plus de mal que Gagne et l'Unitéide. Si ça continue, il suffira dans 10 ans: 1° de n'avoir rien à dire; 2° de le dire en mauvais vers et en vers faux; 3° d'écrire comme un javanais pour être un poète de génie. Et vous, savez-vous . . . que vous aurez votre part de responsabilité.' *Lutèce*, 19 March 1885.

13. 'J'ai insisté sur l'esthétique empirique de la complainte.' August (rather than July) 1885, *Oeuvres*, V, p. 131.

14. *Ethics*, Th. 2, Proposition 7, Post. 1.

15. February 1885, *Lettres à un ami*, p. 74.

16. 'Je reste d'avis qu'enlever la première pièce du volume c'est enlever moralement toute une moitié de ce volume.'

Chapter IX

1. 'Et tout le drôle navrant d'être dans ces îles déchiquetées et venteuses, le premier jour de 86 (année où nous claquerons peut-être). Quoi qu'il en soit nous aurions dit au vent bien des propos relativement immortels.' *Lettres à un ami*, p. 144.
2. *Make it New*, 1935, p. 171.
3. 'En se penchant sur "son propre puits" le poète, avec une clairvoyance aiguë, discerne l'opposition de ses tendances, le conflit de ses instincts, et son "moi" divisé contre lui-même. Son ironie, c'est l'étincelle de magnésium qui jaillit au choc des forces contraires et qui, une seconde, éclaire le chaos de son âme.' Jacques Nanteuil, *L'Inquiétude religieuse et les poètes d'aujourd'hui*, 1925, p. 28.
4. Dumont-Wilden, *Le Crépuscule des maîtres*, 1947, p. 119.
5. *Jules Laforgue, sa vie, son oeuvre*, pp. 143-7.
6. *Principles of Literary Criticism*, 5th edition, 1934, p. 251.
7. 'Complainte à Notre-Dame des soirs.'
8. *Revue blanche*, VIII, 1895, p. 553.
9. *Oeuvres*, III, p. 132.
10. *Moralités légendaires*, 1902, p. 253.
11. 'L'Eternel quiproquo.'
12. 'A Paul Bourget,' *Les Complaintes*.
13. 'Préludes autobiographiques,' *Les Complaintes*.
14. *Revue blanche*, VIII, 1895, p. 552.
15. 'Amours de la quinzième année,' Edition Connaissance, I, p. 32.
16. 'Complainte de l'automne monotone.'
17. *Oeuvres*, III, p. 150.
18. 'Pierrots,' I, *Oeuvres*, I, p. 221.
19. *Oeuvres*, I, p. 181.
20. 'Complainte des mounis de Montmartre.'
21. 'Anticipations des principes de la psychanalyse dans l'oeuvre d'un poète français,' *Journal de psychologie normale et pathologique*, 19e année, 1922.
22. *Jules Laforgue, sa vie, son oeuvre*, p. 85.
23. *L'Evolution dynamique de l'image dans la poésie française du Romantisme à nos jours*, 1943, p. 168.
24. Anna Balakian, *Literary Origins of Surrealism*, 1947, pp. 106-8.
25. To Charles Henry, *Oeuvres*, IV, p. 67.

26. 'Le vrai vers libre est conçu comme tel, c'est-à-dire comme fragment dessiné sur le modèle de son idée émotive, et non plus déterminé par la loi fixe du nombre.' *Esthétique de la langue française*, 1894, p. 229.

27. 'Marie Krysinska a une sensibilité artiste à fond originale, mais tout cela est bien noyé dans le rhéto à la mode, n'est-ce pas?' Letter first published in *L'Art moderne*, 25 March 1888, p. 99. There are other references to Marie Krysinska in letters written 17 July 1883 and 14 July of the same year, *Oeuvres*, v, pp. 27, 38.

28. 'On se demande si c'est Laforgue ou Gustave Kahn qui a fondé le vers libre en France. Pour moi la question ne se pose pas. Je ne sais pas si Kahn est un poète pour d'autres, en tout cas il ne l'est pas pour moi. Par conséquent son vers ne m'intéresse pas, il est inexistant, tandis que Laforgue est toujours là, poète, même quand il se trompe.' Letter of 22 April 1949 to the writer.

29. For Laforgue's translations from Whitman and the order of their publication in *La Vogue*, see Bibliography for the year 1886, p. 265.

30. 'Dans la gde salle vitrée des antiques surtout vers midi, quand il était seul dessinant parmi les statues blanches et calmes. La salle était désertée. C'était le gd silence de midi. On entendait les échos des pas sur les dalles par l'école des élèves qui allaient dîner—Lui restait là oubliant sa faim—Une cloche voisine (St. Sulpice ou St. Germain des Prés) sonnait, mettant une sorte de solennité de plus dans ce gd calme de midi sous le plein jour tombant d'en haut. Dans le recueillement de ce peuple de statues blanches et immobiles. Des conceptions solennelles lui venaient. Il était dans une vie idéale loin de la vie bruyante des rues étroites et boueuses de la rive gauche, loin des mansardes des orgues, des mastroquets graisseux, des tailleurs, des fournisseurs, il était là transporté dans d'autres temps, loin de notre démocratie enfiévrée, jouissant d'une belle vie calme et noble—les bourgeois qui dans la rue vous dévisagent en passant et laissent tomber un regard sur vos souliers—un Jacques de misère à l'arrivée à Paris—dîners à 50c—bottines éculées—la santé menacée—les poignets effilochés dont on coupe les fils—' 'Bonjour cher Jacques! Toujours tes petits soucis cosmiques?' Unpublished prose fragment.

31. 'Et vinrent alors ces étranges Argonautes, comme on n'en reverra plus! Epoques splendides! Jason était leur chef, Hercule suivait, et son ami Thésée, et Orphée qui se faisait fort de me charmer

avec sa lyre (et qui devait avoir plus tard une fin si tragique!)
et aussi les deux Gémeaux: Castor, dompteur de chevaux, et Pollux, habile au pugilat. Epoques évanouies! Oh! leurs bivouacs, et
les feux qu'ils allumaient aux soirs!' 'Persée et Andromède,'
Oeuvres, III, p. 255.

32. 'Guitare,' *L'Imitation de Notre-Dame la Lune*.
33. 'Locutions des Pierrots,' III, *L'Imitation de Notre-Dame la Lune*.

Chapter X

1. *Oeuvres*, V, p. 142.
2. 'les galeries de l'Odéon, les ciels malades que l'on voit du pont
   de la Concorde, les belles flaques de la place de ce nom . . . les
   enterrements à la Madeleine et à Saint-Augustin, et les rosses
   résignées et somnolentes des fiacres.' Letter to Ephrussi, 9 January
   1882, *Mélanges posthumes*, p. 241.
3. *Mélanges posthumes*, p. 318, and *Oeuvres*, V, p. 151.
4. 'Vous savez qu'il y a trois sexes: l'homme, la femme, l'Anglaise.'
   Letter to Henry, 12 August 1882, *Oeuvres*, IV, p. 185.
5. 'Oh! moi, j'épouserai une institutrice anglaise!' Jean-Aubry, Introduction to *Berlin, la cour et la ville*, p. lxiii.
6. 8 September 1886, *Oeuvres*, V, pp. 150-59.
7. 'C'est décidé, archi-décidé. Je vais commencer à expédier mes
   livres et mes bibelots chez Kahn. J'en ai assez. La perspective de
   repasser un autre hiver ici, entre l'Oberwallstrasse, Renz, Bauer
   et la Brandenburger Tor et le Schutzmann devant ma fenêtre et
   les menues carrioles attelées de chevaux faméliques, et le corps de
   garde en face, et toutes les têtes de valets à favoris et guêtre
   café au lait, etc., etc., cette perspective me pousserait des fois à
   m'en aller chez les Mormons ou à me faire châtrer pour la Sixtine.
   C'est mon dernier hiver! . . . plutôt croupir typographe dans un
   sous-sol que de passer un autre hiver ici. Cinq ans en face des
   mêmes têtes, c'est trop pour un homme qui n'est pas toujours
   très sûr d'avoir la sienne.' Unpublished letter to Lindenlaub.
8. Letter to Marie quoted above.
9. Unpublished letter to Vielé-Griffin.
10. Letter of 30 September 1886, *Oeuvres*, V, pp. 162-4.
11. 'le mariage, qu'il considérait comme un aménagement possible de
    la vie, supprimant les pertes de temps, les périodes vagues d'inquié-
    tude, créant une citadelle autour de l'écrivain . . .' 'Les Dernières
    années de Jules Laforgue,' *Nouvelles littéraires*, 26 January 1929.

12. 'Jules Laforgue,' *French Studies*, Oxford, IV, July 1950, pp. 193-207.
13. Henri de Régnier, *Nos Rencontres*, 1931, pp. 95-6.
14. *Symbolistes et Décadents*, 1902, p. 197.

Chapter XI

1. Jules Supervielle, 'Poème,' *Les Dits modernes*, August 1919.
2. Téodor de Wyzewa, *Nos Maîtres*, 1895, pp. 236-7.
3. Alain-Fournier to Jacques Rivière, 10 January 1906, *Correspondance, J. Rivière et Alain-Fournier*, 1926, pp. 220-21.
4. 'La Sensibilité de Jules Laforgue,' *Promenades littéraires*, 1904, I, p. 106.
5. 'Je goûte aujourd'hui une forme plus resserrée, plus concentrée que celle de Laforgue, mais comment ne pas être touché par l'accent de cette poésie. . . Je crois que Laforgue aurait fait des merveilles s'il avait vécu. Tel qu'il est, il a apporté un ton nouveau dans la poésie française et même universelle.' Jules Supervielle in a letter to the writer, 22 April 1949.
6. '. . . un repoussoir pour admirer Laforgue sans restriction.' To Rivière, 13 September 1905, *Correspondance, J. Rivière et Alain-Fournier*, I, p. 100. The remaining quotations in this chapter are taken from this correspondence.

Chapter XII

1. Introduction to *Selected Poems of Ezra Pound*, London, 1928.
2. *Harper's New Monthly Magazine*, LXXXVII, June-November 1893, p. 858.
3. Ibid. p. 863.
4. *The Symbolist Movement in Literature*, 1899, p. 108.
5. Ibid. p. 106.
6. Ibid. p. 114.
7. *Scribner's*, XIII, March 1893, pp. 337-52.
8. *Blue Juniata*, 1929, p. 33.
9. Ibid. p. 37.
10. *The Fugitive*, October 1922.
11. *Letters of Ezra Pound*, edited by D. D. Paige, 1950, p. 41.
12. According to the order established by E. J. H. Greene and corroborated by Eliot, 'Jules Laforgue et T. S. Eliot,' *Revue de littérature comparée*, July-September 1948, p. 369.
13. *Harvard Advocate*, LXXXVIII, January 1910, p. 114.

14. Ibid. p. 103.
15. 'On a Recent Piece of Criticism,' *Purpose*, April-June 1938, pp. 91-2.
16. In a letter to E. J. H. Greene, *Revue de littérature comparée*, July-September 1948, p. 365.
17. *Entretiens politiques et littéraires*, IV, May 1892, p. 207, and Edition Connaissance, II, p. 119.
18. 'L'Aquarium,' *La Vogue*, no. 6, 29 May 1886, p. 193. ('Limules' was misprinted 'linnules').
19. By Elizabeth Drew, *T. S. Eliot: the Design of his Poetry*, 1949, p. 36.
20. *Hamlet*, Act II, Scene II.
21. Introduction to Ezra Pound's *Selected Poems*, 1928.
22. 'The Metaphysical Poets,' *Selected Essays (1917-1932)*, 1932, p. 248.
23. 'The Poetry of Jules Laforgue,' *Scrutiny*, V, September 1936, pp. 128-49.
24. Introduction to Ezra Pound's *Selected Poems*.
25. 'Flint, in return for having been resurrected, has put me on some very good contemporary French stuff: Rémy de Gourmont, de Régnier, etc.' To Isabel W. Pound, 12 February 1912. Letter preserved in the library of Yale University.
26. 'die zusammenstellung, das verhältnis der einzelnen teile zueinander, die notwendige folge des einen aus dem andern kennzeichnet erst die hohe dichtung.' 'Uber Dichtung I,' *Tage und Taten*, Berlin, 1933, p. 85.

Chapter XIII

1. *Hart Crane*, 1948, p. 93.
2. Published complete for the first time in *Inventario*, Autumn-Spring 1946-7, pp. 89-90.
3. *Reactionary Essays on Poetry and Ideas*, 1936.

BIBLIOGRAPHY

I. Works of Laforgue

Published during his lifetime

1880

'Les Fiancés de Noël: Triptyque en prose,' *La Vie moderne*, 2e année, no. 52 (25 December), p. 821.

1881

Review of Huysmans' *En Ménage, Magazin für die Literatur des In- und Auslandes*, May 28. Published in French translation by Olive Jacobs, 'Une Page oubliée de Jules Laforgue,' *Mercure de France*, cccIV (1 November 1948), pp. 460-64.

'Le Public des dimanches au salon,' *La Vie moderne*, 3e année, no. 23 (4 June), p. 359.

'Tristesse de réverbère,' *La Vie moderne*, 3e année, no. 36 (3 September), pp. 575-6.

'Ballade de retour,' *L'Art de la mode*, III (September), p. 34.

1882

'*Albert Dürer et ses dessins.*' Review of the book by Charles Ephrussi, *Gazette des Beaux-Arts*, xxv (1 June), 608-16.

'Expositions de l'Union artistique de Berlin,' *Chronique des Arts et de la Curiosité* (8 July), pp. 185-6.

1883

'Le Salon de Berlin,' *Gazette des Beaux-Arts*, xxVIII (1 August), pp. 170-81.

1884

'Correspondance de Berlin. Expositions de M. Adolphe Menzel à la National-Galerie,' *Gazette des Beaux-Arts*, xxx (1 July), pp. 76-84.

1885

'Complainte propitiatoire à l'Inconscient,' 'Complainte de Faust fils,' *Lutèce*, 8 March.

'Complainte de cette bonne lune,' *Lutèce*, 22 March.

'Complainte des blackboulés,' *Lutèce*, 17 May.

'Complainte sur certains temps déplacés,' 'Complainte des condoléances au soleil,' *Lutèce*, 21 June.

'Complainte-litanies de mon sacré coeur,' *Lutèce*, 19 July.

Les Complaintes de Jules Laforgue, volume of 145 pages with the epigraph, 'Au petit bonheur de la fatalité—*Much ado about Nothing.* Shakespeare.' Vanier.

Letter to Trézenik, *Lutèce*, 4 October.

1886

'Exposition de la cinquantenaire de Menzel à Berlin,' *Chronique des Arts et de la Curiosité* (9 January), pp. 13-14.

'Correspondance de Berlin. Exposition de sculpture polychrome à la National-Galerie,' *Gazette des Beaux-Arts*, xxxiii (1 February), pp. 166-70.

'Menues dragées au camphre,' *La Vogue*, i, no. 3 (25 April), pp. 73-6. Ten reflections:

> Une femme aimée qui a la consolation
> Fruit amer de l'expérience
> Paganisme et Christianisme
> Pourquoi dites-vous une ville
> Il est des moments en amour
> Que penser des classes dirigeantes
> Remarquez que la plupart des femmes
> Autre remarque, et des plus sérieuses
> Rentrez chez soi!
> Vanité! Vanité!

'Préface,' 'Romance,' 'Soirs de fêtes,' 'Les Chauves-souris,' *La Vogue*, i, no. 4 (2 May), pp. 113-17.

'L'Aquarium,' with dedication to Gustave Kahn, *La Vogue*, I, no. 6 (29 May), pp. 192-6.

'Salomé,' first and second parts, *La Vogue*, I, no. 9 (21 June), pp. 295-306; third part, no. 10 (28 June), pp. 329-34; third part, continued, no. 11 (5 July), pp. 380-87.

L'Imitation de Notre-Dame la Lune, selon Jules Laforgue, plaquette of 72 pages with the epigraph, 'Ah! quel juillet nous avons hiverné, *Per amica silentia lunae!*–Ile de la Mainau (Lac de Constance).' Vanier.

'Les Brins d'herbe: Traduit de l'étonnant poète américain Walt Whitman–J. L. (Dédicaces: Je chante le soi-même. Aux nations étrangères. A un historien. A une certaine cantatrice. Ne fermez pas vos portes. Poètes à venir. A vous. Toi, Lecteur),' *La Vogue*, I, no. 10 (28 June), pp. 325-8.

'O Etoile de France,' translation from Whitman, *La Vogue*, I, no. 11 (5 July), pp. 388-90.

'Le Concile féerique,' *La Vogue*, I, no. 12 (12 July), pp. 405-13.

Le Concile féerique. Plaquette of 16 pages, edition La Vogue.

'Lohengrin, fils de Parsifal,' first part, *La Vogue*, II, no. 1 (19 July), pp. 1-12; second part, no. 2 (26 July), pp. 46-54.

'Une femme m'attend,' translation from Whitman, *La Vogue*, II, no. 3 (2 August), pp. 73-6.

'L'Hiver qui vient,' 'La Légende des trois cors,' *La Vogue*, II, no. 5 (16 August), pp. 156-62.

'Dimanches,' *La Vogue*, II, no. 7 (30 August), pp. 226-32.

'Aquarelle,' *Le Décadent littéraire*, no. 23, 25 September.

'Paul Bourget,' *Les Hommes d'aujourd'hui*, VI, no. 285, Vanier.

'Persée et Andromède, ou le plus heureux des trois,' *La Vogue*, II, no. 9 (13 September), pp. 289-301, no. 10 (20 September), pp. 343-55.

'Exposition du centenaire de l'Académie royale des arts de Berlin,' *Gazette des Beaux-Arts*, XXXIV (1 October), pp. 339-45.

'Pétition,' 'Simple agonie,' *La Vogue*, III, no. 11 (18 October).

'Bobo,' *Le Symboliste*, 15 October.

'Le Miracle des roses,' *La Vogue*, III, no. 2 (18 October), pp. 51-64.

'A propos de toiles. Ça et là,' *Le Symboliste*, 20 October.

'A propos de Hamlet,' *Le Symboliste*, 22 October.

'Solo de lune et légende,' *La Vogue*, III, no. 3 (25 October), pp. 82-90.

'Sur une Défunte,' *Revue indépendante*, I, no. 1 (November), pp. 45-7.

'Hamlet,' *La Vogue*, III, no. 5 (15 November), pp. 145-7, no. 6 (22 November), pp. 186-203, no. 7 (29 November), pp. 217-27.

'Les Amours,' with the epigraph: 'Arrêtons-nous, amour, contemplons notre gloire. (Pétrarque)', *La Vogue*, III, no. 3 (6 December), pp. 261-5.

1887

'Bal de gala à la cour de Prusse,' under pseudonym: Jean Vien, *Figaro*, Literary Supplement, 29 January.

'Chronique parisienne,' *Revue indépendante*, II (February), pp. 165-9.

'Bal de l'Opéra de Berlin,' under pseudonym: Jean Vien, *Figaro*, Literary Supplement, 12 February.

'Chronique parisienne,' *Revue indépendante*, II (March), pp. 340-45.

'L'Empereur d'Allemagne,' under pseudonym: Jean Vien, *Figaro*, Literary Supplement, 12 March.

'Chronique parisienne,' *Revue indépendante*, III (April), pp. 24-31.

'Pan et la syrinx,' *Revue indépendante*, III (April), pp. 121-51.

'Chronique parisienne,' *Revue indépendante*, III (May), pp. 214-20.

'Mésaventure berlinoise,' under pseudonym: Jean Vien, *L'Illustration*, 7 May.

'Chronique parisienne,' *Revue indépendante*, III (June), pp. 341-4.

'Chronique parisienne,' *Revue indépendante*, IV (July), pp. 30-34.

'Chronique parisienne,' *Revue indépendante*, IV (August), pp. 158-61.

Posthumous works

1887

'Les Amours de la quinzième année,' *La Vie moderne*, 27 August.

'L'Impératrice d'Allemagne,' under pseudonym: Jean Vien, *Figaro*, 17 September.

'Le brave, brave Automne,' 'Complainte des crépuscules célibataires,' *L'Art moderne*, VII (9 October), pp. 321-2.

Moralités légendaires, published by the *Revue indépendante*, 231 pages.

'Lettres inédites de Jules Laforgue à un de ses amis,' (Charles Henry), *L'Art moderne*, VII (December), pp. 386-9, 396-7, 403-5, 411.

1888

'Lettres inédites de Jules Laforgue à un de ses amis,' (Charles Henry), *L'Art moderne*, VIII, pp. 20-21, 36, 59, 91, 99, 107, 228, 259, 282, 291, 306, 364, 372, 419.

'Les deux pigeons,' *Revue indépendante*, VI (January), pp. 1-6.

'Des Fleurs de bonne volonté,' with bibliographical note by Edouard Dujardin, *Revue indépendante*, VII (April), pp. 5-53.

> Mettons le doigt sur la plaie
> Maniaque
> Rigueurs à nulle autre pareilles
> Je fais la cour à ma destinée
> Dimanches (O Dimanches bannis . . .)
> Dimanches (Oh! ce piano . . .)
> Flûte (L'Espace . . .)
> Quiproquo (Droite en selle . . .)
> Petite prière sans prétentions
> Dimanches (Le ciel pleut sans but . . .)
> Cythère (Quel lys sut ombrager ma sieste . . .)
> Dimanches (Je m'ennuie, natal!)
> Albums (On m'a dit la vie . . .)
> Dimanches (Je ne tiens que des mois . . .)
> Petites misères d'octobre
> Gare au bord de la mer
> Impossibilité de l'infini en hosties
> Ballade (Oyez, au physique . . .)
> Petites misères d'hiver
> Dimanches (Quand reviendra l'automne,)
> Dimanches (N'achevez pas la ritournelle,)
> L'Existence qu'elles me font mener
> Dimanches (Mon sort est orphelin,)
> Petites misères d'automne (Je me souviens,)
> Dimanches (J'aime! oh! de toute ma misère!)
> Des Crépuscules célibataires
> Petites misères (On dit: l'express!)
> Air de Biniou
> Passants, n'm'induisez point en beautés d'aventure
> Espoir d'aurore (Vois, les steppes stellaires)

     Dimanches (Une qui me parlait,)
     Guitare (Pour un coeur authentique,)
     Et la coiffure, l'art du front

'Le Gemuth, etc. etc.,' *Revue libre*, May, pp. 38-42

'Complainte du libre arbitre,' *La Cravache parisienne*, 26 May.

'Vers inédits de Laforgue,' *Revue indépendante*, IX (December), 466-80.

     Célibat, célibat, tout n'est que célibat (Sucer la Chair . . .)
     L'Ile (c'est l'île, Eden entouré d'eau de tous côtés . . .)
     Le Vaisseau fantôme (Il était un petit navire . . .)
     Dimanche (Le dimanche on se plaît . . .)
     Dimanche (Ils enseignent . . .)
     La mélancolie de Pierrot (Le premier jour . . .)
     Cas (Ah! notre âme a sept facultés)
     Signalement (Chair de l'autre sexe . . .)
     Noire bise, averse glapissante

'Lettres [quatre] à Max Klinger,' *La Cravache parisienne*, 8 September.

1890

Les Derniers Vers de Jules Laforgue, 'des Fleurs de bonne volonté, le Concile féerique, Derniers vers, édités avec toutes les variantes, par Mm. Edouard Dujardin et Felix Fénéon,' Tours.

1891

'Dragées grises,' thirty-four aphorisms, *Entretiens politiques et littéraires*, II (January), pp. 1-10

     Première entrevue d'aveux (*Mélanges posthumes*, p. 63)
     Mariage d'amour (*M.p.*, p. 64)
     La femme merveilleux suppôt du Progrès (*M.p.*, p. 65)
     Histoire de femmes (*M.p.*, p. 66)
     La Femme achalande l'Ennui (*M.p.*, p. 66)
     Ce qui fait pour moi le charme du passé (*M.p.*, p. 67)
     Relevé sur le livre (*Connaissance* II, p. 79)
     Tu reviens de votre voyage de noces (*M.p.*, p. 67)
     Si j'étais femme (*M.p.*, p. 67)
     L'éternelle formule (*M.p.*, p. 68)
     Les femmes me font souvent l'effet de bébés (*M.p.*, p. 68)

La vie a beau être réaliste (*M.p.*, p. 69)
Pour toucher irréparablement une femme (*M.p.*, p. 69)
De même qu'on finit (*C.* ii, p. 60)
La civilisation (*C.* ii, p. 60)
Devant un visage de femme (*C.* ii, p. 45)
La vie est un amour de tête (*C.* ii, p. 61)
Voyage de noce (*C.* ii, p. 106)
Etre heureux (*C.* ii, p. 50)
Les communiantes (*C.* ii, p. 59)
On a chanté leurs mollets (*C.* ii, p. 42)
Chercher les raisons physiologiques (*M.p.*, p. 70)
Pourquoi est-elle heureuse (*M.p.*, p. 70)
Nous avons à la posséder (*C.* ii, p. 58)
Edgar Poe (*C.* ii, p. 76)
Je ne trouverai beau et pur (*M.p.*, p. 70)
L'Innocence (*C.* ii, p. 59)
D'ailleurs la fin de l'homme approche (*M.p.*, p. 71)
Quelles réflexions font-elles (*M.p.*, p. 71)
Je croupis dans les Usines du Négatif (*C.* ii, p. 52)
La douleur (*M.p.*, p. 72)
Je viens de gagner une gageure (*M.p.*, p. 42)
Dans un bal blanc (*M.p.*, p. 72)
Je voudrais trouver des pensées

'Notes inédites de Laforgue sur Baudelaire,' *Entretiens politiques et littéraires*, ii (April), pp. 97-120.

'Notes inédites de Laforgue sur Corbière, Mallarmé, Rimbaud,' *Entretiens politiques et littéraires*, iii (July), pp. 1-17.

'Ennuis non rimés,' *Entretiens politiques et littéraires*, iii (September), pp. 81-93.

Poèmes en prose datés de partout (*C.* ii, p. 85)
Ecrire une prose très claire (*M.p.*, p. 23)
Poèmes en prose—Le chat (*C.* ii, p. 86)
Il pleut à verse (*C.* ii, p. 19)
Ce sentiment de *mélancolie* (*M.p.*, p. 21)
Tu n'es plus là (*M.p.*, p. 22)
Qu'il était de tous le plus adonné aux songeries
Et à Montevideo les semaines (*C.* ii, p. 33)
Il était temps d'en finir
Complainte du faux convalescent (*M.p.*, p. 45)

Toute l'incompréhensible, l'insaisissable désolation d'exil (*C.* II, p. 43)
Ces dimanches de février en province (*M.p.*, pp. 36-8)
Après dîner, torride et stagnante (*M.p.*, p. 38)

'Notes inédites de Laforgue,' *Entretiens politiques et littéraires,* III (November), 153-9.

Un grain de cachou parfumé (first stanza), (*M.p.*, p. 61)
Les Fleurs du bon
Elle le premier jour (*C.* II, p. 92)
Eve—Elle très-jeune (*M.p.*, p. 63)
Seuls bijoux permis (*C.* II, p. 19)
Victoria-theater (*C.* II, p. 25)
La Littérature: la Légende de la vie (*C.* II, p. 40)
Bade—Cet éternel orchestre (*C.* II, p. 17)
Je cesserai de vivre (*M.p.*, p. 15)
Se marier à mort (*C.* II, p. 45)
Note: l'air figé à blanc
Cette frousse animale, réflexe
Aimé jamais pour moi (*C.* II, p. 48)
L'âme s'affine-t-elle
Le gras suffète Hannon
De Bordeaux à Paris (*M.p.*, p. 41)

1892

'Notes inédites de Laforgue,' *Entretiens politiques et littéraires,* IV (January), pp. 1-12.

Genre d'esprit à trouver (*C.* II, p. 86)
Ecrire un roman (*C.* II, p. 93)
Elle me bouche l'horizon (*C.* II, p. 47)
Franchement un vol. de méditations (*C.* II, p. 93)
Analyser un mariage (*C.* II, p. 87)
Un volume intitulé Nihil (*C.* II, p. 93)
Pour écrire mon roman (*C.* II, p. 99)
Un sage de la planète Lune (*C.* II, p. 87)
Roman—Je ne veux pas raconter cet amour
Mon roman. Elle (*C.* II, p. 97)
Roman—et pourtant (*C.* II, p. 97)
Ah! tu finiras (*C.* II, p. 46)
O rêve caressé des anges

On se roule les uns les autres
Seins tièdes
Berlin—la française est trop habituée (*C*. II, p. 24)
Avis à mourir (*C*. II, p. 18)
La poignance lointaine de ces valses (*C*. II, p. 19)
Il n'y a que la jeunesse (*C*. II, p. 61)
Je sais des cloches en province
Les Anglais n'admettent pas de plaisanterie
Triste et matelas aux enchères
10 h du soir (*C*. II, p. 20)
Je suis infiniment plus triste
Berlin—ici elles s'échauffent plus vite (*C*. II, p. 25)

'Notes inédites de Laforgue,' *Entretiens politiques et littéraires*, IV (February), pp. 49-57 and IV (May), pp. 198-207.

pp. 49-57:

La rage de vouloir se connaître (*C*. II, p. 41)
Aujourd'hui tout préconise (*C*. II, p. 64)
Le nu nous affole (*C*. II, p. 55)
La tête seule est nue (*C*. II, p. 56)
Tout cela est voilé (*C*. II, p. 111)
Les ongles longs (*C*. II, p. 119)
Rappelle-toi—autrefois seul (*C*. II, p. 51)

pp. 198-207:

Chapitre. Voyons; pourquoi suis-je fou d'elle (*C*. II, p. 104)
Le Désir est tout (*C*. II, p. 109)
La possession dégoute (*C*. II, pp. 107-9)
Les mouettes blanc d'argent satin (*C*. II, p. 22)
La rue est ces jours-ci un chantier (*C*. II, p. 11)
Leur système, voyager de façon (*C*. II, p. 106)
Le surlendemain de ce dimanche (*C*. II, p. 102)
Juillet—8 h—du matin (*C*. II, p. 15)
Fredonnant cette phrase de Mendelssohn (*C*. II, p. 101)
Le type de l'adorable (*C*. II, p. 46)
Comme elle est belle (*C*. II, p. 118)

'Pierrot fumiste,' *Entretiens politiques et littéraires*, IV (June), pp. 247-61.

'Cinq poèmes,' ('Nuage,' 'Solutions d'automne,' 'On a des principes,' 'La Complainte des montres,' 'Moeurs,') *Entretiens politiques et littéraires*, V (October), pp. 173-9.

1893

'Inédits de Laforgue: Notes,' *Revue anarchiste*, 1 November, pp. 65-8.

Oui, l'Idéal de la liberté
C'était un caractère cousu d'incertitudes (*M.p.*, p. 19)
Nous disons: humains (*M.p.*, p. 47)
La concurrence vitale est terrible
D'autres de parfaites cavales blondes (*M.p.*, p. 48)
Sa poitrine est remarquable (*M.p.*, p. 49)
Elle est délicate et frêle (*M.p.*, p. 50)
Elles causent avec des jeunes gens
L'homme n'a qu'un but (*M.p.*, p. 50)
Poètes et écrivains
Elles sont bêtes comme des enfants gâtés
Les femmes, ces êtres médiocres et magiques (*M.p.*, p. 47)
Comédie éternelle (*M.p.*, p. 59)
La femme—la légende féminine
Au fond la femme (*M.p.*, p. 47)
Homme ou femme (*M.p.*, p. 51)
La femme est un être vaillant (*M.p.*, p. 51)
C'est la femme qui sauvera le monde (*M.p.*, p. 52)

1894

'Pauvre petit coeur sur la main,' *Les Ibis*, IV.

'Inédits de Laforgue: Notes,' *Revue blanche*, VII (October), pp. 295-307.

Le Soleil torride à son apogée (*M.p.*, p. 25)
J'aime, j'aime (*M.p.*, p. 40)
Un crépuscule frileux (*M.p.*, p. 27)
Des femmes les bras nus (*C.* II, p. 39)
Dans sa rue perdue (*C.* II, p. 47)
Chair présente (*C.* II, p. 100)
Le bonheur (*M.p.*, p. 13)
Nous n'avons pas, mêmes malades (*M.p.*, p. 13)
En pleine effervesc. d'amour (*C.* II, p. 50)
Je suis fiancée (*C.* II, p. 105)
Oh! qu'elle fût blessée (*C.* II, p. 46)
Un Enterrement (*C.* II, p. 29)
Cette odeur (*C.* II, p. 103)
Je sais qu'il en est qui s'étalent

Le montré de la denture des Anglaises (*M.p.*, p. 59)
Une toute jeune
Tout cela—lettres et journal brûlé (*C.* II, p. 49)
En fait de religion (*M.p.*, p. 14)
Le bonheur positif (*C.* II, p. 63)
Je suis dans une année (*C.* II, p. 44)
Une histoire de Jeanne d'Arc (*C.* II, p. 93)
Passé une fin de journée en province (*M.p.*, p. 36)
A buddhist catechism (*C.* II, p. 123)
Sous ses fenêtres, ô trésor (*C.* II, p. 16)
Voyez un clair de lune (*M.p.*, p. 28)
Quand on a passé un mois malade (*C.* II, p. 62)
L'action est le débouché naturel (*M.p.*, p. 16)
Dans un parc (*C.* II, p. 35)
Mourir suffoqué dans l'extase (*C.* II, p. 49)

Poésies complètes: les Complaintes, l'Imitation de Notre-Dame la Lune, le Concile féerique, Derniers Vers, with a preface by Edouard Dujardin, Vanier.

1895

'Inédits de Laforgue,' *Revue blanche,* VIII (15 June), pp. 549-60.

Novembre (*M.p.*, p. 29)
Un jour au séquestre (*C.* II, p. 34)
Dans le roman (*M.p.*, p. 41)
Orgies d'orange (*C.* II, p. 80)
Central hôtel (*M.p.*, p. 41)
Fond de tiroir (*C.* II, p. 80)
C'est comme si tu disais
Un jeune sectaire naturaliste
Je suis pour une matinée (*C.* II, p. 20)
Le calme du Rhin plat (*C.* II, p. 15)
Ah! se disait-il (*C.* II, p. 128)
Elle avait ceci et cela
Luxueux: en allemand *luxuriöse* (*C.* II, p. 67)
Les fiacres pris en automne (*M.p.*, p. 42)
Un cabinet de travail (*M.p.*, p. 42)
Monsieur que voici (*C.* II, p. 61)
Dimanche soir—10 h. . . . Comme elle est pure (*M.p.*, p. 56)
Elle ne me dit ni des voluptés (*M.p.*, p. 57)
Crépuscule de mi-juillet 8 h (*M.p.*, p. 35)
A l'aquarium de Berlin (*M.p.*, p. 35)

Contes pour la jeunesse (*C.* II, p. 87)
S'abandonner à cette force unique (*M.p.*, p. 16)
Dimanche, le Rhin (*C.* II, p. 16)
Enfant au lycée (*C.* II, p. 33)
La Revue (*C.* II, p. 94)
Souvenirs–Puvis de Chavannes (*C.* II, p. 74)
L'Ile (*M.p.*, p. 79)
Et les nuits d'orage (*M.p.*, p. 80)
Et la lourdeur des jours (*M.p.*, p. 80)
Enlevée (*M.p.*, p. 82)
Les premiers temps (*M.p.*, pp. 82-4)
Et des tapisseries (*M.p.*, p. 84)
Lac de Constance
Et la mélancolie des marines (*C.* II, p. 28)
De la terrasse (*C.* II, p. 21)
Guizot–a dit en public
Et ma liberté d'allures (*M.p.*, p. 30)
Effet de neige légère–Après l'extase (*C.* II, pp. 23, 40)

'Lettres et Vers,' *Revue blanche,* IX (August), pp. 110-18.

Letters to Madame Mullezer ('Sandah Mahali'):
From Coblenz 2 July 1882, containing the poem 'Sieste éternelle'
(*Oeuvres,* IV, pp. 173-5)
From Coblenz 13 July 1882, containing the poem 'N'allez pas
devant ces vers-ci' (*Oeuvres,* IV, pp. 176-7)
Letter headed 'Dimanche matin, Spleen,' February 1882 (*Oeuvres,*
IV, pp. 121-4)
Letter headed 'Mercredi' March 1882, containing the first two
verses, with variants, and the beginning of the third verse of
the poem 'Encore à cet astre' (*Oeuvres,* IV, pp. 125-31).
From Tarbes, September 1882 (*Oeuvres,* IV, pp. 195-6).
From Tarbes, 13 October 1882 (*Oeuvres,* IV, pp. 197-8).
Poems:
'La Chanson du petit hypertrophique'
'Spleen des nuits de juillet'

'L'Art moderne en Allemagne,' *Revue blanche,* IX (1 October), pp.
291-300.

1896

'Un carnet de notes,' *Revue blanche,* X (15 March), pp. 241-9.

Un ouvrage . . . Palettes et factures
Négligez les chefs-d'oeuvre finis (*M.p.*, p. 173)

Clarifier sa peinture (*M.p.*, p. 175)
Les matins d'éreintement (*M.p.*, p. 39)
Ce qu'Herbert Spencer appelle (*C.* II, p. 71)
L'éternel dualisme (*M.p.*, p. 175)
Ils disent: le principe esthétique (*M.p.*, p. 176)
C'est à remiser (*M.p.*, p. 177)
Dire: L'émotion esthétique
Dans la jouissance d'une toile (*M.p.*, p. 177)
Pour le monde de l'oeil (*C.* II, p. 72)
L'Eglise de l'avenir (*C.* II, p. 75)
Les statues de nos gloires (*C.* II, p. 75)
La femme prendra (*M.p.*, p. 178)
Les virtuoses en musique (*M.p.*, p. 178)
Les médaillons de cire (*C.* II, p. 75)
François del Sarte (*C.* II, p. 124)
L'hôtel Drouot (*C.* II, p. 123)
La forme et l'idéal dans l'art (*C.* II, p. 123)
Pendant mes vacances (*C.* II, p. 85)
Esthétique—Allemagne (*C.* II, p. 71)
Réhabiliter Lebrun (*C.* II, p. 93)
Avant il y a eu l'Ecole des nobles lignes (*M.p.*, p. 179)
Ciel bleu de Sèvres (*C.* II, p. 23)
La ville (*C.* II, p. 24)
On trouve naturels les uniformes (*C.* II, p. 17)
Nisard
N'est-ce donc pas un bonheur (*C.* II, p. 128)
Quel est donc ce fonds
Il me semble (*C.* II, p. 128)
Avec un peu plus de respect (*C.* II, p. 128)
Aller chez sa maîtresse (*C.* II, p. 56)
Le sceau de l'adoption (*C.* II, p. 127)
Un de nos hommes (*C.* II, p. 127)
Le ciel pour dédommager les femmes (*C.* II, p. 127)
La triste nécessité du vice (*C.* II, p. 127)
J'abordai toutes les voluptés (*C.* II, p. 127)
Sentant distinctement (*C.* II, p. 127)
Tout, autour de moi (*C.* II, p. 127)
J'étais aimé (*C.* II, p. 128)
Relier—étoffes d'été (*C.* II, p. 74)
Rubens (*C.* II, p. 80)
La singulière abondance (*C.* II, p. 79)

La Grammaire de l'ornement (*C.* II, p. 123)
William Hunt (*C.* II, p. 123)
Esthétique (*M.p.*, p. 179)
L'Inconscient (*C.* II, p. 66)
Et dans les sensations (*C.* II, p. 67)
Elle est belle en soi (*M.p.*, p. 58)
Le Marché Saint Martin (*C.* II, p. 72)
Cultiver la fraîcheur du premier jet
Caldecott (*C.* II, p. 74)

'Feuilles volantes,' *Revue blanche,* x (15 April), pp. 367-77.

Le paysage d'en face (*C.* II, p. 12)
A Chevreuse (*M.p.*, p. 31)
Des jours de soleil (*C.* II, p. 36)
Comme on est bien (*M.p.*, p. 17)
Voici le crépuscule (*M.p.*, p. 43)
Autre type de chanteur dans les cours (*M.p.*, p. 44)
L'horloge sonne gravement (*C.* II, p. 38)
Fête de nuit—inauguration (*C.* II, p. 13)
Un soir de printemps (*M.p.*, p. 32)
Au mur de sa petite chambre (*C.* II, p. 34)
Les folles rages de l'amour (*C.* II, pp. 25-8)
Boulevard Bourdon (*M.p.*, p. 33)
En juin quand l'astre (two quatrains with variants)
Un sage contemporain (*C.* II, p. 91)
L'inévitable anthropomorphisme (*C.* II, p. 65)
Nous avions même un garçon nègre (*C.* II, p. 61)
Une preuve que le Mal (*M.p.*, p. 19)
Aux Indifférents (*M.p.*, p. 20)

'Notes sur le Musée du Luxembourg en 1886,' *Revue blanche,* xi (June), pp. 556-62.

'Lettres de Jules Laforgue à M.*' (Charles Ephrussi), *Revue blanche,* xi (1 September), pp. 219-28.

From Paris, 20 November 1881 (*Oeuvres,* IV, p. 19)
From Paris, 28 November 1881 (*Oeuvres,* IV, p. 23)
From Coblenz, 30 November 1881 (*Oeuvres,* IV, pp. 27-30)
From Berlin, 5 December 1881 (*Oeuvres,* IV, pp. 40-44)
From Berlin, 7 December 1881 (*Oeuvres,* IV, pp. 51-5)
From Berlin, 13 December 1881 (*Oeuvres,* IV, pp. 60-64)
From Berlin, 24 December 1881 (*Oeuvres,* IV, pp. 69-71)

From Berlin, 31 December 1881 (*Oeuvres*, IV, pp. 79-82)
From Berlin, 9 January 1882 (*Oeuvres*, IV, pp. 85-9)

'Lettres de Jules Laforgue à M.*' (Charles Ephrussi), *Revue blanche*, XI (15 September), pp. 271-6.

From Berlin 13 January 1882 (*Oeuvres*, IV, pp. 94-7)
From Berlin 29 January 1882 (*Oeuvres*, IV, pp. 106-9)
From Berlin, 2 February 1882 (*Oeuvres*, IV, pp. 110-12)
From Berlin, 12 February 1882 (*Oeuvres*, IV, pp. 113-17)
From Berlin, 13 March 1882 (*Oeuvres*, IV, pp. 118-20)

'Lettres de Jules Laforgue à M.*' (Charles Ephrussi), *Revue blanche*, XI (1 October), pp. 313-20.

From Berlin, 31 March 1882 (*Oeuvres*, IV, pp. 132-4)
From Berlin, 9 April 1882 (*Oeuvres*, IV, pp. 138-41)
From Wiesbaden, 26 April 1882 (*Oeuvres*, IV, pp. 147-9)
From Baden-Baden, 1 May 1882 (*Oeuvres*, IV, pp. 150-52)
From Baden, 12 May 1882 (*Oeuvres*, IV, pp. 158-60)
From Baden, 5 November 1883 (*Oeuvres*, IV, pp. 203-6)
From Berlin, 24 December 1882 (*Oeuvres*, IV, pp. 214-17)
From Berlin, December 1883 (*Oeuvres*, V, pp. 59-62)

'Notes d'esthétique,' *Revue blanche*, XI (1 December), pp. 481-8.

Le règne de la statuaire (*M.p.*, p. 146)
Traiter Cornélius
Sculpture (*M.p.*, p. 147)
M. Taine de même que M. Renan
Le but et le critérium
V. Hartmann (*M.p.*, p. 147)
Selon Renan, l'art (*M.p.*, p. 148)
Taine—Esthétique (*M.p.*, p. 150)
Les puissances souveraines de la nature (*M.p.*, pp. 151-6)
De la peinture sans spasme d'oeil (*M.p.*, p. 156)
Selon la formule de Bourget (*M.p.*, p. 156)
Taine—Tout cela (*M.p.*, p. 157)
L'opinion de Taine
Comment s'est passée notre puberté (*M.p.*, pp. 156-7)
Bienfaisance de caractère (*M.p.*, pp. 158-63)

'Plans de nouvelles et notes,' *Revue blanche*, XI (15 December), pp. 543-7.

Nuit d'août (*M.p.*, pp. 74-9)
Dans la scène de la prairie (*C.* II, pp. 36-8, 80)

1897

'Histoire de femmes (Plans de nouvelles et notes),' *Revue blanche*, XII (1 May), pp. 518-24.

Dès le premier rendez-vous (*C.* II, p. 103)
J'ai honte que tu me demandes si peu (*C.* II, p. 117)
Son amour (si raisonneur) (*C.* II, p. 118)
Le cauchemar lui étreignait les gencives
Elle dormait (*C.* II, p. 115)
Réfléchissons (*C.* II, p. 110)
Une de ces passions platoniques (*C.* II, p. 87)
Les levers—les lits défaits (*C.* II, p. 88)
Cherchez la femme, cherchez l'Inconscient (*C.* II, p. 88)
Un refrain lui mélopéait (*C.* II, p. 88)
Je ne puis pas la planter là (*C.* II, pp. 89-91)
Il était né . . . d'une bretonne (*C.* II, p. 113)
Eh bien! la table est mise (*C.* II, p. 113)
Ils ne se donnaient jamais le bras (*C.* II, p. 114)
Je sens le passé (*C.* II, p. 115)

1901-1902-1903

Oeuvres complètes de Jules Laforgue, Edition du Mercure de France.

I *Moralités légendaires* ('Hamlet, ou les suites de la piété filiale,' 'Le Miracle des roses,' 'Lohengrin, fils de Parsifal,' 'Salomé,' 'Pan et la syrinx, ou l'invention de la flûte à sept tuyaux,' 'Persée et Andromède, ou le plus heureux des trois,' 'Les Deux Pigeons.')

II *Poésies.*

Part I, *Le Sanglot de la terre*, twenty-nine poems:

Complainte de l'organiste de Notre-Dame de Nice
Soir de carnaval
La chanson du petit hypertrophique
Spleen des nuits de juillet
Farce
Apothéose
Encore à cet astre
Sieste éternelle
Médiocrité

Curiosités déplacées
Marche funèbre
Fantaisie
Rosace en vitrail
Litanies de misères
Pour le livre d'amour
Hypertrophie
Crépuscule de dimanche d'été
Couchant d'hiver
Noël sceptique
Petite chapelle
L'impossible
Devant la grande Rosace
Sonnet pour éventail
Méditation grisâtre
Les têtes de mort
Eclair de gouffre
La dernière nuit
Intarissablement
La cigarette

followed by *Les Complaintes* and *Le Concile féerique.*

Part II, *L'Imitation de Notre-Dame la Lune, Derniers Vers,* and *Des Fleurs de bonne volonté.*

III *Mélanges posthumes*

Part I, 'Pensées et Paradoxes,' 'Paysages et impressions,' 'Notes sur la femme,' 'Pierrot fumiste.'

Part II, 'Littérature,' 'Critique d'art.'

1903

'Correspondance inédite de Jules Laforgue. Lettres à sa soeur,' *Occident,* III (January), pp. 18-23; (February), pp. 78-85; (March), pp. 168-78.

1918

Oeuvres choisies de Walt Whitman: poèmes et proses traduits par J. Laforgue, L. Fabulet, A. Gide, V. Larbaud, J. Schlumberger, F. Vielé-Griffin, with an introduction by Valery Larbaud, Edition N. R. F. Translations by Laforgue (reprinted from *La Vogue,* 1886), pp. 52-60, 68, 250.

1920

'Agenda de 1883,' communicated to the N. R. F. by Jacques-Emile Blanche, *Nouvelle Revue Française*, 1 October, pp. 511-38.

Chroniques parisiennes, Ennuis non rimés, Textes inédits, edited by André Malraux, Edition Connaissance, Vol. 1:

'Les Fiancés de Noël,' 'Le Public des dimanches au salon,' 'Tristesse de réverbère, 'Amours de la quinzième année,' 'L'Aquarium,' 'Bobo,' 'A propos de Hamlet,' pp. 11-57.

'Chroniques parisiennes' (1887), pp. 63-120.

Dragées, Charles Baudelaire, Tristan Corbière, textes inédits, edited by André Malraux, Edition Connaissance, Vol. 11: Fragments arranged under completely arbitrary headings, pp. 9-128. Notes on Baudelaire not published by the Mercure Edition, pp. 135-56. Notes on Corbière not published by the Mercure Edition, pp. 161-8. Drawings by Laforgue, on five unnumbered pages.

1921

Exil, Poésie, Spleen, textes inédits, Edition Connaissance, Vol. 111:

'Lettres à un poète,' Madame Mullezer, pp. 17-35.

Facsimile of three letters, pp. 41-52.

'Lettres à un ami,' Charles Henry, pp. 53-160.

'Le Gemuth, etc. etc.,' pp. 165-71.

Verse Portrait of Charles Henry, *La Connaissance*, 2e année, no. 5 (June).

'Une Vengeance à Berlin' (originally entitled 'Mésaventure berlinoise'), *Revue de Genève*, 111 (October), pp. 460-67.

1922

Berlin, la cour et la ville, with an introduction by Jean-Aubry, Editions de la Sirène.

Oeuvres complètes de Jules Laforgue, Edition Mercure de France.

I. *Poésies: Le Sanglot de la terre; Les Complaintes; L'Imitation de Notre-Dame la Lune.*

II. *Poésies: Des Fleurs de bonne volonté; Le Concile féerique; Derniers Vers; Appendice.*

1923

Les Complaintes. Cent vingt-huit lithographes de Georges A. Drains, Edition Kra.

'Seize lettres inédites de Jules Laforgue,' *Cahiers idéalistes,* no. 8 (May).

1924

Oeuvres complètes, Edition Mercure de France.

   III. *Moralités légendaires* ('Hamlet, ou les suites de la piété filiale,' 'Le Miracle des roses,' 'Lohengrin, fils de Parsifal,' 'Salomé,' 'Pan et la syrinx,' 'Persée et Andromède, ou le plus heureux des trois.'

Hamlet et quelques poésies, with a biographical note by Georges Duthuit, Les Contemporains, no. 37.

1925

Oeuvres complètes, Edition Mercure de France.

   IV. *Lettres*–I (1881-2). Introduction and notes by G. Jean-Aubry.
   V. *Lettres*–II (1883-7). Notes by G. Jean-Aubry.

1927

Pierrot fumiste de Jules Laforgue, with engravings by Charles Martin.

1930

Oeuvres complètes, Edition Mercure de France.

   VI. *En Allemagne: Berlin. La Cour et la ville; Une Vengeance à Berlin; Agenda.* Introduction and notes by G. Jean-Aubry.

1932

Les Plus Belles Poésies de Jules Laforgue, with a preface by Jean Proix and an original etching by Jean Demailly.

1941

Lettres à un ami (1880-86), with the facsimile of an unpublished letter to S. Mallarmé, introduction and notes by G. Jean-Aubry, Mercure de France.

Feuilles, plaquette of unpublished fragments by Jules Laforgue edited by 'Nous Quatre,' (G. Jean-Aubry, Jean Gabriel Daragnès, Jules Laloux, Lucien Jaïs), Montmartre, 20 copies only.

1943

Poésies complètes, 2 volumes, edited by G. Jean-Aubry. Edition de Cluny.

1944

Poésies, Edition Viau, Buenos Aires.

1945

Le Miracle des roses, suivi par Lohengrin et les Deux Pigeons, Edition Cultura Moderna, Rome.

1946

Stéphane Vassiliew, avec une introduction de François Ruchon et l'iconographie complète de Jules Laforgue, edited by Pierre Cailler, Geneva.

II. TRANSLATIONS

ARENSBERG, W. C.
  'Complaint of Lord Pierrot' ('Autre Complainte de Lord Pierrot'), 'Conceits' ('Jeux'), *Poems,* 1914, pp. 100-103.
BATTISTESSA, ANGEL DE.
  Two prose fragments in which Laforgue recalls his Montevidean childhood, *Nosotros,* Buenos Aires, April 1923, pp. 517-21.
  'Cantilena del pobre joven,' *Verbum,* Buenos Aires, 1932, pp. 145-7.
BITHELL, JETHRO.
  'For the Book of Love,' *Modern Book of French Verse,* 1920, p. 240.
BLEI, FRANZ.
  'Pierrot, der Spassvogel,' 'Uber die Frauen,' *Pierrot, der Spassvogel, Eine Auswahl von Franz Blei und Max Brod,* Berlin, 1908, pp. 21-39, 71-6.
BROD, MAX.
  'Das Lied des kleinen Hypertrophischen,' 'Die erste Nacht,' 'Die Zigarette,' 'Beklagung dieses guten Mondes,' 'Beklagung der Pianos die man in den wohlhabenden Stadtvierteln hört,' 'Beklagung des Foetus eines Poeten,' 'Beklagung der Schiffswache in

polaren Minuten,' 'Beklagung der Hochzeitsförmlichkeiten,' 'Solo des Mondes,' 'O, käme eine . . . ,' 'Mondschein,' 'Pierrots,' 'Reden des Pierrots XII, XV,' 'Das Wahre an der Sache,' 'Sonntage' ('Es regnet ungerührt und ohne Sinn, Es regnet in der Strom, O Schäferin! . . .'), 'Festabende' ('Ich bin die Gondel, die zu spät . . .'), 'Unsere kleine Gefährtin' ('Wenn mein Blick euch etwas sagt'), 'Sonntage' ('Man sagt in Sontags Glanz'), *Pierrot, der Spassvogel, Eine Auswahl von Franz Blei und Max Brod*, Berlin, 1908, pp. 40-70.

'Eine Augustnacht,' 'Die beiden Täubchen,' ibid. pp. 77-81, 82-99.

CRANE, HART.

'Locutions des Pierrots I, II, III,' *The Double Dealer*, May 1922.

DIEZ-CANEDO, ENRIQUE.

'Encore un livre,' 'Ton geste,' 'Je ne suis qu'un viveur lunaire,' 'Solo de lune,' *La Poesia francesca del romanticismo al superrealismo*, Buenos Aires, 1945.

DRAKE, WILLIAM A.

'Another Complaint of Lord Pierrot,' *Poet Lore*, XXXIV, 1923, p. 460.

LEGGE, J. A.

'Another Book,' 'Certain ennuis,' *Chanticleer: A Study of the French Muse*, 1935, pp. 257-60.

LEVIN, HARRY.

'Two Pigeons,' *Accent*, Spring, 1944, pp. 131-9.

LEWISSOHN, L.

'Encore un livre,' *The Poets of Modern France*, 1918.

MACKWORTH, CECILY.

'Complainte de la fin des journées,' 'Complainte de l'oubli des morts,' *A Mirror for French Poetry, 1840-1940*, London, 1947.

NEWMAN, FRANCES.

'The Miracle of the Roses,' *The Short Story's Mutations*, 1924, pp. 146-63.

Six Moral Tales from Jules Laforgue: 'Lohengrin, Son of Parsifal,' 'The Miracle of the Roses,' 'Pan and the Syrinx, or the Invention of the Flute with Seven Reeds,' 'Hamlet, or the Consequences of Filial Piety,' 'Salomé,' 'Perseus and Andromeda, or the Happiest One of the Triangle,' 1928.

POUND, EZRA.

'Scène courte mais typique' (After the Pierrots of Jules Laforgue), *Little Review*, IV, May 1917, pp. 11-12 (Under the pseudonym 'John Hall'). Reprinted in *Pavannes and Divisions*, 1918, pp. 43-4.

RED, D.
'Impressionismus von Jules Laforgue,' from the 'Critique d'Art' (*Mélanges posthumes*), Kunst und Künstler, Berlin, 1905, pp. 501-6.

SAMARANI, PAOLO.
La Malinconia di Jules Laforgue (Poems from Laforgue's five collections), Milan, 1945.

SHIPLEY, JOSEPH T.
'Our Little Helpmeet,' ('Notre Petite Compagne'), *Poet Lore*, XXXVI, 1925, p. 626.

SMITH, WILLIAM JAY.
'The Clowns' ('Pierrots' i-v), *Poetry*, July 1951, pp. 210-15.
'Complaint of that Lovely Moon,' 'The First Night,' 'The Impossible,' 'Complaint of the King of Thule,' 'Another for the Sun,' 'Funeral March for the Death of the Earth,' 'Foreword,' 'Unparalleled Severity,' 'Romance,' 'Carnival Evening,' 'The Phantom Vessel,' 'Complaint of the Moon in the Provinces,' 'Spleen of July Nights,' 'Complaint of the Organist of Our Lady of Nice,' 'Apotheosis,' *Wake* 10, 1951, pp. 37-50.

WIEGLER, P.
Sagenhafte Sinnspiele (*Moralités légendaires*), Berlin, 1905.

III. MUSICAL ARRANGEMENT

NINO AND IBERT, J.
'Persée et Andromède, ou Le Plus Heureux des Trois,' Opera in two acts by Nino, from the *Moralités légendaires*, with music by Jacques Ibert, 1928. The same, with text translated into German by André G. Bloch, 1929.

IV. CONCERNING LAFORGUE (Selective)

L'Art moderne.
VIII (8 January 1888), unsigned essay on the *Moralités légendaires*, pp. 10-12.
X (30 November 1890), unsigned essay occasioned by the 1890 edition of *Derniers Vers*, pp. 377-9.

JEAN-AUBRY, G.

'Jules Laforgue,' *Revue de Hongrie*, XI (15 May 1913), pp. 379-95.

'Jules Laforgue,' *La Pluma*, Madrid, February 1921, pp. 79-83.

'Jules Laforgue et la musique,' *Revue de Genève*, III (October 1921), pp. 443-59.

'La Nostalgie de Jules Laforgue,' *Revue de l'Amérique latine*, I (February 1922), pp. 130-37.

Introduction and notes to *Berlin, la cour et la ville*, 1922; pp. ix-xcii, Life of Laforgue; pp. xciii-cx, Bibliographical description of the tale 'Une Vengeance à Berlin.'

Exchange of letters with Jean Pérès, 'Au Sujet de Jules Laforgue,' regarding Aubry's idea of Laforgue's 'nostalgia,' *Revue de l'Amérique latine*, I August 1922, pp. 351-2.

'Montevideo, Parnasse français,' *Figaro* (probably February), 1923.

'Au Berceau de Laforgue,' *Les Nouvelles littéraires*, September 1926.

Notes, *Oeuvres complètes*, II, III, IV, V, VI; especially II, pp. 220-47 on the poetry and variants; III, pp. 275-319 on the *Moralités légendaires*; VI, v-xi, pp. 5-7.

'Jules Laforgue au travail, avec un texte inédit,' *Mercure de France*, CCXCVIII (July 1940-December 1946), pp. 112-17.

Introduction, pp. 5-16, and notes to *Lettres à un ami*, 1941.

BALAKIAN, ANNA E.

Literary Origins of Surrealism: a New Mysticism in French Poetry, 1947.

BARRE, ANDRÉ.

Le Symbolisme, 1911; on Laforgue, pp. 344-7.

BATTISTESSA, ANGEL J.

'Güiraldes y Laforgue,' *Nosotros*, Buenos Aires, February 1942, pp. 149-70.

BAUËR, GERALD.

'Le "Berlin" de Jules Laforgue,' *Echo de Paris*, 18 January 1923.

BEAUNIER, ANDRÉ.

'La Poésie nouvelle, Jules Laforgue,' *Revue bleue*, XVI (August 1901), pp. 238-43.

BLIN, GEORGES.

'A la Recherche de l'infini: Laforgue et Baudelaire,' *Revue hebdomadaire*, 5 November 1938, pp. 84-93.

BOLGAR, R. R.
'Jules Laforgue,' *French Studies*, Oxford, July 1950, pp. 193-207.
BROD, MAX.
'Jules Laforgue,' introduction to *Pierrot, der Spassvogel*, Berlin, 1908, pp. 5-20.
CARRIÈRE, J. M.
'Jules Laforgue and Leopardi,' *Romanic Review*, XXXIV (February 1943), pp. 50-53.
CHAMBERLAIN, HOUSTON S.
Lebenswege meines Denkens, Munich, 1919, pp. 332-4.
CLOUARD, HENRI.
'La Poésie de Jules Laforgue,' *Le Divan*, XV (May 1923), pp. 261-9.
La Poésie française moderne, 1924, pp. 118-26.
Histoire de la littérature française, du symbolisme à nos jours, 1947, pp. 70-75.
CROS, GUY-CHARLES.
'Strophes pour ceux qui se sont tus,' *Vers et Prose*, XV, 1908.
CUISINIER, JEANNE.
Jules Laforgue, Paris, 1925.
DERÈME, TRISTAN.
'Jules Laforgue,' *Vers et Prose*, XXX (1912), pp. 211-16 and XXXI, pp. 104-7.
DOYON, RENÉ-LOUIS.
'Lettres de Jules Laforgue,' *Exil, Poésie, Spleen*, Edition Connaissance, II, pp. 7-14.
La Canne de Jules Laforgue et la statue de Bobillot, Les Livres du Mandarin, 4° série no. 2, November 1939.
DUFOUR, MÉDÉRIC.
Etude sur l'esthétique de Jules Laforgue, 1904.
DUJARDIN, EDOUARD.
'Bibliographie d'un volume de vers inédits par Jules Laforgue,' *Revue indépendante*, VII (April 1888), pp. 1-4.
'Les Premiers Poètes du vers libre,' *Mercure de France*, CXLVI (15 March 1921), pp. 577-621. The same in book form, 1922.
DURRY, MARIE-JEANNE.
Jules Laforgue. Poètes d'aujourd'hui, 1952.
EIGELDINGER, MARC.
L'Evolution dynamique de l'image dans la poésie française du Romantisme à nos jours, Neuchâtel, 1943, pp. 163-170.

ELIOT, T. S.
'London Letters,' *Dial*, April 1921, p. 452.
'The Metaphysical Poets,' *Homage to John Dryden*, London, 1924, pp. 24-33.
'Donne in Our Time,' *A Garland for John Donne*, Harvard University Press, 1931, pp. 2-19.
'On a Recent Piece of Criticism,' *Purpose*, April-June 1938.
'Propos,' *Une Semaine dans le Monde*, 1 May 1948.

FARGUE, LÉON-PAUL.
'Jules Laforgue,' *Revue de Paris*, 42e année (April 1935), pp. 783-90.

FOWLIE, WALLACE.
'Jules Laforgue,' *Poetry*, Chicago, Vol. 78 (July 1951), pp. 216-222.

GOLFFING, FRANCIS.
'Jules Laforgue,' *Quarterly Review of Literature*, III (Summer 1946), pp. 55-67.

GORREN, ALINE.
'The French Symbolists,' *Scribner's*, XIII (March 1893), pp. 337-52.

GOURMONT, RÉMY DE.
Le Livre des masques, 1896, pp. 203-9.
Promenades littéraires, 4e série, 1910, pp. 105-10.

GREENE, E. J. H.
'Jules Laforgue et T. S. Eliot,' *Revue de littérature comparée*, 22e année (July-September 1948), pp. 363-97.
T. S. Eliot et la France, 1951.

GUICHARD, LÉON.
Jules Laforgue et ses poésies, Grenoble, 1950.

HUNEKER, JAMES.
'A Masterpiece of Irony, the Hamlet of Jules Laforgue,' *New York Sun*, 11 January 1903.
'Jules Laforgue,' *North American Review*, CII (July 1915), pp. 80-91. The same, reprinted as 'The Buffoon of the New Eternities: Jules Laforgue,' *Ivory Apes and Peacocks*, 1915, pp. 32-51.

HURET, JULES.
Enquête sur l'évolution littéraire, 1891.

KAHN, GUSTAVE.
'Jules Laforgue,' *Les Hommes d'aujourd'hui*, VI, no. 298 (1886).
'Jules Laforgue,' *Revue blanche*, X (1896), pp. 122-6.
'Les Origines du symbolisme,' *Revue blanche*, XXVI (1901), pp. 321-48. The same, reprinted in *Symbolistes et Décadents*, 1902.

'Jules Laforgue,' *Symbolistes et Décadents,* pp. 181-99.

'Jules Laforgue,' *Mercure de France,* CLX (December 1922), pp. 289-313.

'Jules Laforgue,' *Le Figaro,* 25 August 1923.

'Trente Ans de symbolisme; Jules Laforgue en Allemagne,' *Les Nouvelles littéraires,* 12 January 1929.

'Trente Ans de symbolisme; les dernières années de Jules Laforgue à Paris,' *Les Nouvelles littéraires,* 26 January 1929.

LALOU, RENÉ.

Histoire de la littérature française contemporaine, editions since 1922.

LANSON, GUSTAVE.

Review of the Mercure de France edition of the *Moralités légendaires, Revue universitaire,* II (1903), p. 424.

Review of the Mercure de France edition of the *Oeuvres complètes, Revue universitaire,* I (1904), p. 322.

LEHMANN, A. G.

The Symbolist Aesthetic in France, Oxford, 1950.

MARTINO, PIERRE.

Parnasse et Symbolisme, 1925: 'La Poésie décadente: Jules Laforgue,' pp. 147-50; 'Note complémentaire,' p. 161.

MAUCLAIR, CAMILLE.

'Une Causerie avant des poèmes,' *L'Ermitage,* 7e année (January 1896), pp. 12-21.

'Essai sur Jules Laforgue,' *Mercure de France,* XVII (February 1896), pp. 159-78 and (March) pp. 302-27. The same in volume form, 1902.

'Le Cinquantenaire de Jules Laforgue,' *Revue de Paris,* 15 July 1937, pp. 341-51.

MESIRCA, G.

'Laforgue e l'impressionismo,' *Rassegna d'Italia,* nos. 11-12 (1947), pp. 25-34.

MICHAUD, GUY.

Message poétique du symbolisme, II (1947), pp. 299-314.

MIOMANDRE, FRANCIS DE.

'Jules Laforgue,' *Mercure de France,* XLV (1903), pp. 289-314.

'Notes et impressions sur Jules Laforgue,' *Revue de Paris,* 44e année (August 1937), pp. 666-71.

MOORE, GEORGE.
'Two Unknown Poets: Rimbaud and Laforgue,' *Impressions and Opinions*, London, 1891, pp. 95-102.
MORIER, HENRI.
Le Rythme du vers libre symboliste, II (1943-4), pp. 142-5.
MORRISSETTE, BRUCE A.
Les Aspects fondamentaux de l'esthétique symboliste, 1933, pp. 105-130.
MUÑOZ, GERVASIO AND ALVARO.
Lautréamont et Laforgue, Montevideo, 1925, pp. 69-93.
NEWMAN, FRANCES.
The Short Story's Mutations, 1924, pp. 144-5.
Six Moral Tales from Jules Laforgue, 1928, pp. 9-26.
PÉRÈS, JEAN.
'Antécédents Franco-Américains d'un poète français,' *Bulletin de l'Amérique latine*, March-April 1918, p. 198.
'Anticipations des principes de la psychanalyse dans l'oeuvre d'un poète français,' *Journal de psychologie normale et pathologique*, 19e année (1922), pp. 921-7.
'Sur Laforgue: Idées et souvenirs,' *Revue de l'Amérique latine*, June 1922, pp. 130-35.
Exchange of letters with Jean-Aubry, 'Au sujet de Jules Laforgue,' *Revue de l'Amérique latine*, 1 August 1922, pp. 351-2.
'Notes sur Jules Laforgue. Une époque, un âge de la vie, une philosophie vécue,' *Revue bleue*, 63e année (1925), pp. 300-306.
POUND, EZRA.
'Irony, Laforgue and some Satire,' *Poetry*, XI (November 1917), pp. 93-8.
'A Study of French Modern Poets,' *Little Review*, February 1918.
'A Study in French Poets' (the *Little Review* article with minor changes and a concluding essay on Laforgue), *Instigations*, 1920, pp. 7-19. The same reprinted in *Make it New*, 1935, pp. 159-247.
QUENNELL, PETER.
Baudelaire and the Symbolists, London, 1929, pp. 131-51.
RAYMOND, MARCEL.
De Baudelaire au surréalisme, 1933.
RÉGNIER, HENRI DE.
Faces et profils; souvenirs sur Villiers de l'Isle-Adam, Jules Laforgue, Stéphane Mallarmé, 1931. The same essay, 'Jules Laforgue,' in *Nos Rencontres*, 1931, pp. 85-96.

RIVIÈRE, JACQUES.

Correspondance, J. Rivière et Alain-Fournier, 1905-1914, 1926-8.

'Alain-Fournier,' *Nouvelle Revue Française,* XIX (December 1922), pp. 643-68. The same reprinted as introduction to *Miracles* by Alain-Fournier, 1924, pp. 11-89.

RUCHON, FRANÇOIS.

'Jules Laforgue,' *La Semaine littéraire,* Geneva, 13 January 1923, pp. 15-17.

Jules Laforgue, sa vie, son oeuvre, Geneva, 1924.

Introduction to *Stéphane Vassiliew,* 1946, pp. 7-21.

SCHMIDT, A.-M.

La Littérature symboliste, 1942, pp. 42-50.

SOUZA, ROBERT DE.

Etudes sur la poésie nouvelle. Le Lyrisme sentimental et la poésie populaire, 1895.

'Un Cinquantenaire: Jules Laforgue, l'homme et l'oeuvre,' *Mercure de France,* CCLXXIX (1 November 1937), pp. 453-87.

SYMONS, ARTHUR.

'The Decadent Movement in Literature,' *Harper's New Monthly Magazine,* LXXXVII (November 1893), pp. 858-67.

The Symbolist Movement in Literature, London, 1899, especially pp. 101-11.

TAUPIN, RENÉ.

L'Influence du symbolisme français sur la poésie américaine (de 1910 à 1920), 1929, especially pp. 150-55, 225-32.

THIBAUDET, ALBERT.

Review of *Chroniques parisiennes, Ennuis non rimés,* Edition Connaissance, III, *Nouvelle Revue française,* XV (1 December 1920), p. 952.

Histoire de la littérature française de 1789 à nos jours, 1936, pp. 468, 488.

TURNELL, G. M.

'Introduction to the Study of Tristan Corbière,' *Criterion,* XV (April 1936), pp. 393-417.

'The Poetry of Jules Laforgue,' *Scrutiny,* V (September 1936), pp. 128-49.

'Jules Laforgue,' *Cornhill Magazine,* London, no. 973 (Winter 1947-8), pp. 74-90.

TRÉZENIK, LÉO.

Review of the *Complaintes, Lutèce,* 9-16 April 1885.

WILSON, EDMUND.
  Axel's Castle, 1931.
WINTERS, YVOR.
  Primitivism and Decadence, 1937.
WYZEWA, TÉODOR DE.
  Nos Maîtres, études et portraits littéraires, 1895, pp. 235-40.

INDEX